B + T

Also by William H. Gass

Life Sentences

LIFE SENTENCES

Literary Judgments and Accounts

William H. Gass

ALFRED A. KNOPF

NEW YORK

2012

THIS IS A BORZOI BOOK
PUBLISHED BY ALFRED A. KNOPF

www.aaknopf.com

Knopf, Borzoi Books, and the colophon are registered trademarks of Random House, Inc.

Grateful acknowledgment is made to the following for permission to reprint previously published material:
Alfred A. Knopf: Excerpt from *The Tunnel* by William H. Gass, copyright © 1995 by William H. Gass. Used by permission of Alfred A. Knopf, a division of Random House, Inc.
University of Chicago Press: Excerpt from *Gnomes and Occasions* by Howard Nemerov, copyright © 1973 by Howard Nemerov. Used by permission of the University of Chicago Press.

Library of Congress Cataloging-in-Publication Data
Gass, William H., [date]
Life sentences : literary judgments and accounts / William H. Gass
p. cm.
"This is a Borzoi book."
ISBN 978-0-307-59584-3
I. Title.
PS3557.A845L54 2012
814'.54—dc23   2011033577

Jacket design by Barbara de Wilde
Manufactured in the United States of America
First Edition

For Mary, Catherine, and Elizabeth

The women in my life

CONTENTS

Contents

ACKNOWLEDGMENTS

Earlier versions of these essays have appeared, often with different titles than they have here, as well as significantly altered texts, in the following venues: "The Literary Miracle," delivered as an acceptance speech for the 2007 Truman Capote Award for Literary Criticism, Iowa City, October 25, 2007, and published in the *Iowa Review,* Spring 2008; "Slices of Life in a Library," delivered as an acceptance speech for the St. Louis University Library Literary Award, 2007, and published in *St. Louis Magazine,* December 2007; "The First Fourth Following 9/11," in *The American Spirit* (New York: Life Books, 2002); "A Wreath for the Grave of Gertrude Stein," a presentation at the 92nd Street Y, published in *PEN America,* issue 4, 2004; "Reading Proust," a presentation at the 92nd Street Y, published in *PEN America,* issue 2, 2001; "Nietzsche: In Illness and in Health," *Harper's Magazine,* August 2005; "Half a Man, Half a Metaphor," *Harper's Magazine,* August 2006; "Unsteady as She Goes: Malcolm Lowry's Cinema Inferno," *Harper's Magazine,* January 2008; "Henry James's Curriculum Vitae," *Harper's Magazine,* August 2008; "Introduction" to *Nickel Mountain* (New York: New Directions, 2007); "Katherine Anne Porter's First Fiction," *Harper's Magazine,* January 2009; "Kinds of Killing," *Harper's Magazine,* August 2009; "Norway's Nobel Nazi," *Harper's Magazine,* March 2010. "Form,"

Acknowledgments

"Mimesis," and "Metaphor" were the Biggs Lectures in the Classics, given in 2004 at Washington University, St. Louis. "Mimesis" was published in *Conjunctions* 46, 2006. "Lust" was published in *Wicked Pleasures*, edited by Robert Solomon (Lanham, MD: Rowman and Littlefield, 1999). "The Esthetic Structure of the Sentence," was the Dotterer Philosophy Lecture at Penn State and was published in *The Review of Contemporary Fiction*, fall 2008. "Narrative Sentences" was presented at Michigan State University in April 2002 and was published in *The Yale Review*, Winter 2011.

The Personals Column

THE LITERARY MIRACLE

An acceptance speech for the 2007
Truman Capote Award for Literary Criticism

I have already participated in the Truman Capote Prize for Criticism, first as a nominator, then as an evaluator, so I am familiar with many of the texts which have been considered for it in the past. They comprise a company I should be proud to say I keep, and I am grateful that you have now encouraged me to that immodesty.

I have always been interested in miracles—not just in the one we are presently celebrating, but especially in the secular kinds. A miracle is something that cannot happen, and shouldn't, and won't again, but has occurred all the same, despite laws, odds, expectations. A miracle is also something fortunate for somebody, and suggests the influence of a higher power—doubtless a holdover from its sacred use. We don't say, "Wow, five hundred people died from eating the same ice-cream cone. It's a miracle!" though it is remarkable, even deplorable, depending upon the flavor.

There is another sort of miracle, though, equally unlikely, equally difficult to explain, but one that occurs with satisfactory frequency despite enemies almost as persistent as mortality itself, and that is a phenomenon called consciousness and its tendency toward individuation.

Hume, I think, was right in insisting that any event that deserved to be classified as a miracle should be examined by a host of competent observers who had nothing to gain if Lazarus, to take a famous example, were to wake from his death to boast that now only his belly ached. Suppose dispassionate and qualified observers could be found in Beijing, Berlin, and Boston. Then Lazarus would have to oblige by dying (when he wasn't booked elsewhere) in front of gathered specialists in these varied cities, who might attest then to his pre- and postmortem condition. Of course, if his revival was used to support the claims of any religion, political party, or upcoming movie, it would be immediately disqualified for violating the impartiality rule, and if it passed all tests it would simply become another exceptional break in an otherwise impeccable regularity, like black swans or albino squirrels, and no longer a miracle at all. Footnotes would merely mention that a few folk, each one named Lazarus and owning a mole on his left cheek, occasionally returned to life after their deaths, if their deaths occurred on the second of February, and they performed their demises in public before qualified officials for the edification and amusement of many. This kind of circular begging of the question is okay if Hume does it.

Not content, we would explain the anomaly by showing that—whatever the exemplary occurrence was—some subatomic particle, not the butler, had done it, and further that this surprising breach of the laws of nature formed a pattern with others of a similar sort (like albinism), and was, in fact, establishing a February second, mole-cheeked regularity of its own. If black swans can do it, why can't the Lazarites?

The finer works of art are miracles in the sense that they are so unlikely to have emerged from the ignoble and bloody hands of man that we stand in awe of them, and that they have been written or built or composed at the behest of superstitions so blatantly foolish as to embarrass reason, and cause common sense to snicker, is itself wondrous and beyond ordinary comprehension. However, the fact that a gay guy painted the Sistine ceiling is not nearly as dumbfounding as the papacy's protection of pederasts in spite of their official attitude toward such "objectionable" practices—one of which ought to be the ceiling itself, for if anything is unnatural, for them, genius is.

The secular miracle is an incomprehensible juxtaposition of events, not a rare or occasional break in the order of things, but a paired regularity that persists in making no sense: the first being the creation of inspired art, and the second requiring a wonder equal to it, namely, that such astonishments are accomplished, often, by quite ordinary or even subpar human beings. For a long time I have been trying to understand these two things—the miracle of their appearance and the unlikely nature of their cause. Moreover, some of these artists are required to perform their miracles many times, for patrons and audiences everywhere, something we know Lazarus could not manage.

No wonder the Muses worked overtime, and inspiration, itself inexplicable, was often offered as an explanation. As cognitively empty as the concept has always been, there was this much to it: when inspiration struck, the vain slow-witted poet of commonplaces left his body like someone removing a soiled shirt, and the spirit of a higher power took his place. Pete the poet didn't do it, any more than Paul the prophet had the vocal cords to speak for God, but simply lip-synched the deity's messages, which had been conveniently prerecorded for this purpose.

Yeats writes amazing poems on behalf of a personal mythology; Blake also roars at the wind like a hound at the moon; dozens and dozens of other poets, ditto; Wagner rises to unheard-of—or rather heard—heights despite a character that would not be chosen by a jackal; Mozart often played the fool; Marlowe was a murderer; some artists are bigots, some are thieves, far too many were Tories. Out of the mouths of sewers fine wine flows; out of bitter British laureates, truths sneak like thieves. What is to be made of all this? What are the contents of these revelations?

Are we really to suppose that Dante was right about the afterworld? Is that why his Comedy is so compelling? Or that he was just such a fine chap he should have been canonized by the Church as well as the academy? And his genius pours out of him like wine from a bottle he couldn't stopper? Ah . . . it's because it is a handsome tale of revenge and redemption. Well, an act of revenge it surely is. No one ever got even as unfairly or as often as Dante.

Gertrude Stein (not one of the slow wits) said: "Let me recite you what history teaches. History teaches." And painters paint, musicians compose, and writers put one word next to another, as we all do when we write, so what is the difference? But Shakespeare had profound thoughts, deep feelings, a proud incorruptible pen . . . didn't he? We wish we knew. What we do know is that his words, led by their music, rich in range and reference, a remarkable image in every line, expressed ideas with the force of a fist, evoked passions more profound than the abyss (not the pits which are easily provoked but as shallow as a saucer), and, to consider that proud pen's problems . . . well, it probably made humiliating accommodations to stagecraft, actors, donors, and the political weather.

What works of art testify to is the presence in this world of consciousness, consciousness of many extraordinary kinds. Not that of the artists themselves, for theirs are often much the same as any other person's. They are merely partaking of the evolutionary miracle found most obviously in man, but not necessarily any more useful to his survival than a raven's, or a cat's, or a chimp's is to its. It is not the writer's awareness I am speaking of but the awareness he or she makes. For that is what fine writing does: it creates a unique verbal consciousness. And how it happens, and what value it has, has been a persistent question in my little essayistic exercises.

Emerson's essays build the mind that thinks them. It is that mind that is the miracle that interests me. Did he think the thinker who then thinks his thoughts? "The eye is the first circle; the horizon which it forms is the second; and throughout nature this primary figure is repeated without end. It is the highest emblem in the cipher of the world." I don't believe he began by having "the eye is the first circle" arrive in his own inward office like a parishioner with a problem, and that, subsequently, he copied this thought down exactly the way it appeared when it knocked, and as he would have been required to had the words come from Allah or from God. He wrote them down so he could think their thought. And when he thought, "the eye is the first circle," I'll bet he didn't know what the second circle was. But writing notions down means building them up; it means to set forth on a word, only to turn back, erasing and replacing, choosing and refusing alternatives, listening to the language, and watching the idea take shape like solidifying fog.

"Dream," he writes . . . "Dream delivers us to dream, and there is no end to illusion. Life is a train of moods like a string of beads, and, as we pass through them, they prove to be many-colored lenses which paint the world their own hue, and each shows only what lies in its focus." Apparently life is a train made of metaphors: life is just a bowl of cherries, life is rosy as a cheek, life is alum, stinging nettles, a bog, a lawn, a log on which we may sit in good company while we converse beneath another, not yet fallen, tree. I feel fulfilled and ripe today, rich with juice, but yesterday I was as sour as a grape. In essays like "Circles" and "Experience," Emerson takes the measure of our moodiness, our vagaries, in different sentences, other images, changing speeds. It is not the idea, but an awareness of it that he catches. "What I write, whilst I write it, seems the most natural thing in the world; but yesterday I saw a dreary vacuity in this direction in which now I see so much; and a month hence, I doubt not, I shall wonder who he was that wrote so many continuous pages. Alas for this infirm faith, this will not strenuous, this vast ebb of a vast flow! I am God in nature; I am a weed by the wall."

Thoughts are assembled, worried like a cat with its mouse, armed against enemies, refined and refashioned, slid forth into the world like a christened ship. Perceptions, feelings, energies, and images are parts of the same verbal enterprise that creates, for instance, a poem. "For it is not metres, but a metre-making argument, that makes a poem—a thought so passionate and alive, that, like the spirit of a plant or an animal, it has an architecture of its own, and adorns nature with a new thing."

To adorn nature with a new thing: that is the miracle that matters. Most prose flows into an ocean of undifferentiated words. To objectify through language a created consciousness, provide it with the treasured particularity we hope for for each human being—that is the cherished aim of the art.

What does make a sentence or a line of verse rise from the dead and walk again, run for a record, and even dance as dancers do when blessed? It is important for the reader to respond to these miracles with belief when they occur, because two or three inspired lines can turn a sonnet into a masterpiece, or make what might have been a rather slight little song into an arresting aria. It is equally crucial for the critic to be aware of those who merely mimic greatness through grandeur's empty gestures, and not be taken in by inarticulate simplicity's pretense to profundity, or answer to the trumpets that announce the coming of deep feeling as they might the queen. In addition, the critic should remain suspicious of imaginative sweeps more suitable to a broom, or a rhetoric that's about to ride long-haired but bareback through the streets.

Matthew Arnold called genuine poetic moments "touchstones," since it seemed to him they were exemplary instances of inspiration, and Paul Valéry, who liked to think artistry was an arm of intellect, confessed that some lines, images, or phrases appeared suddenly, inexplicably, from who knew what embarrassingly irrational depths, and between these glistening peaks were the dull unambitious gullies that the skills of the poet had to fill with intelligence and technique, as you might try to level a road. In short, between these rare and wonderful gifts from the gods, a chain gang's labor.

Though the three greatest masters of English prose—Thomas Hobbes, Jeremy Taylor, and Sir Thomas Browne—came to their loose syntax and noble music by way of Latin, they were capable of some resounding Anglo-Saxon when those notes were needed, and it is among their sentences that the miracles I have been speaking of can be most frequently found. Emerson may have had passages from

Browne's *Urn Burial* in mind when he wrote "Circles"—especially the one by Sir Thomas that begins:

> Circles and right lines limit and close all bodies, and the mortal right-lined circle must conclude and shut up all. There is no antidote against the opium of time, which temporally considereth all things; our fathers find their graves in our short memories, and sadly tell us how we may be buried in our survivors. Grave-stones tell truth scarce forty years. Generations pass while some trees stand, and old families last not three oaks.

I can repeat these clauses with the same appreciation I have for the greatest poetry: "our fathers find their graves in our short memories"; "grave stones tell truth scarce forty years", "old families last not three oaks."

But the sons and daughters of such sentences—Virginia Woolf, for instance, Henry James—aspire always to, and often realize, such heights. From their eminence they urge even us, with our lesser talents, to make the climb, because, though we must halt at a ledge halfway, the view of the valley below is still sublime.

SLICES OF LIFE IN A LIBRARY

I live in a library.

When I was a youngster, eager to leave the nest although flightless as a dodo, I would imagine a magical new life for myself in New Zealand. Since I knew nothing about New Zealand except that it was at both ends of the earth and had rules against bringing bad habits into the country, my Zealand could be dreamed as I chose, made safe from all family connections and therefore without resident illness or anger, its days sweet, its nights serene. There, trees bore books instead of fruit, and one drank sodas tapped from gourds whose juices had been blessed by the native gods. I would sail there as a deckhand on a ship whose description came from Joseph Conrad and whose course was plotted by Robert Louis Stevenson. Getting away was cheaper by the book than by the ticket, and when you went by book you were always home in time for dinner.

Then, during the Second World War, I actually sailed the ocean blue. The sea was all that had been written of it. It was never blue; it was moody; there was a lot of it; and it was, every ship's bell, more beautiful than the bells before. On calm days its surface was the skin of a sleeping creature. I would wash my skivvies by tying them to the end of a rope and letting the ship pull them through the water as though I was fishing for a bigger catch, perhaps a dress suit. There they gathered salt while being thoroughly scoured, so that wearing them was no longer advisable. I decided to go without underwear, something I managed for a brief time, till a tell-all told all to my superiors, of whom there were many. Several years later, packed away in drawers at home, my skivvies still smelled of salt.

I was a passively disobedient officer, often confined to my quarters, where I read whatever readable books were aboard. This lot consisted of a handful of Hemingway and a pinch of Faulkner. Otherwise I played chess with another miscreant, who was never confined to quarters but was always there anyhow. Because of my exemplary incompetence I was promoted (such is the navy way) to top-secret officer. I was therefore entrusted with the combination to the ship's walk-in safe, where books of codes and ciphers, printed on dissolvable paper and weighted with lead, dwelt in silent isolation except for the company they kept with the ship's medicinal booze. To this secure space, the size of a bedroom at the Red Roof Inn, I regularly repaired, closed its heavy armored door, nipped a bit of brandy, and read the same Hemingway and Faulkner I had already repeatedly enjoyed, but with my ease uninterrupted and my attention undistracted—a lot like my dreamy New Zealand—until some tell-all told all to my superiors, of whom there were many. They immediately removed the brandy. I could still lock myself in and read or snooze. My superiors seemed content to miss me.

While in graduate school at Cornell, I spent hours in the university library, as PhD drudges are required to do. I had a carrel—a small nick in the wall of the stacks that held a mean metal chair and a bulb, a sheet of steel to write or rest a book on, a rack in front of my face for volumes taken from the shelves (but on one's honor not to be removed from the building), and a jar of hard candy whose contents were dangerous when wet. To take notes, pencils-only was a rule I was willing to observe, since, unlike those of the navy, it made sense. The building resembled a ship in some ways and bore me off smoothly. Not only were the stacks made of metal, the floor was of steel mesh that let an already worn out light sink toward a basement as distant as a bilge. Steps naturally rang a little unless you were in sneakers, but there were areas so removed from human interest (nutrition, for instance . . . it was a different era) that the only sounds you were likely to hear were those of the watchmen, who were apparently heavy men in boots. Nevertheless, sitting there day after day in dusky light, Eden's image began to change. It had no location on a map, but was a destination determined by the Dewey decimal system.

When I wasn't reading or falling asleep over a page of Lovejoy's *The Great Chain of Being,* I roamed. Up and down the metal steps. Up and down the metal aisles. I stalked like a hunter through a dim light deemed beneficial for any volume's long interment, but barely feasible if you desired to read one, my fingers sometimes slipping along the edges of the books as a kid passing a fence might run a stick, my gaze on spines and their titles, a gaze full of wonderment that there were so many, as dead to me as those rows and rows of skulls in the catacombs were unless I removed one from their ranks, and opened it, and read the way Hamlet examined the skull of Yorick: Jean Henri Fabre's *Book of Insects* or *The Worst Journey in the World* by Apsley Cherry-Garrard. Who could resist an author whose name was Apsley Cherry-Garrard? I would check out the Henri Fabre for a son of my thesis director, Professor Max Black, since I had been asked to find worthwhile but entertaining texts for one of his boys. Unfortunately, the young man loved my selections and Professor Black prolonged my service. The Apsley Cherry-Garrard too, was a hit. Therein was one of the most harrowing accounts of Antarctic adventure ever penned, pages of cold and snow, pain and uncertainty, plus a stubborn unintended heroism that I would try to remember when I wrote *The Pedersen Kid,* a novella set in a snowdrift. Since I was a philosophy student I tried to make into a paradox the fact that *The Worst Journey* was really the best trip I'd ever taken.

The heavy-footed guys guarding the darkness didn't like readers to stay the night. You could nod over John Locke all afternoon, they wouldn't mind, but come ten o'clock they'd begin to sweep us out.

Slices of Life in a Library

First they came scouting to see who was in their carrels. They would mark you by your light. Since our little nooks were as open as a supermarket, if they didn't see you sitting there, they would turn off your lamp. Hiding at the right time by making yourself thin at the end of an aisle or fleeing to another level like an amused draft, we would wait to return only after closing.

Dodging the gestapo's heavy tread became a game, but our abilities (and I was certainly not alone in this practice) were put to serious use each year when the library had its book sale. I knew succession, secession, recession, possession, concession, depression, and now I was to enjoy deaccession. A room on one of the lower levels would be set aside and furnished with several large library tables. Upon them rows of books, spines up, would be packed. The humanities filled more tabletops than the sciences did, which was not a surprise, because the scientists didn't read; they tested. And reported their results in magazines that cost more than books. Rumors accused persons unknown of hiding overnight in the stacks in order to be first in line when the sale began the next morning. But that was not the worst these sneaks would sink to. They would actually take the books they wanted from one table (literature, philosophy, history) and hide them among economics or statistics, and one person I know was accused of taking volumes entirely away to another part of the building for the night, only bringing them back as if freshly chosen the following morning. Some tell-all told all once again.

The competition was fierce and friendship had no standing. Every book belonged to each of us, and often there were juicy prizes to be taken, since our teachers sometimes had the decency to die and their heirs, in ignorance or indifference, to dump the bulky part of the inheritance in the bins of the library. But these books would never reach the shelves. They'd be denied admittance ("we already have this edition of *The Maid of Orleans*"). A writer once said about editors that out of refusal comes redemption, in this case because the sale books would not have been disfigured by the library's boastful black footprint (PROPERTY OF THE CORNELL UNIVERSITY LIBRAR-

IES), or pricked by the university's embossed seal, or pasted with a withdrawal and return record, or embarrassed by a tattoo inked on their spines as if they were headed for the boxcars. We busy buyers said we were rescuing the books that we were eagerly pulling out of the pack from who knew what calamitous destiny. Not death. That was nothing. The bleakest fate was to be always available but never molested.

I have been to many library sales since, and can vouch for the fact that these duplicates are rarely examined, or their source respected, for out of them have fallen, as out of book-fair books, treasures that sometimes surpass even their pages: not just the debris readers normally leave behind to keep their place—paper clips, kitchen matches, rubber bands, foil, curls of hair, bookmarks, bills, sucker sticks, lists, letters of love, post cards, postage stamps, gum wrappers—but photographs and threatening notices, greenbacks, checks, and a draft of a telegram to be sent to the Allied High Commissioner asking him to expedite the transport of Werner Heisenberg out of Germany, which fluttered to my floor when I riffled one of Arthur Holly Compton's books after purchasing it for fifty cents at a Washington University purge.

Collectors who do not care for books but only for their rarity prefer them in an unopened, pure, and virginal condition, but such volumes have had no life, and now even that one chance has been taken from them, so that, imprisoned by stifling plastic, priced to flatter the vanity of the parvenu who has made its purchase, it sits out of the light in a glass-enclosed humidor like wine too old to open, too expensive to enjoy.

Whereas Mister Tatters has his economic failure marked on his flyleaf, as a character in Dickens might, by virtue of the quality, wear, and soilage of his hat, cane, and coat. He has an enriched history: sold new in 1932 for $3.95, as used from the Gotham Book Mart in 1947 for two bucks, and marked down successively in pencil and then in crayon from seventy-five to fifty, from thirty-five cents to a quarter during the decades since—owned by at least two who signed their names, one who added an address in Joliet—until it completed its journey to St. Louis, where it is picked from a barrow or a box at a garage sale or out of a bin in a Goodwill the way I found my copy of George Santayana's *The Sense of Beauty* in 1982. It survived its adventures as admirably as Odysseus. I am rather free with my books and will let anyone who wants to kiss *The Sense of Beauty*'s cover in hopes for a bit of good luck in life, kiss its cover.

This is how I learned to live in the library, what routes to take to the bathrooms, what provisions to smuggle in by briefcase, how to cushion a hard seat, the skill to size up swiftly what is on the reshelver's trolley or to find the books they put back out of place like a dime gone missing at the beach, how to mourn the loss of the card catalog, where it is easiest to read, where it is safe to sleep.

It would be a decade before I would encounter my first great library. By "great library" I mean a library whose holdings are so huge that no one quite knows what is in its basements; a library in which Vivaldi scores may lie hidden for a hundred years; a library of density as well as scope; a library that will turn no book away—trash or treasure—for a good library is miserly, proud of its relics as a church, permitting even a cheap novel to be useful to the study of the culture it came from; an institution, consequently, that won't allow ephemera to ephemerate and is not ashamed of having the finest collection of bodice rippers in existence; a library that has sat safely in the same place and watched like a sage its contents age, consequently a library whose dust is the rust of time; a library that never closes on cold days and will allow the homeless to rest in its reading room; a library that will permit me to poke about in its innards as long and as often as I like; and finally a library that makes generous awards, and then lets me win one.

The University of Illinois library is such an institution and I spent a joyous year in it rescuing valuable first editions from the open stacks, and, tempted to slip away with them by personal greed and literary love but prevented by honesty's cultural concerns and a love of literature, bringing them to the attention of the rare-book people whom I knew would condemn them to purdah. But could a copy of *Tender Buttons* in the so-called Plain Edition be placed in public jeopardy? I knew Gertrude would not mind if a student puzzled over it, carrying it about in the same backpack as *Small Farm Management Practices*. But . . . was it safe even in my reverent hands because I had taken it home to exult with my wife about my prize and self-righteously complain of the staff's carelessness, only to nearly spill—my God—Gallo (it was a different era) on a corner of its flimsy cover during dinner? I decided that it was better to have a cheap copy to work from (I was writing on Gertrude Stein at the time), and so I returned *Buttons* posthaste to the rare-book room, where I suspect it hasn't been seen since.

I realize now that I began my life in the library as an enemy of the institution, having troublesome run-ins with the shushing hair-knotted sour-faced spinster at the checkout desk . . . (stereotypes are accurate more often than not, and profiling essential to the art of the novel, or where would Trollope and Thackeray and Dickens be without their caricatures, and how would Roger Tory Peterson sell his bird guides, because spotting a cowbird in my garden is like finding an Irishman in a pub? and none of the jokes about a priest, a rabbi, and an imam trying to explain the bitters in their pints to a Scot called David Hume, none of those jokes would be funny—and who would want to give up a good laugh?) . . . as I was saying . . . when I tried, as a high school kid, to take out James Joyce's *Ulysses* and was told (a) I was too young, and (b) it was anyhow a dirty book, and (c) if I persisted in trying to obtain nasty books of this kind she would inform all my superiors, of which there were many.

While I was still in college, though now also a conscript for the navy, I was asked by my literature professor to write on *Lady Chatter-ley's Lover*, and received a note from him asking that I be permitted to withdraw such work from Special Requests (a holding cell, I supposed, for seditious books), but the whey-faced lady who guarded the guilty lot refused, contending that the work in question contained descriptions of unnatural acts. This response provoked an eagerness for the project that I had not previously had, but it was no go. Acting on a hunch, I hunted up the library's copies of *Canterbury Tales,* only to find (actually to my delight) that some of the Wife of Bath's story had been razored out. I found similar damage had been done to copies of Boccaccio, Catullus, Petronius, and Aristophanes. There was no Henry Miller, but, had there been, his then scandalous texts would surely be doing jail time. I told all to her superiors, of which there were many. The whey-faced razor lady declared that it was her duty to protect the students from smut. I thought their own ignorance a sufficient safeguard. The navy moved me on to midshipman school, and I don't know what happened to this particular guardian of public morals. They always look ill but live forever.

Now in my own home I am surrounded by nearly twenty thousand books, few of them rare, many unread, none of them neglected. They are there, as libraries always are, to help when needed, and who knows what writer I shall have to write on next, what subject will become suddenly essential, or what request arrive that requires the immediate assistance of books on . . . well . . . libraries, or the language of animals, or the pronunciation of Melanesian pidgin, since my essays tend to be assigned, not simply solicited, and because I am easily seduced by new themes. I can actually say a few things in Melanesian pidgin, none of them polite.

So they are there to keep my curiosity awake and working, to inform me who the notable American writers were considered to be in 1894, when Henry C. Vedder published his book on that subject (I have just this moment pulled it at random from my shelves), and consequently to make the acquaintance of Charles Egbert Craddock and Elizabeth Stuart Phelps, but also to learn that Henry James is "too clever by half" and his theory of fiction disgraceful because he dares to suppose that "a novel is good when it is well written" and "bad if it is ill written," an opinion that suggests a deplorable indifference to the novel's moral dimension. Oh, how badly I should fare at Mr. Vedder's hands! Of course, Henry James did not, for a moment, ignore the novel's moral dimension. I try to suppress a smile at these confusions, and my indignation at this judgment, in order to enjoy John Quincy Adams's definition of luncheon (quoted by Mr. Vedder) as "a reflection on breakfast and an insult to dinner."

Before Mr. Vedder went back into the obscurities he came from, and so justly deserves, I managed to find out that the notable Egbert Craddock was a pseudonym for M. N. Murfree, and that the postbox from which his first story was mailed to the *Atlantic Monthly* was in St. Louis (as journalists do, we have gotten in our local reference). Reading on in the chapter devoted to him, I was informed that our mystery author is Mary Noailles Murfree, that she comes from "the best American stock" and was, when first seen by the *Atlantic* editors, a young slip of a thing. What her ultimate fate, and that best American stock was, you shan't know, because I own the book and you don't.

But book dipping is great fun, and not a day passes that I don't blindly pick a prize and then read a page of it to be mystified, informed, surprised, delighted, and affronted.

When you live in a library you are constantly being solicited by good-looking texts to leave your present love for their different, more novel, pleasures. New volumes are always arriving, perhaps a present from a friendly press of a fine fresh translation from its sixteenth century French of Maurice Scève's emblem sonnets, or Charles Rosen's *Piano Notes,* which you ordered over the Internet, or a roughly used collection called *Songs My Mother Never Taught Me* that you picked up at an estate sale; or a book you've had since you were young, and forgotten, takes hold of your eye and then pulls open your memory to the days it saved from sadness, and its patient silence since.

My books are there to comfort me about the world, for only the wicked can be pleased by our present state of things, while the virtuous disagree about the reasons for our plight and threaten to fall to fighting over which of us is responsible for the misery of so many millions, and in that way steadily increasing the number of hypocrites, jackals, and rogues.

Among them, writers of books. No occupation can guarantee virtue the way hard labor makes muscle, and only sainthood requires it as a part of its practice. So the writers write, perhaps improving their texts from time to time, but only rarely themselves.

But the books . . . the books disagree quietly, as the minds of the many readers in the library may, without the least disturbance; and in that peace we can observe how beautiful, how clever, how characteristic, how significant, how comically absurd the ideas are, for here in the colorful rows that make bookcases seem to dance, the world exists as the human mind has received and conceived it, but transformed into a higher realm of being, where virtue is knowledge, as the Greeks claimed, where even knowledge of the worst must be valued as highly as any other, and where events as particular as any love affair, election, or battlefield are superceded by their descriptions—by accounts like Apsley Cherry-Garrard's cold white journey across the cold white page—for these volumes are banks of knowledge, and are examples, carefully constructed, of our human kinds of consciousness, of awareness that is otherwise momentary, fragile, and often confused. Among the shelves, where the philosophers tent their troops, there is a war of words—a war of the one supportable kind—a war of thoughtfully chosen positions, perhaps with no problems solved, but no blood spilt; shelves where human triumph and its suffering are portrayed by writers who cared at least enough about their lives and this world to take a pen to paper. Thucydides knew it when he said, concerning the conflict that occurred on the Peloponnesus, in effect: this war is mine. History happens once. *Histories* happen repeatedly in reader after reader.

Every one of these books is a friend who will always say the same thing, but who will always seem to mean something new, or something old, or something borrowed, something blue. A remark that reminds me that I must go and see Queen Victoria. I've promised her a visit. She's in the stacks that stand in my basement now. In Lytton Strachey's biography. Still plump, a bit dowdy. Still queen.

SPIT IN THE MITT

Every spring, as the season drew near, my father would speak more frequently of the days when he had played minor-league baseball in the Northern League, and especially of the disgraced Black Sox and other barnstormers he had batted against, but most particularly of the pitcher Chick Hafey, a legendary figure, according to his account, as well as others named Moose and Sly and Bull. He had known some of the great ones, and he still remembered the diamonds of Fargo and Grand Forks, and how the grass so softly reflected the summer sunlight it would seem to stain a lowered palm. He could recall the higher numbers of the grandstand seats, how bats would sound and how cheering echoed from the outfield walls. He knew, he said, the specific break of the great lefties' sliders, balls so often spit upon they sank like torpedoed ships.

They were the pride of his life, those encounters, and he had a cap he could still pull down over his encircled eyes, and did pull down when we went to Indians games, even though the players Cleveland had performing for them had no aura, nor the sparkle to make him wink in wonder at their play. From under its bill he would holler at the pen: "Bagby, you bastard, you're throwing with your nose." Jim Bagby pitched for Boston and had a nose as broken as his curve. The cap stood for my father's professional past, and although others might swear from the stands, their obscenities were empty, my father claimed, while his were full of observation and advice. The subtlety of this distinction was beyond my years. On the field, when a player bobbled a ball, my father would cup his hands and shout: "Spit in your mitt, Yawkey, spit in your mitt."

Boston was, for him, the big enemy. I don't know why. I hated the Yankees. Their lineup was called the Murderers' Row because of the way they killed my team. Anyway, the Red Sox were owned by some beantowner whose name sounded like Yawkey when yelled, hence the content of that catcall. My father described himself as a yipper—a player given to constant taunts and chatter. Even when, in our backyard, he would toss a baseball high in the air in hopes I would catch it, he would murmur as I ran around under it, "Hey hey hey go get hey go hey go get . . ." It did not help my concentration.

My father also had a book of scraps from those times when he won medals in the dash, medals in the broad jump, and trophies in boxing and basketball. Old photos of him in his blouse and baggies were pasted alongside accounts of his prowess with fist and hoop which he'd clipped from local papers. These provincial rags had names like the *Larimore Pioneer,* or the *Devils' Lake News*—names I found as strange and otherworldly as Nap's name, and Chick's. He entered the pros on the brink of the Depression and would make more in a few months playing pickup or bandit ball in the Northern League than he would in two years teaching high school in Ohio.

We listened to ticker re-creations together—always the Indians, always blowing a lead. You could hear the click of the wireless sometimes as the announcer turned the tape's dry and sullen information—F8—into a long drive which Earl Averill pulled down against the wall after a mighty run. Later, I would realize that those radio matches were more interesting than games seen on TV or from a poor seat in some vast modern stadium, because they were conveyed in symbols, created in words, and served to the field of the imagination.

The cap was the cap of the St. Louis Browns, and it was my father's

repeated story that he had been a Brownie—a utility infielder, for
one catastrophic season—but with the Browns what other kinds
of seasons were there? After settling his cap and carefully leafing
through his newsprint past, my father would take his glove from a
cardboard box. It looked like something run over on the road: flat,
thin, torn, stiff, a dark disagreeable brown. "No padding, look," he'd
say. "The bums these days try to catch balls with a pillow." You could
no longer put your hand into it, the leather was so stiff and stuck
together, so brittle and torn. "A good glove was supposed to be loose
and flexible in those days so you could get your whole hand around
the ball when you caught it." He would demonstrate by making a
fist already crabbed by arthritis. "Then we'd put a little chew in our
cheek and now and then spit in the glove so the ball would stick
there like it'd fallen in a bog." That was why the glove was so stiff,
stained from his youthful saliva. "Pitchers didn't mind if the ball
came out of your mitt as damp as peed pants. Pock," he'd say. "When
you caught a tall foul. Pock."

So he'd shout, "Spit in the mitt," after every error, or to warn a
player to be ready to go and get it, or simply to suggest a little concentration was advisable. "Get in the game! Spit in the mitt!" And
he would lift the glove in the palm of his hand to show me how you
wore it when expecting a bunt, or a pop, or to scoop up a grounder.
Hot smashes were another matter—line drives. The spit in the mitt,
he claimed, cooled off the ball. "That's the way to cool one," he'd
yell after Kenny Keltner had snared a liner along the third base line.

The last clipping we came to, the last story in his set, was an
account of his play for the Browns one day. The clipping was real and
the headline amusing, but the story may have been about another
time, another team, than I was told it was. I still wish to think my
father had made the grade, a grade that lofty, even though it led to a
sickening humiliation. It seemed my father tripped over something
while chasing a foul beyond third base, where he was occasionally
stationed, and fell, wet mitt and all, swallowing his chew when he
hit the ground. He did manage, nevertheless, to get a good pock from

the ball, which he held in the air while the tobacco went down. A moment later, dizzy and green, as the newspaper gleefully reported, my father threw up on the field.

My father always told this story for my amusement, but I could see he felt a little sorry, a little sad—not because he'd fallen, or been sick, but because those good sweet years were now so far away, as are the small parks, the ardent crowds, and the grass which would shine its green shade on a player's palm.

THE FIRST FOURTH
FOLLOWING 9/11

In my boyhood, the Fourth of July was a day set aside for noise. It was, I thought, such a suitable idea that no one I knew could be thanked for it. The Fourth was for small towns as well as for small boys. Things went bang at odd moments all day, but during the late afternoon people often gathered in the local park for a pot-luck picnic. Tables were customarily covered with white paper, but the bandstand would be decked out in red and blue bunting. There the town band would play robustly sentimental and patriotic tunes, badly but with beery energy, and a politician or two might speech-ify, making sounds as meaningless as the caps that went off for no reason other than exuberance. There would be a softball game, sack races, and, on the meditative side of the picnic grounds, horseshoes carefully tossed to collar a problem as if they were weighty thoughts. Their clang always seemed calm and immensely reassuring to me, and the men who tossed them at least serious, if not wise. They offered, before and after every turn, thoughts, briefly put, on the state of crops, morals, and the nation.

The women cleaned up after the men had eaten their hamburg-ers, beans, and potato salad, then sat about the tables gossiping, fanning away warmth and flies. I saw nothing the matter with any of this . . . I was busy being a boy, and I saw nothing the matter with that either. I threw cherry bombs into the pond where there had been ducks that morning. Too excited to eat sensibly, I rushed from one activity to another, a large red firecracker in my left fist, as real as if it had been drawn by Norman Rockwell, a glorious burst that I was saving for the day's end, which I knew would otherwise be marked by girls waving sparklers and shrieking with glee as they ran to make tracers within the darker environment of the trees.

Sports, food, speeches, music, noise: each a gift of the day that marked our independence, the day that was supposed to repuff our pride and reaffirm our loyalties. My father was an athlete but he had duties beyond the field of play. He was a veteran of the First World War and a member of the American Legion, so on the morning of the Fourth he would dress himself in puttees, a Sam Browne belt, and a shiny tin helmet, then oil the valves on his cornet, which would have stuck since last fingered, and make a few soft-mouthed toots to hear whether his lips were still strong enough to do it. The Legion's small band would turn out for deaths and patriotic anniversaries, either to sound taps or tire out a few Sousa tunes. Then, as the sun set, it would conclude its part in the ceremonies by marching briskly behind the strains of "It's a Grand Old Flag" till both band and flag left the park and were out of sight.

I was in awe of my father's uniform, especially the shiny tin hat I was allowed to fondle, as much as I was of the photographs that showed him in his professional baseball stripes. They were memories for him, symbols for me, full of mystery, for he had been in a world I never knew and fought his war in advance of mine—an improbability that became reasonable only when I pushed my way out of my own past, fleeing my memories as if I had already been in battle a few times before I got decked out as an ensign by Saks Fifth Avenue and wore my one and only tailor-mades on leave, hoping to appear a person of accomplishment.

The Fourth was more military and more masculine than Memorial Day. Memorial Day was for moms and old men, but on the Fourth we rattled our ceremonial sabers and shot off our toy guns and proclaimed our might and main, resolving to resolve. I eventually learned that such festivities rarely meant a great deal. The holiday was as much about our nation's independence as Christmas was about Christ. On such occasions we were to spend money and have a good time.

The first Fourth following Pearl Harbor I remember as too serious to be noisy. The Japanese had attacked our fleet as it lay asleep on a sunny Sunday before church. By the time Independence Day arrived we were at war in the full sense, already making many sacrifices, mobilizing our forces, our resources, and suffering humiliating losses every day. I remember being as shocked when Singapore fell as I was about the destruction at Pearl Harbor. The families of the sailors who died received the thanks of a grateful nation, but these sons had been sailors, after all, not civilians, and had signed a contract that endangered them. Still, when we were drafted we were insured for $10,000 apiece—a policy that I haven't permitted to be cashed yet.

People stayed on their porches that Fourth. There were gas-rationing regulations and rubber tire conservation rules that warned folks from the roads; trains were occupied by soldiers and their freight; and no one gave a thought to planes. Kids were sent to summer camps, though, because so many moms wanted to be near their husbands while the army bases could still be visited. Miniature golf got popular again, and Manhattanites sailed 'round their island on slow boats or bicycled in packs through startled parks. You had to put a lid on fireworks along the coast, because who knew when a bomb burst might be real and the beginning of a German or a Jap attack. Of course, we held parades and waved flags. The war had broken the Depression's drought. There were quarters, not pennies, in our pockets. And more of them stayed in those pockets, because there was less to be bought. The war forced Sears Roebuck to drop antifreeze and accordions from its catalog, along with alarm clocks, wheelbarrows, sheets and pillowcases. Books were a popular item, though soon restrictions on paper would lessen their life span. In most cities the best seller was Wendell Wilkie's *One World,* with 1,700,000 copies purchased, except in St. Louis, where *The Joy of Cooking,* by the city's own Irma Rombauer, led the list, and would eventually circle *One World*'s sales several times.

The Japanese had blown up warships at a naval base because warships were what you fought a war with and they didn't want us to have ours, but the usurping passengers who were piloting their first aircraft that other dreadful morning had symbols as their targets and were borne aloft by the names United and American toward twin towers that stood for World Trade on a day that would be written "911" in unintended irony. They may have hoped, but they could not have counted on, a photographic coverage so vivid and complete it would bring dismay to a nation and joy to their cause in almost identical moments, and maybe in matching amounts.

The more dismay was ours, the more joy was theirs, for hate has an insatiable appetite, and will eat whatever's offered it. Though thousands died, casualties were not the purpose of the attack. There were no islands to be won or lost, no towns to be taken. The World Trade Center had been wounded before; this time they killed it. And the towers fell of their own released weight, so that the head was the destroyer of the feet. No Pearl Harbor here. The target was what they believed we stood for: money—money and its power; greed— greed and what it served; arrogance—the arrogance of the rich.

The terrorists, as we decided to call them, did not smile wryly at the money of the wealthy men who funded them, or at the scams, the lies, the treacheries, the drug sales and robberies that were committed to support their cause. Nor did they examine their own ills, except to blame us for them. They are, and were, the least independent of all men. In exchange for our burning towers, they sent us images of boys throwing rocks and men firing guns at God. They became the bombs that blew up at their festivals. Such shells burst into the only stars their celebrations make: bloody wall spatter and street stain.

Now we have guards at every significant gathering. They peer suspiciously in purses, in bags, at packages that are usually recent purchases, the soles of shoes, at IDs where the poorest possible pictures of ourselves tell them—these strangers—of our harmless hearts, our benevolent selves. At this huge joke no one is allowed to laugh. What bridge, dam, public building, bank, arena, school; what plane, bus, purification plant, or power station will be picked on next? Yet terrorists did not set the West on fire. We did. In St. Louis, where I live, thousands gathered at the arch to listen to Western tunes or rock schlock in the early evening, and subsequently to ooh and ahh at the fireworks, as they have done in the past, though this year there were plastic fences in a vulgar orange everywhere, police busy being noticeable, park rangers searching sacks, National Guardsmen who would have looked natty in their camouflage suits had we been able to see them, and, as a consequence of this protection, far fewer people.

In the weeks after 9/11, the homes that line my street were strewn with flags. They hung from attic windows; they rose up on poles stuck in yards; they fluttered like wash from improvised lines. On this Fourth three small grave-size flags were posted in flower boxes near my house. At the last minute, two more were hung down the block. But decals, once prominent on cars, are soiled; banners that flew from antennae have been shredded to indistinctness, bumper stickers have worn out their welcome. It's only a small sample, I know, but it strikes me that the spirit of the Fourth, this year, was used up by September's end and fell like an early leaf.

Instead of fresh defeats, which weekly headed our news after Pearl Harbor, and which refueled our anger and renewed our resolution, other types of towers have fallen, not cities in Asia or islands off Alaska, but those that many corporate entities and financial markets form, with consequences of a different kind: thousands whose jobs have been lost or are now in doubt, savings looted, pensions dissolved, smug and greedy members of small-town gambling clubs who have been left holding their handbags while businesses built of money-lust collapsed from moral decay, as nearby, steeples standing for God's good family enterprises sagged from similar fears: tarnish of reputations, drops in contributions, huge losses in civil suits. The terrorists could not have dreamed of luck like the luck they've had, because, though it sometimes seems so, 9/11 was not the cause of our present consternations, our tepid patriotism, our anxieties about the future, our massive mistrust of our leaders, or the weakening of our faith in mammon, the god, as our money ought to say, in whom we bank and trust.

The symbol our enemies chose was an appropriate one, and our failure to own up, even now, to what we often fly our flags for—how we are likely to seek justice mainly through litigation, or how our generosity and concerns tend to exhibit themselves by the size of our monetary contributions—is our defenseless underbelly, our possibly incurable weakness, because the fireworks and the crowds are made of money, too; the funnel cake vendors will complain when our custom declines; we shall celebrate as much in shops as at potlucks; our spirits will rise with the markets; we shall win this war without losses, endangering mostly drones; and crab-voiced codgers like me can sweeten the sour taste in our mouths by eating patriotically packaged cookies, available in sacks from machines, born and baked, they say, in the USA, to be offered to the palate in the shape of Uncle Sam himself, or his hat, or Lady Liberty, or the letters USA, and even the Grand Old Flag itself, though I notice, as the cookie commences its crumble, that the flag boasts but nine stars . . . well . . . now six. I wonder which states they stood for.

WHAT FREEDOM OF EXPRESSION MEANS, ESPECIALLY IN TIMES LIKE THESE

Winnie, the housewife of Samuel Beckett's play *Happy Days,* appears, as the curtain rises and her day begins, to be buried nearly to her armpits in earth, in the monotonous routines of her English life. Winnie may be partly immobilized, but she still has her comforts: her parasol, for instance, which she can open against the glare of an incessant light, and her shopping bag, from which she can still remove her possessions: a toothbrush and a tube of paste, cosmetic mirror, small revolver, handkerchief, pair of specs. And, of course, she can still speak, still pray. "Begin, Winnie," she says. "Begin your day."

When the curtain rises again for the second act, Winnie is imbedded (Beckett's suggestive word) like a post in the ground to the precincts of her chin, so that she cannot move her head either from side to side or up and down, but can only wiggle her lips, wrinkle her nose, blink her lids, swivel her eyes; while in place of her parasol a hat sits on her head, and her bag lies out of her reach, out of her sight, and comfortless. "Hail, holy light," she says, undeterred.

Suppose we were to take Beckett's symbolism a stage further. Imagine yourself to be without a body and thus incapable of any effect. Imagine yourself aware of the world without any part of yourself active in it, so that you saw without eyes, felt surfaces, heard sounds, identified scents, tasted sweets, without the use or need of a single sense; that you thought and felt and longed and hoped and loved and feared without a skin to sweat or pore to prickle, brow to crease or sex to tingle. You were a consciousness in a capsule, your dreams and desires like boats in a bottle, your ideas stuck where they were issued like collected stamps. Winnie has a smile that goes on and off as if it were a switch on a wall, but your laugh has no lips and shows no teeth and pleases no ear. As an image, you have everything, but in being denied a body, you have been denied expression. You are a lost life, a ghost who can never affright, or groan, or beg of a son that he remember you; you are a movie without a screen, a sound track which provides rails for silence to run on.

There are so many types of tyranny. There is the tyranny of your own routines—your own habits—that rise around you like the sides of your grave. There is the castle where we keep the girl with the golden hair. Beauty set in stone becomes only a diamond. There are the cries of the crows and other customs of society. There are the demands of decorum. There is ideology lying over us like a smog that stings any eye that dares to stay open.

Swaddle the woman like a baby then; squeeze her feet; bury her in confining conventions like Winnie is buried whenever she takes the stage. Pound her into her housewife life like a post into the ground.

The tyrant ties tongues in knots. Speech is so easy it takes more than snow to slow its course. The tyrant must frighten people from their freedom; beat the soles of their feet till they mince their step in time to his goose-wide stride. Stagger after me; the best is yet to be. The tyrant can make men line up as though they were made of tin or lead to tip over for this week's war, because pain is a great big persuader, and their lead-headed patriotism is petty and made of hatred; because, after all, though a war may topple their obedient rows, the tyrant can, in any case, melt them down, these tin-lead men, mold them anew, and paint their britches pretty. He can encourage kids to tattle on their folks; he can set friend against friend, family against family; for the fear of punishment and the promise of reward do for men what they do for the donkey. Be fruitful, multiply, the tyrant says benignly. I must have a larger army.

What is always offered us? The truth like a stuffed bird. But even if the real word were given, given in all honesty, given with good intention, given as tradition claims it gives everything, with absolute accuracy and serene assurance, it will not be our word until it is allowed freely to live in us and freely to issue from our mouths, even poorly pronounced, inadequately stated, open to the risk . . . the terrible risk . . . of misstep, misstatement, of error . . . or . . . horror! . . . change of mind. Because we have the right to be wrong. We have the right to be mistaken. We have the right to travel the long low potholed road instead of the high. We have the right to dawdle when called, to dance instead of march, to make vulgar sounds and embarrass society, embarrass ourselves.

Our tyrants always feel in need of excuses. Our enemies are always spying, undermining, arming, plotting, seizing the high ground, inventing new horrors, inventing flashier weapons. This mole, or that rat, is smarter than we ever imagined, and it is working day and night against us—cunning and conniving—out of sight, in secret—because beneath deep undergarments it holds a gun, a knife, a bomb, or a book full of dreadful ideas.

We must monitor our phones, watch our neighbors—note, film, record, trace, follow, measure every movement, scrutinize every public meeting, overhear every private one, rifle records, ponder every purchase, search through garbage, twist dumb tongues till they scream with the pain of prying pliers.

Tyrannies do not come in ones or twos; tyrannies come in battalions: there is Mother's heart you mustn't break or Father's hopes you dare not dash; there are the reprisals taken by society because you sniffed when you should have sneezed; there are all those looks delivered like blows from someone sitting on his high horse and wielding his scorn like a whip. It does not matter what the party motto is, what flag flies, what history pretends to teach, what rewards will be yours, what hurt feelings will follow; we need to be free to choose our own errors, our own myths, to furnish our souls as we see fit.

Of course, what we believe is important, but that we believe it freely, that we can speak of it openly, that we fear neither disapproval nor contradiction, is essential to the humanness of our being. This freedom—if it is to be freedom and not another fraud—comes at a cost. It is a cost that those who have rarely been free are often reluctant to pay, because they are as unused to the presence of liberty in others as they are of freedom when granted to themselves.

We can be real only when others are allowed to play their radios. It's odd, but our liberty lies in the liberty of our neighbors. They will be rude; they will cross the street against the light; they will eat offal; they will entertain tyrants at tea; they will be tasteless; they will be other; they will be . . . That's it . . . they will be. They will speak strangely, dress oddly, live quaintly, worship a deity they found in a dime store. Worse: they won't like Bach or Henry James. Worse: they will live like gnats in annoying clouds. Worse: for us they will have no particular esteem. Worst: they will want us to be nice to them, share our rights, give them room. Worse than worst: they will deny us our desires if they can; they will blame us for their plights; they will give evidence, everywhere, of the same mean-spirited insecurities that have soiled our souls from our birth.

When we deny to others their interior life, we deny ourselves all knowledge of it. We are unaware of what, unhindered, they would choose to do, how they presently feel, the strength of their resolve, what may in consequence ensue. The naive, the innocent and open, may allow us to read their minds and hear their hearts as though they were television news, and this may merely amuse us for a moment or endanger them for life; but at least they turned the tube on, they chose their own exposure, they told us what sort they were.

Freedom of expression is, like that of speech, a freedom to conceal, to dupe, to put on an act; it is also the freedom to be a jerk; yet I should prefer that the bigots who now pretend to be my buddies, because they don't want to lose their jobs or get sued, were rude to my face, and crude as a crowd, because then I should know who they really were, and what creeps were crawling up the columns of the courthouse to take from me my bill of rights.

It is a tough life, living free, but it is a life that lets life be. It is choice and the cost of choosing: to live where I am able, to dress as I please, to pick my spouse and collect my own companions, to take pride and pleasure in my opinions and pursuits, to wear my rue with a difference, to enjoy my own bad taste and the smoke of my cooking fires, to tell you where to go while inspecting the ticket you have, in turn, sent me. I shall make my Hail Marys, my happy hallelujahs, my bows and scrapes, to whom I wish and when I want; I shall wear my cap and gown with an arrogant swagger or with deceptive modesty; I shall practice foolishness day and night until I get it right.

And if we are free to express ourselves, we are bound to give offense: a joke, a gesture, a point of view, a choice of words, a jeer. Some tyrannies are made of toes. And if you move you'll step on twenty. Yet who is really hurt by boorish behavior but the boor? No, the tyranny of the one, the few, the many: each must be opposed, as must be resisted all brutal, all subtle, all soft, all comfortable, all easy and agreeable suppressions of the self. There are both murderers and mufflers among them.

Nothing is older than this issue. No one has spoken more vigorously in the defense of free expression than the nonconformist John Milton. "The whole freedom of man consists either in spiritual or civil liberty," he wrote. The free commonwealth should be most concerned to protect, above all things, our liberty of conscience, since, as a government, it ought to be the "most fearless, and confident of its own fair proceedings."

It is not the strength of convictions that must worry us, but their weakness: the doubts, the fears, the insufficiencies inside them, that make us take up the sword on their sad behalf, to shut all mouths not shouting for our side, to try to cow the slightest opposition and send it quietly to pasture. When one is confident of the truth, slurs are simply shaken off, remonstrance is calmly observed and duly noted, while one awaits the counterargument that cannot come— because the truth, before the contest began, was already a winner.

I don't have to like what you stand for, but I must stand for it all the same; and stand up for it, too, even if someone were to try to take away what I can't stand about you without your leave, since we both ought to be resolved not to stand for that. We should not permit any tyranny over consciousness; we should not allow any move to squelch the soul's sense of itself. Such suppression is in no one's interest, for if I silence the sound of your heart, I shall surely sour the sound of mine.

RETROSPECTION

"Don't look back," Satchel Paige is supposed to have said; "someone may be gaining on you." Don't look back, Orpheus was advised; you may find your earlier poems better than the ones you will write tomorrow. Lot's wife looked back at Sodom and was so shaken by the sight of the Red Sea swallowing the city she became salt. Look back only if the mess you have made of your life leaves you eager to reach a future that will offer a fairer prospect. Otherwise cover your eyes before blame blinds them the way Oedipus's pin put out his. However, Paul Valéry warns us that no one "can deliberately walk away from any object without casting a backward glance to make sure he is walking away from it."

For anyone who has reached eighty-seven years, as I have, only the past is likely to have much duration; greed and regret will have eaten the present, which is at best a sliver of cake too small for its plate, while the future fears it may cease before having been. I hear it running to get here, its labored breathing like an old man—eighty-seven—on the stairs. Lust and rage, Yeats rightly said, attend one's old age.

So it is in a spirit of disobedience that I look back at what I may have done rather than toward all that remains to be encountered, coped with, perhaps yet accomplished. I say, "may have done" because what one has really done is never clear and certainly never comforting. Rarely does one say, "I may have married her but only time will tell."

Your station in the literary world, whatever that might be, does not matter much if you've spent your life chasing words with Nabokov's net. That's still where the results of your life went, into the killing jar, sentenced to a verbal smother, pinned in place, a display that's initially a cause of mild indifference, and then evermore ignored.

Looking back I find it less painful to concentrate on the *kind* of thing that concerned me, rather than on the messes I made or on the few fragile triumphs I may have enjoyed. Looking back I find I fit the epitaph Howard Nemerov once wrote for himself in *Gnomes and Occasions* (1973).

> Of the Great World he knew not much,
> But his Muse let little in language escape her.
> Friends sigh and say of him, poor wretch,
> He was a good writer, on paper.

It turns out that these preoccupations, these bad habits, these quirks number at least seven, though I am sure I am ignoring the ones that really matter. They are: naming, metaphoring, jingling, preaching, theorizing, celebrating, translating.

First: naming.

Critics still write of me as if my interest in words was an aberration. Yet Adam's task has always seemed to me to be, for a writer, the central one: to name, and in that way to know. It wasn't true for Adam, for whom all names were fresher than the daisy, but it is true for us now: a name no longer merely points something out and distinguishes it in that manner from the rest of the world; every name stands for all that has been thought, felt, said, perceived, and imagined about its referent, and represents all that has been discovered during explorations of its indigenous concepts during two thousand years. And since we humans have the deplorable yet entrancing habit of naming things that do not exist, the realm of names is larger than the realm of things as much as the population of China exceeds that of New York State. This passage about naming trees comes from my first novel, *Omensetter's Luck* (New York: New American Library, 1966), and concerns my unfortunate character Henry Pimber, who will end up hanging himself from one of the branches of the trees he sings about.

The path took Henry Pimber past the slag across the meadow creek where his only hornbeam hardened slowly in the southern shadow of the ridge and the trees of the separating wood began in rows as the lean road in his dream began, narrowing to nothing in the blank horizon, for train rails narrow behind anybody's journey; and he named them as he passed them: elm, oak, hazel, larch and chestnut tree, as though he might have been the fallen Adam passing them and calling out their soft familiar names, as though familiar names might make some friends for him by being spoken to the unfamiliar and unfriendly world which he was told had been his paradise. In God's name, when was that? When had that been? For he had hated every day he'd lived. Ash, birch, maple. Every day he thought would last forever, and the night forever, and the dawn drag eternally another long and empty day to light forever; yet they sped away, the day, the night clicked past as he walked by the creek by the hornbeam tree, the elders, sorrels, cedars and the fir; for as he named them, sounding their soft names in his lonely skull, the fire of fall was on them, and he named the days he'd lost. It was still sorrowful to die. Eternity, for them, had ended. And he would fall, when it came his time, like an unseen leaf, the bud that was the glory of his birth forgot before remembered. He named the aspen, beech, and willow, and he said aloud the locust when he saw it leafless like a battlefield. In God's name, when was that? When had that been?

I have never been able to break the denominating habit. In a relatively recent piece, "Emma Enters a Sentence of Elizabeth Bishop's," I managed to cram the names of 110 weeds into one paragraph.

Writing has almost always been difficult for me, something I had to do to remain sane, yet never satisfying in any ordinary sense, certainly never exhilarating, and never an activity that might satisfy Socrates' admonition to find a *Logos* for my life, as I felt it surely had for the authors I admired: even Malcolm Lowry's dissolutely drunken sprees; even Hart Crane's beatings at the hands of sailors, beatings he sought out as he ultimately sought the sea; even Céline's meanness, a bitterness that ate through his heart before it got to his shoes and ate them too; even these malcontents, though nothing justified their wasted ways, their anger, their multiplication of pain, might be, by their works, somewhat saved, their sins hidden under sublime blots of printers' ink.

Number two: whoring and metaphoring.

One aspect of writing was easy, was unstoppable, and that was the flow of imagery that ran through my head like a creek in flood— no—like the babble of voices around a bar at happy hour—no—like a stream of ants toward a source of sugar—oh, no—like carp rise to a dimple of bread—oh, no—oh, no—a cloud of gnats—a giggle when tickled. An attack of bats. I could swat away six and still write eight. It was a curse disguised as a blessing. I was always looking at the world from another word. The wolf spider roams at night from field to field in search of prey, while the mantis sits still as a twig by a flower's sweetened cup until some sucker comes to nose it, and then she, the madam mantis, sups. But these facts interested me mainly because I knew people like that. I was one—a waiter—the sort of waiter who is always looking the other way. So I wanted, when I named a tree, to invoke a plant equal to every phase the plant had seen. I didn't simply want to make a tree with roots, bark, branches, trunk, twigs, nesting birds, needles, and leaves; I wanted to imagine ones that were telly poles too, bore lynch limbs, and had branches to which possums were driven by packs of unpleasant dogs; I wanted trees with doors in them, clothes trees where dress suits were hung; trees that had family histories dangling from their diagrams.

I am not observant of persons, so if I imagine someone whose skin is as smooth and pale as a grocery mushroom, it is the mushroom that did it. Among the thousands of my photographs there may be three (the fairy-tale number) that misinclude people, and even then they look like barely promising piles of rags. Recently, in an essay on François Rabelais, I wrote that while his work looked woolly, its sense was consistent, unified, pure yet iridescent, as though silk had swallowed water. That last image was a simple pun on watered silk that let me gloat a quarter of an hour before its time on the meter was up.

I am an octogenarian now and should know better, but I recently let a sentence reach print so embarrassingly bad its metaphors seemed frightened into scattered flight like quail. I meant to shame myself by reciting it to you, but I find I cannot, sparing myself, not you. Instead I'll quote something that's perhaps passable, from a story called "Order of Insects" in the collection *In the Heart of the Heart of the Country* (New York: Harper & Row, 1968). For this piece I did indeed study cockroaches, and came to admire them immensely (few humans measure up: haven't the humility, the wiles, the longevity or body armor, the moves), but it was as a metaphor made into a symbol that I wanted to use them. A housewife, who narrates the story, has begun finding dead roaches on her downstairs carpet in the morning, apparently killed by her murderously playful cat. As she inspects them she finds a beauty in their construction that imperils her opinion of her own life. She wonders what would happen if we wore our skeletons on the outside, like a costume for Halloween, and concludes this way:

> I suspect that if we were as familiar with our bones as with our skin, we'd never bury dead but shrine them in their rooms, arranged as we might like to find them on a visit; and our enemies, if we could steal their bodies from the battle sites, would be museumed as they died, the steel still eloquent in their sides, their metal hats askew, the protective toes of their shoes unworn, and friend and enemy would be so wondrously historical that in a hundred years we'd find the jaws still hung for

the same speech and all the parts we spent our life with tilted as they always were—rib cage, collar, skull—still repetitious, still defiant, angel light, still worthy of memorial and affection. After all, what does it mean to say that when our cat has bitten through the shell and put confusion in the pulp, the life goes out of them? Alas, for us, I want to cry, our bones are secret, showing last, so we must love what perishes: the muscles and the waters and the fats.

Number three: jingling.

When you are a cowed and confused kid you say to the stupid question grown-ups always ask with such condescension that you want to bruise their shins: I hope to be a fireman when I grow up. But of course you really want to be a poet. Everyone wants to be a poet. It is the beckoning inaccessible peak. How many poets have told us? At twelve I wrote awful Edgar Allan Poe, much as Poe had—jingle all the way; at fourteen I was as interminable as Walt Whitman; I extolled the groceries and made lists of buffalo hunters and Indian scouts. I did patriotism, I'm ashamed to say, and praised mothers. My God, I was even against drink. Most of all, what I wrote was bad. Not just youthful. Not just undisciplined. Bad beyond excuse. After years of futile wondering, I think I now know why. My irreverence, my hatred for authority, my distrust of tradition, my enjoyment of the comforts of middle-class life and my contempt for its philistine values, my habitual "up yours" and "in your eye" attitude, also inhibited my ability to absorb conventional poetic forms. Instead I was attracted to the urchins among them, indecorous lines and unruly stanzas. Ezra Pound, an early hero, too melodious and poetical by half much of the time, would nevertheless burst out, to my delight, with, "Damn it all! all this our South stinks peace," a sestina in praise of bloodshed and war, while at other times condemn such belligerence, as he does in *Hugh Selwyn Mauberley*'s unforgiving anger at the First World War:

> There died a myriad,
> And of the best, among them,

> For an old bitch gone in the teeth,
> For a botched civilization. . . .

Or when, in the same poem, he wrote that "his true Penelope was
Flaubert," I was immediately moved, because Flaubert has always
been my favorite hater, and I was grateful to Pound too, though
absurdly, because he was the first poet I knew to use the word *fuck-
ing* in a poem. Even if they were panthers that were up to it.

I despised pop tunes, yet I imbibed their forms. When Gertrude
Stein wrote: "I am Rose, my eyes are blue, I am Rose and who are
you? I am Rose, and when I sing, I am Rose like anything," I was
perhaps more pleased than was reasonable. I practiced the limerick
in secret and dallied with other cheapjack devices. My career as a
poet ended in doggerel and japery. Yet I found a use to which I might
put them—these dogs. For my novel *The Tunnel* (New York: Knopf,
1995), I invented a historian named Culp, whose subject, I meanly
said, was the American Indian, and I claimed that he was energeti-
cally engaged in writing a limerickal history of the world, as well
as a cycle of such rhymes that shared the same first line: "I once
went to bed with a nun." I got good at it—at the limerick, I mean—
and began to do to it what I couldn't do to the sonnet—torture its
type.

Here are three from the Carthaginian period.

> Over the Alps on an elephant
> went Hannibal out of his element,
> for the elephant's motion
> was so like the ocean,
> he continually punic'd
> upon his best tunics,
> and his slaves had to wash off the elephant.

Earlier:

> Dido wrote to Aeneas,
> Why don't you sail by and see us,

Retrospection

I'm here all alone
with my lust and no phone,
half dead of desire,
my crotch quite on fire,
which I've heard you'd put out with your penis.

Later yet:

Dido said to Aeneas,
Surely you're not going to leave us?
you wouldn't flee home
just to found Rome,
which will fall anyway,
so you might as well stay
to enjoy all my sweet panaceas.

Some nuns:

I once went to bed with a nun
by pointing a pistol at one;
said she, with a quaver,
that's a good big persuader,
but what is the point of the gun?

Lastly, my favorite:

A nun went to bed with the pope,
who tied her four limbs with a rope.
It's not that, my dear,
you have something to fear,
but I want you quite still
so nothing will spill
when your holiness is filled by the pope.

The compulsive doggerel syndrome does not confine itself to dirty verses, otherwise it would not be called "compulsive," but turns up in almost every line of my prose, in sound patterns that get pushy, even

43

domineering. The narrator of *The Tunnel,* when a child, is caught by his father stealing pennies to play the punchboards so popular in the Depression era, and this is what happens as judgment is made:

Low, dry, slowly formed, the pronouncement came, my father's voice full of pause and consideration, like maybe a judge's, with a kind of penal finality even in midsentence, midphrase, and unlike the rather pell-mell stridency of his customary dress-me-downs and more commonplace curse-outs, those scornful accounts of my character which always included disclaimers of responsibility for my failures, for my laziness (not a whiff in his family), my shiftiness (in contrast to the stand-up nature of the relatives around me), my myth-making, my downright lying (whose cause could not be anywhere discerned), my obstinacy too, and my prolonged stretches of pout, sulk, and preoccupied silence which I seemed to take an inordinate joy in inflicting upon my undeserving family, who had always done their level best

> . . . and all the rest . . .
fed me, washed me, made sure I was dressed,
repaired what I broke, cleaned what I messed
> . . . and all the rest . . .
so I could live like someone blessed,
and bow my head at God's request
> . . . and all the rest . . .
but I had fouled my own sweet nest,
and cracked the hearts in their fair chests
> . . . and all the rest . . .
so they would treat me, henceforth, as a guest
until such time as I went west
> . . . and all the rest . . .
to seek my skuzzy fortune or confessed
my crimes, with remade mind, and soul distressed

Retrospection

> . . . and all the rest . . .
> whereupon, with sins redressed,
> they might—of my presence—make the best:

charges which were rapidly related, as if memorized, and hurled headlong at my head, between my eyes, as I always thought, causing my knees to bend a bit each time as if to duck, though ritually, a shower of stones.

Back in the days when there were inner tubes—items none of you now will remember—air would bubble up in the rubber like a rhyme, just before it burst.

Number four: preaching.

I have been characterized as—accused of—sentenced to—sentences. Well, it is easier to study the sentence than the story, and you do have to write a lot of sentences if you want to pretend to write prose. But I have always been equally interested in paragraphs. I like, for light reading, texts on rhetoric: not just those of Aristotle, Cicero, and Quintilian, but also those of George Campbell, Richard Whately, Joseph Priestley, Hugh Blair, and Thomas De Quincey. In such works, and only in them, is the question of the form of the paragraph as well as the shape of the phrase addressed, and the lost art of eloquence taken seriously.

Any plowboy can become a father, Mencken famously remarked; and, "Every man, as he walks through the streets, may contrive to jot down an independent thought, a shorthand memorandum of a great truth," De Quincey says. "Standing on one leg you may accomplish this. The labour of composition begins when you have to put your separate threads of thought into a loom; to weave them into a continuous whole; to connect, to introduce them; to blow them out or expand them; to carry them to a close." Just as De Quincey carries his own paragraph to a close by carrying it to the word *close*.

So I have tended, when conceiving characters, to prefer fulminators—preachers and teachers—and allowed them to consider the misfortune, more important to me than any other, apparently: that of missing the opportunities and obligations offered you by the luck of having life. Here is one such preacher, Jethro Furber, speaking to his rural Ohio congregation in *Omensetter's Luck*.

"I ask you now to ask yourselves one simple foolish question—to say: was I born for this?—and I ask you please to face it honestly and answer yea if you can or nay if you must.

"For *this*?

"You rise in the morning, you stretch, you scratch your chest.

"For this?

"All night, while you snored, the moon burned as it burned for Jesus or for Caesar.

"You wash, you dress.

"For this?

"At breakfast there are pancakes with dollops of butter and you drip syrup on your vest.

"So it's for this.

"You lick your lips.

"Ah, then it's this.

"You slide your pants to your knees and you grunt in the jakes.

"It's for this?

"Light's leaving a star while you stare at the weeds; centipedes live in the cracks of the floor; and the sun, the Lord says, shines on good and evil equally.

"So you were meant for this? You've your eyes, your human consciousness, for this?

"Well, you're not entirely easy in your mind. The weather's been poor. There are the crops to get in, payments to make on the farm, ailing calves to tend. Friends have promised to help with the haying, but they haven't, and you've got to keep your eldest son somehow away from that bargeman's daughter—a bitch with cow's teats.

"The mind's for this?

"Wipe yourself now. Hang your pants from your shoulders. There are glaciers growing. But you wish your wife weren't so fat and given to malice, and your thoughts are angry and troubled by this.

"This?

"Very well—you can complain that I've chosen trivialities in order to embarrass you.

"Eat, sleep, love, dress—of course you were born for something better than this."

I carry this refrain on into *The Tunnel,* a novel finished thirty years later, where it turns out that men were made by their alleged creator to murder one another, and to invent the bulldozer in order to dig mass graves.

Along with hundreds of others, I was once asked by a French newspaper to state, in a word, why I wrote. I replied in a sentence suitable for a courtroom. I write to indict mankind. I suppose I could have said: I write to convict mankind, but man has already done that without my help, and, besides, I wanted the use of the pun.

So—on to number five: evidence for a theory. This is my account, the bald facts taken from Holocaust documents, of the death pit at Dubno, and my narrator of *The Tunnel*'s characteristic double-edged use of it.

We read, and therefore see before us a great mound of earth which bulldozers have gouged from the ground. . . . In front of the mound: a mile of naked strangers. In groups of twenty, like smokes, they are directed to the other side by a man with a truncheon and a whip. It will not help to ink in his face. Several men with barrows collect clothes. There are young women still with attractive breasts. There are family groups, many small children crying quietly, tears oozing from their eyes like sweat. In whispers people comfort one another. Soon, they say. Soon. No one wails and no one begs. Arms mingle with other arms like fallen limbs, lie like shawls across bony shoulders. A loose gray calm descends. It will be soon . . . soon. A grandmother coos at the infant she cuddles, her gray hair hiding all but the feet. The baby giggles when it's chucked. A father speaks earnestly to his son and points at the heavens where surely there is an explanation; it is doubtless their true destination. The color of the sky cannot be colored in. So the son is lied to right up to the last. Father does not cup his boy's wet cheeks in his hands and say, You shall die, my son, and never be remembered. The little salamander you were frightened of at first, and grew to love and buried in the garden, the long walk to school your legs learned, what shape our daily life, our short love, gave you, the meaning of your noisy harmless games, every small sensation that went to make your eager and persistent gazing will be gone; not simply the butterflies you fancied, or the bodies you yearned to see uncovered—look, there they are: the inner thighs, the nipples, pubes—or what we all might have finally gained from the toys you treasured, the dreams you peopled, but especially your scarcely budded eyes, and that rich and gentle quality of consciousness which I hoped one day would have been uniquely yours like the most subtle of flavors—the skin, the juice, the sweet pulp of a fine fruit—well, son, your possibilities, as unrealized as the erections of your penis—in a moment—soon—will be ground out like a burnt wet butt beneath a callous boot and disappear in the dirt. Only our numbers will be remembered—not that you or I died, but that there were so many of us. And that we were

. . .—orderly, quiet, dignified, brave. On the other side of the mound, where two young women and the grandmother are going now, the dead have placed themselves in neat rows across an acre-square grave. The next victims clamber awkwardly to the top of the pile where they'll be shot by a young man with a submachine gun and a cigarette. Some of the dead have not yet died. They tremble their heads and elevate their arms, and their pardons are begged as they're stepped on; however, the wounded worry only that the earth will cover their open eyes; they want to be shot again; but the bullets bring down only those above them, and for a few the weight is eventually so great it crushes their chests . . .

Sometimes a foot slips on the blood-wet bodies, and a fat woman slides face forward down the stack when she is hit. Climbing up, there are quiet words to the wounded, and an occasional caress. From the gunman's end, of course, the mound looks like a field full of false hair. Millions die eventually, in all ways. Millions. What songs, what paintings, poems, arts of playing, were also buried with them, and in what number? who knows what inventions, notions, new discoveries, were interred, burned, drowned? what pleasures for us all bled to death on the ice of a Finnish lake? what fine loaves both baked and eaten, acres of cake; what rich emotions we might later share; how many hours of love were lost, like sand down a glass, through even the tiniest shrapnel puncture?

Of course one must count the loss of a lot of mean and silly carking too. Thousands of thieves, murderers, shylocks, con men, homos, hoboes, wastrels, peevish clerks, loan sharks, drunkards, hopheads, Don Juans, pipsqueaks, debtors, premature ejaculators, epileptics, fibbers, fanatics, friggers, bullies, cripples, fancy ladies, got their just deserts, and were hacked apart or poisoned, driven mad or raped and even sabered, or simply stood in a field and starved like wheat without water; and we shall never know how many callow effusions we were spared by a cut throat; how many slanderous tongues were severed; what sentimental love songs were choked off as though in mid-note by the rope; the number of the statues of Jesus, Mary, or the pope, whose making was prevented by an opportune blindness or the breaking of the right bones; what canvases depicting mill wheels in moonlight, cattle at dawn, children and dogs, lay unexecuted on their easels because of the gas, talent thrown out as if it were the random pissing of paint into a bedpan; so that, over all, and on sober balance, there could have been a decided gain; yet there is always the troublesome, the cowardly, midnight thought that a Milton might have been rendered mute and inglorious by an errant bullet through the womb; that some infant, who, as a precocious young man, might conceive a Sistine ceiling for the world, and humble us all with his genius, as he made us proud of our common humanity . . . well, there is always the fear that this not-yet youth has been halved like a peach; that Vermeer, Calderón, or Baudelaire, Frege or Fourier . . . could conceivably, oh yes, just might possibly . . . have . . . been . . . gently carried to his death between a pair of gray-haired arms, which, otherwise, were no longer even strong enough to disturb a clear soup.

I wrote *The Tunnel* out of the conviction that no race or nation is better than any other, and that no nation or race is worse; that the evil men do every day far outweighs the good—the goods being great art and profound knowledge scientifically obtained.

The poet who has been my unwitting companion in this enterprise, Rainer Maria Rilke, similarly wondered, as his own career grew to a close, whether mankind had justified its reign of terror with some offsetting achievements. He thought about the grandeur of cathedrals. But, really, was it enough? I quote from my translation of the Seventh Elegy:

> Wasn't it miraculous? O marvel, Angel, that we *did* it,
> we, O great one, extol our achievements,
> my breath is too short for such praise.
> Because, after all, we haven't failed to make use
> of our sphere—*ours*—these generous spaces.
> (How frightfully vast they must be,
> not to have overflowed with our feelings
> even after these thousands of years.)
> But one tower was great, wasn't it? O Angel, it was—
> even compared to you? Chartres was great—

and music rose even higher, flew far beyond us.
Even a woman in love, alone at night by her window . . .
didn't she reach your knee?

That *but*—"but one tower was great, wasn't it?"—that plaintive,
despairing *but*—as if anything played or painted or built or composed or inscribed—or a little love, honest for a change, and felt
by another—could weigh as much as a sigh in the balance against
Dubno's pit and its high pile of corpses, or any massacre, even if it is
that of fish in a poisoned lake.

I have taught philosophy, in one or other of its many modes, for
fifty years—Plato my honey in every one of them—yet many of those
years had to pass before I began to realize that evil actually *was*
ignorance—ignorance chosen and cultivated—as he and Socrates
had so passionately taught; that most beliefs were bunkum, and that
the removal of bad belief was as important to a mind as a cancer's
excision was to the body it imperiled. To have a head full of nonsense
is far worse than having a nose full of flu, and when I see the joggers
at their numbing runs I wonder if they ever exercise their heads or
understand what the diet of their mind does to their consciousness,
their character, to the body they pray to, the salvation they seek.

Yet I had to admit, wondrous as he often was, that D. H. Lawrence was a fascist chowderhead, Eliot an antisemitic snob, Yeats
fatuous, Blake mad, Frost a pious fake, Rilke—yes, even he—wrong
more often than not, and that even Henry James . . . well . . . might
have made a misstep once alighting from a carriage. But—there it
was again, that *but*, that *yet*—yet Henry was great, surely, if anyone
was. How did the artist escape the presumably crippling effects of
his intellectual idiocies? Here I had activity number five to help me.
It was theorizing. Not about truth. About error. Skepticism was my
rod, my staff, my exercise, and from fixes, my escape.

What is critical to the artist is not the fact that he has many
motives (let us hope so), or that their presence should never
be felt in his canvases, or found in the narrative nature of his

novels, or heard amid the tumult of his dissonances. In the first place, our other aims won't lend their assistance without reward, and they will want, as we say, a piece of the action. No; the question is which of our intentions will be allowed to rule and regulate and direct the others: that is what is critical. It is a matter of the politics of desire, or, as Plato put it when he asked this question of the moral agent: what faculty of the soul is in control of the will?

I believe [I use this word here with the greatest irony] . . . I believe that the artist's fundamental loyalty must be to form, and his energy employed in the activity of making. Every other diddly desire can find expression; every crackpot idea or local obsession, every bias and graciousness and mark of malice, may have an hour; but it must never be allowed to carry the day. If, of course, one wants to be a publicist for something; if you believe you are a philosopher first and Nietzsche second; if you think the gift of prophesy has been given you; then, by all means, write your bad poems, your insufferable fictions, enjoy the fame that easy ideas often offer, ride the flatulent winds of change, fly like the latest fad to the nearest dead tree; but do not try to count the seasons of your oblivion. (*Finding a Form*, 1996)

Life may be a grim and grisly business, but the poet's task and challenge remains unchanged. Rilke wrote:

> Tell us, poet, what do you do?
> —I praise.
> But the dreadful, the monstrous, and their ways,
> how do you stand them, suffer it all?
> —I praise.
> But anonymous, featureless days,
> how, poet, can you ask them to call?
> —I praise.
> What chance have you, in so many forms,

under each mask, to speak a true phrase?
—I praise.
And that the calm as well as the crazed
know you like star and storm?
—because I praise.
[*"Oh sage, Dichter, was du tust?"*]

Celebrating is the sixth preoccupation then. Because to write well about anything, and it might be mayhem, is to love at least the language that you are attaching to it, and therefore to give it glory. This result can be disconcerting, and there are readers, writers, critics, who feel that such attention as the artist often gives to the awful is itself awful. Even those anonymous, featureless days should be left where they lie, like idle waste, idly discarded—unphrased.

I am sometimes accused of retreating into language, of being a good writer—on paper. It is certainly where I often send my characters—villains or whores, most of them—into a world of words. Is there happiness, fulfillment, to be had from the canvas, the stone, in the score, on the page? Nope, I wrote:

> So even if you hope to find some lasting security inside language, and believe that your powers are at their peak there, if nowhere else, despair and disappointment will dog you still; for neither you nor your weaknesses, nor the world and its villains, will have been vanquished just because now it is in syllables and sentences where they hide; since, oddly enough, while you can confront and denounce a colleague or a spouse, run from an angry dog, or jump bail and flee your country, you can't argue with an image; in as much as a badly made sentence is a judgment pronounced upon its perpetrator, and even one poor paragraph indelibly stains the soul. The unpleasant consequence of every such botch is that your life, as you register your writing, looks back at you as from a dirty mirror, and there you perceive a record of ineptitude, compromise, and failure. (*Finding a Form*)

Translating (number seven) allowed me to get close to poetry in a way my own feeble efforts would never permit, and—yes—when I had finished a poem of Rilke's I would sometimes imagine I had written it, and that his sounds were mine (as, in English, they had to be), that he was once more alive in me, in all of us who could hear him—say him—be him. I concluded my book *Reading Rilke* (1999) with this paragraph and one poem, as I shall conclude this reading and these remarks.

The poem is thus a paradox. It is made of air. It vanishes as the things it speaks about vanish. It is made of music, like us, "the most fleeting of all" yet it is also made of meaning that's as immortal as immortal gets on our mortal earth; because the poem will return, will begin again, as spring returns: it can be said again, sung again, is our only answered prayer; the poem can be carried about more easily than a purse, and I don't have to wait, when I want it, for a violinist to get in key, it can come immediately to mind—to my mind because it is my poem as much as it is yours—because, like a song, it can be sung in many places at once—and danced as well, because the poem becomes a condition of the body, it enlivens our bones, and they dance the orange, they dance the Hardy, the Hopkins, the Valéry, the Yeats; because the poem is a state of the soul, too (the soul we once had), and these states change as all else does, and these states mingle and conflict and grow weak or strong, and even if these verbalized moments of consciousness suggest things which are unjust or untrue when mistaken for statements, when rightly written they are real; they themselves *are* as absolutely as we achieve the Real in this unrealized life—*are*—are with a vengeance; because, oddly enough, though what has been celebrated is over, and one's own life, the life of the celebrant, may be over, the celebration is not over. The celebration goes on.

Retrospection

The Death of the Poet

He lay. His pillow-propped face could only stare
with pale refusal at the quiet coverlet,
now that the world and all his knowledge of it,
stripped from his senses to leave them bear,
had fallen back to an indifferent year.

Those who had seen him living could not know
how completely one he was with all that flowed;
for these: these deep valleys, each meadowed place,
these streaming waters *were* his face.

Oh, his face embraced this vast expanse,
which seeks him still and woos him yet;
now his last mask squeamishly dying there,
tender and open, has no more resistance,
than a fruit's flesh spoiling in the air.

Old Favorites and Fresh Enemies

A WREATH FOR THE GRAVE OF GERTRUDE STEIN

A small boat crowded to the gunwales with journalists met the docking of Gertrude Stein's steamship in New York. Her name ran like an illuminated rabbit around Times Square. Her picture appeared above columns of newspaper copy that made a place for both quotes and those feeble but funny imitations of her style. *The Autobiography of Alice B. Toklas* had been a big hit, and pieces of it had come out in *The Atlantic Monthly*. Now her caricature was flaunted in *Vogue*. There was money in nearly every mail. *Three Lives* had been reborn in the Modern Library. Strangers smiled when they met her figure on the street, moving like a stately teepee, and nodded to Miss Toklas too. College students were charming; lecture halls were full; attentions were paid. She was called Gertrude because Americans were chummy, then Gertie because GIs were chummier. And Gertrude flew, for the first time, over mountains, deserts, lakes, plains, seeing American history through the scope of its geography. Reaching, like Balboa, the Pacific, Stein went west, as she said, in her head, as we each did, obedient to our destiny, though San Francisco, where her father had investments in a cable car company, felt as strange as foreign money. She liked to sample regional food and be fed by the rich, although in Iowa she asked for Vichy water and got tap.

Let me quote: "Then we arrived in Saint Louis. We ate very well there. I was interested in Saint Louis, and it was enormous the houses and the gardens and every way everything looked, everything looked enormous in Saint Louis. They asked us what we would like to do and I said I would like to see all the places Winston Churchill had mentioned in The Crisis." (This Winston Churchill's ten novels sold about five hundred thousand copies each. The British press reviewed him as if their Winston, not ours, had written them. The two Churchills met once but did not get on.) To continue: "They were very nice about it only it was difficult to do because naturally they should have but they really did not know a lot about what Winston Churchill mentioned in The Crisis. . . . we found the Mississippi River . . . and some of the homes and then we gave it up and went on to see something that they could find . . . the house of Ulysses Grant."

Gertrude Stein had begun—she liked to begin things in February—as a pampered baby girl whom her father described as "a little schnatterer . . . She talks all day long and so plainly. She's such a round little pudding, toddles around the whole day and repeats everything that is said or done." At least she hadn't been a boy. "What is the point," she said, "of being born a boy when you're only going to grow up to be a man." She grew herself into a homely girl, a homely Jewish girl, a queer homely Jewish girl, in time a queer homely Jewish woman, and finally into a bizarre avant-garde gay Jewish woman writer known in Paris, her hometown abroad, as the Mother Goose of Montparnasse.

She was homely, but also disinclined, so she got out from under men. "Menace" was made of men with an ace up their sleeve. Her father finally died and she was freed of her family. "Then our life without a father began," she said, "a very pleasant one." Her overbearing brother Leo took her under his smotherly wing until Alice Toklas, who could cook, came along, whereupon her bossy brother left for Florence with Cézanne's apples and a lot of lovely drawings.

So when, nearly sixty, she shook the hand of her fame in New

York, she knew she had arrived. The identity she had worked on for so long was complete: she was Gertrude Stein; she had a wife; she drove a motorcar; she had a fortune invested in Picasso and company; she had her own course of life and could tell Ernest Hemingway where to get off. Yet all the applause, the circulating lights, those nervous hosts and earnest meals, made her uneasy. "I write for myself and strangers," she had once said, but now there were too many strangers who cried hi! who knew what she wore and the waddle of her walk, but didn't know what Vichy water was. "I am I," she wrote with some disgust, "because my little dog knows me." Well, the nose was enough for the mastiff of Ulysses. Yet the self she had struggled so long and hard to define could be pictured on an ID: her passport and her driver's license proved she was she, the way our credit card does now, the dog tag our corpse, as our social security number certifies us, or our mother's maiden name. She had become—for she knew her philosophy—the sum of her adjectives, like an apple being peeled by Bishop Berkeley, and she could be duplicated by anyone who claimed to have the same set of properties the way a spy assumes another's identity.

Suddenly she was no longer certain who had written her books, for the Gertrude Stein on their spine was but a bit of history, a tabloid tidbit; her snows of yesteryear would be carted away in dump trucks; dust would close her eyes as well as it had Helen's; and brightness would fall from the air to run down drains. Had this overweight gay girl written *The Making of Americans?* Was *Tender Buttons* Jewish? *Three Lives* a stop on a Baltimore bus? How could such a local lady fall under the spell of Henry James or Sophocles—genders, nations, ages, worlds away? In an essay she called "What Are Masterpieces and Why Are There So Few of Them?" she addressed the problem. Why would her work, which had circulated only when friends gave away their copies, manage to endure, when the novels of St. Louis's Winston Churchill, whose sales were in millions, would scarcely survive two decades?

Because they had been written, not by Human Nature and all the causes and conditions of our Identities, but by the Human Mind. "I am not I any longer when I see" was a better way to put it. To understand is to step into eternity. All flesh is grass, Isaiah wrote, where pigeons light occasionally, but the spirit is immensely and immeasurably present in every word of a masterpiece, which is why we—when we read—are spirits too, and recognize our kin. Human nature was incapable of objectivity, she decided. It is viciously anthropocentric, whereas the human mind leaves all personal interest behind. It sees things as entities, not as identities. . . . The human mind makes lifetimes out of moments, particulars into generalities, quirks into characters. The human mind can entice human nature into Elysium; though it can do nothing with the quaint, for, as Stein said, quaint ain't . . . yet we are all witness to that transformation, when the human mind sips the tea and tastes the biscuit, to turn the simple offer: have some? into a summation; for we've seen how a paltry pun, a phrase, those perceptions personal to style, how the right writing can drag daily life in its drudgery and exhilaration, with its restless elevators, its solemn ceremonies, from one present tense to another and another and another—for today my little dog did deign to know me, and though I was not a warrior returning in rags, I *was* a warrior returning in rags; a saucer enabled my cup to warm my fingers, and I felt an old friend on the lip of a story, for Gertrude Stein, as so often, was right: every rhyme in Mother Goose is still well with us, and so, for that matter, is the Mother Goose of Montparnasse.

READING PROUST

Was it in the summer? It probably was . . . when you thought you had enough time on your hands to fill them with a book, when an unappointed space had appeared in your life . . . the summer when you decided to read Proust. Perhaps the impossible purpose appeared to you in late afternoon, at an hour customarily assigned to tea and to fingering volumes by Henry James. You would have had to have been—hear the toll of those terrible tenses?—you would have had to have been young. Or recently retired. Ambitious. Or convalescent. Feeling the need, sensing the opportunity, to improve yourself.

When André Gide first looked into *Swann's Way* (1913), it must have seemed a stack of sheets like any other, so his mind would not have been filled with the kind of foreboding that faces the climber of a mountain while still in the foothills looking up at his goal, a blanched peak whose slopes are already dotted with many a failed ambition. Gide's encounter with the name "Proust" would not be like any of ours. He would remember the frivolous social snob, while we would be ready to regard that same person as bearing a title, perhaps like others so often in the literary news—Joyce and Kafka and Mann—so that if we didn't positively love what of Proust we finally read we would never let on, for some small sins are more shameful to the soul than many a public crime.

Yet that's the way we should have got into it—unaware—when it first came out—into *Swann's Way*—because during every decade after, in addition to the rambling work itself, books of commentary and criticism would begin to surround it like a barricade, adding to one's trepidations. Not to mention idle conversations about the great work's length, its difficulties, and laughable place in summertime's hammock—attitudes that built its popular reputation. Am I ready? Am I worthy? Couldn't I settle for Colette or even Sagan, each equally French?

This hunt, this search, this reclamation of the past, is not like one for mislaid keys, or tickets, or even a lost weekend, since such searches end willy-nilly when Sunday comes, the curtain falls, or the locksmith is called. It aims at the recovery of a life, an entire society even—not in ruins like an ancient city hitherto hidden by sand—but one realized in its interiors as well as its trappings—fully fledged, freshly painted—something impossible in every sense of *can't*—especially since it is only a fictive aim: to bring everything that life has touched from the shady side where it snoozes—and depending upon the tree's endurance and solidity—to realize the beauty and the bounty of its leaves.

If it were keys, we should be in a hurry, with an office to reach, a plane to catch. Then we had better read Dumas and get a move on. But no hurry here. The book wakes up as eagerly as a teen on Sunday. What has happened to the narrative drive? It is in reverse. The significant modern novel—those of Joyce, Mann, Musil, Malcolm Lowry—drills for oil, seeks treasure in its depths—*in* is the operable preposition, not *on*. *Around* is another, for the circle has replaced the arrowed line as fiction's favorite figure. And when Proust describes the Hôtel de Guermantes as a castle medievally located in the center of Paris, he surrounds it with small shops—a shoemaker's, a tailor's—and imagines a porter who keeps hens and grows flowers, then an elderly self-appointed "comtesse" who, when she drives out in her rickety carriage, flaunts on her hat a few nasturtiums stolen from the porter's garden plot, and greets the children of the metaphor with a wave and a flounce.

What is the reader to do? She might open her own store next to the tailor's, and take care, when the comtesse bears her vague smile by, to be briskly brooming the steps.

Unlike Balzac's less mediated and exterior world, Proust's society lives like snow in a paperweight, inside the novel's structural imagery. As the narrator says: "To strip our pleasures of imagination is to reduce them to their own dimensions, that is to say to nothing." (601) To Balzac, matter has a weight all its own; to Proust, matter has weight only when metaphored by mind. Musil, another great meditator, is too positivistically inclined to mix the ore with its assessor.

When we begin Henry Fielding's *Tom Jones,* how much of the story does the author expect us to keep in mind as we read along? He expects us, I think, to remember about as much of Tom Jones's history as Tom Jones does; for instance, to remember that Tom broke his leg, but not to remember all that was said by the visitors who appeared at his bedside. The text is meant to dwindle away as past times do, and if some element is supposed to be retained for future use, we can be confident that Fielding will prompt us.

How otherwise it is with Joyce, to name the guiltiest. He would have us recollect Bloom's orangeflower water hundreds of pages after its first appearance, while recognizing that the soap with which it is associated is even more important. The text is not a boat's wake, meant to subside behind us; instead it rises up like a tidal wave and pursues us as we read, ready to flood each and every succeeding page with previous meanings, and altering all that has gone before the way Henry James's predicates surprise and abash their subjects with an ultimate turn of phrase.

How can past time be found if the text in which its discovery is meant to be made is itself as forgetful as Smollett or Fielding or Scott or Trollope? Nor must a text that is the result of dauntless revisions be read as the skater skates, at the sharp edge of blade and the blunt of ice. Proust's novel remembers more fully than any memory might; moreover it remembers in words redolent with sensation and rich with reflection. What has taken place in this novel, what has been rendered into such a verbal vision, it now remains for us to seek and realize and serve. That **M**, the hidden Marcel, whose world I read of there, also stands for me. So much less was once required.

The ultimate narcissist loves to be called "king" and see his stools saved in silver boxes.

When the world is remembered in writing, it alters almost utterly in its density, in its absence of detail. "It, my body," **M** says about waking, subsiding, waking up again, "would recall from each room in succession what the bed was like, where the doors were, how daylight came in at the windows, whether there was a passage outside, what I had had in my mind when I went to sleep, and had found there when I awoke." And the Master makes certain that the reader has **M**'s sense of fullness, as if nothing has been or will be overlooked. ". . . and my body . . . brought back before my eyes the glimmering flame of the night-light in its bowl of Bohemian glass, shaped like an urn and hung by chains from the ceiling . . ." Yet it is only the suggestion of completeness that is given, not its reality, for those chains are darkening their brass with dust, the blue in the flame is rhythmically retreating before the orange, and in the chimneypiece of Siena marble that **M** mentions, there is a noticeable nick that I just put there—in short, no description possesses as much "this and that" as a camera might catch in the flicker of a finger, not to omit the states of mind that furnish a room from time to time with longing, appreciation, and panic.

Things and creatures in the real world buzz and blossom by the billions and we know to beware of their brevity, because decay and death are as continuous as being born or burgeoning. Reading Proust we are constantly sadly, guiltily, reminded of the paucity of our own recollections: life went on around us and we missed it; we might have pondered our place but we did not; we might have discerned connections, for they were there in Jamesian numbers, yet we failed to follow; we might have indulged an obsession, but we were too distracted by the trivial; we might have retained a fond touch, a glimmer of insight, a bit of wit; we might have; we might . . . have . . .

If the distance between what happens and what we have understood about it is dismaying, what of the difference our memory makes on the third day thence, the fifth week after, the seventh year just passed? A habitual victim of his body, Proust knew how great the chasm between the mind and body was. Outside Monsieur Teste's and Paul Valéry's theater of the head, there was a reality indifferent to the plays put on by consciousness. We knew that world in part; it supplied our senses; it gave us occasion for concern, for delight, for desire; it gave us our place—Balbec, Paris, Combray— yet of us that world of matter in motion remained utterly unaware. Our lungs knew their air, but not our aspirations. Speaking of his grandmother's failing health, **M** says, "It is in moments of illness that we are compelled to recognize that we live not alone but chained to a creature of a different kingdom, whole worlds apart, who has no knowledge of us and by whom it is impossible to make ourselves understood: our body."

To remember, to imagine, to dream (all specialties of this house) is to depart the body for a land through which the body cannot travel. To read is to leave the library. Yet it is the body, as it stirs restlessly through the opening pages, that remembers **M**'s rooms; it is the body that prompts him; it nudges him without knowing he is there; its posture reminds him; his stiffened side reminds him, but his muscles do not feel the cramp they bear. So when we assume the position we habitually assume when we read, we ready our departure; our body must know, like a pet from the smell of our luggage, that we are off, and our eyes will see no more floor or wall or ceiling, because we, as the true Proustian performer always does, will adopt another body, that of the type-furrowed field—the conceptual page—and become its syllabic music.

The real world is full of pointless purpose, inattentiveness, confusion, pain, and perplexity, as well as the hazards of its satisfactions.

Yet in Proust's pages it is perceived, it is felt, it is contemplated, in a manner so utterly satisfying that those pains, in their depiction, become pleasures; confusions are given an order only we are permitted to understand; defeats are now worth every word of their accounts; failures victories if only in their voicing.

That is why . . . to live for a while as we ought, in a fully realized world—though its understanding will be forever incomplete and quite beyond us . . . that is why we read Proust.

NIETZSCHE: IN ILLNESS AND IN HEALTH

Perhaps it is the fate of intellectuals who incautiously trust their thoughts to a wider public that those thoughts should be abducted and abused like a child of rich parents; or, because these ideas are sometimes attractive to the intellectually ambitious, they are subjected to obfuscation and misuse: defended by their friends, but traduced, lied about, and maligned by their enemies as if theories were politicians campaigning for office. Maybe no such thinker gets picked on more than another, Walter Kaufmann politely wondered at the beginning of the third edition of his book on Friedrich Nietzsche; nevertheless he found it necessary to whack many a knuckle on the philosopher's behalf for just those depredations and incursions that any fertile but defenseless intellectual territory invites, especially when it displays, as its ideas develop, one threatening or inviting aspect after another.

The opinions of philosophers are not always greeted with yawns. Socrates was expected to execute himself, Bruno was burnt, Spinoza's life threatened, a fearful Descartes seduced to Sweden, where he froze. David Hume's name, famously demonized by Samuel Johnson, was used by pestered parents to cow their children, and his grave on Edinburgh's Calton Hill was expected to burst open at the devil's summons some dark and stormy night so that the notorious disbeliever's soul could fly to its master. For many, Nietzsche has always been a bugaboo, though some regard him as a heroic destroyer of idols, the invigorating voice of skepticism, and a revealer of those embarrassing actualities that the pieties and protestations of the bourgeois have customarily concealed. Others said that behind the bug there was no true boo. Nietzsche doubted, as Descartes did, only to restore an honest ethic to its radiant place; he embraced a genuine spirituality, and wished for a kind of—a sort of—illuminated grace. Whatever their persuasion, Nietzsche's devoted followers are like followers always are: they deplore their leader's revisions of mind and falls from faith; consequently they reinterpret or ignore his changes of heart, while what are felt to be weaknesses of character are concealed. Bertrand Russell regularly left his fellow aerialists grasping air and hoping for a net; Ludwig Wittgenstein made a huge U-turn in midcareer, thereby creating rival factions representing the Early or the Late; and Friedrich Nietzsche sometimes recolored his mind between tea and Tuesday. This is tiresome. A single unified system is required if one is to propagandize for it properly. At least there must be a final, definitive position for the mind, as though the writer were fighting a last-ditch action and was willing to die before surrendering a yard of argument. But in Nietzsche, if such a thing were to be found, it would have to be skeletal, submerged, in code, because the body of his work certainly dips up and down and turns around enough to bear a coaster full of riders who have paid mostly for the thrill. A tone of jubilant acrimony is perhaps its most consistent quality. My teachers saw no reason to speak of Nietzsche at all. In his early biography (1940) Crane Brinton suggested that, apart from his contribution to an evolutionary account of ethical ideals, he would have "a continued use among adolescents as at once a consolation and a stimulus" (*Nietzsche,* New York: Harper & Row, 1965).

Gnomic utterances, poetic outcries, hectoring jibes, oracular episodes, diatribes, and rhapsodic seizures—personality—style: these are not characteristics which are usually thought to suit the philosophical temperament, and add to them the habit of attacking the profession and then reason itself, especially on behalf of primitive urges, instinct, or animal vitality, and they shall be quickly scraped from any academician's plate as if a passing bird had despoiled the serving.

Anthologies of essays allegedly representing the most recent opinions of their elusive subject seasonally appear. There is *Nietzsche: A Collection of Critical Essays,* edited by Robert Solomon: "Our first encounter with Nietzsche typically offers us a caricature of the 'mad philosopher,' a distant yet myopic glare of fury, leaden eyebrows and drooping moustache, the posture of a Prussian soldier caught out of uniform by a French cartoonist of the 1870s"; *The New Nietzsche,* edited by David Allison (1985): "Nietzsche's biography is uninspiring, to say the least. Nonetheless, this subject appears to have been the principal source of inspiration for the tiresome array of books that has followed him"; *Why Nietzsche Now?* (1985) compiled by Daniel O'Hara in the same year, and the year I stopped collecting them: "Friedrich Nietzsche is not a serious writer" . . . but his playfulness is profound, O'Hara is careful to add; while there are explanations of these conflicting opinions in George Morgan's *What Nietzsche Means* (1941): "Can anything be good which attracts so many flies?" a judgment well put, I think (3); Arthur Danto tries to straighten the paper clip that describes the philosopher's course of thought with *Nietzsche as Philosopher* (1965), while *What Nietzsche Really Said* (2000) written by Robert Solomon and Kathleen Higgins, would keep the curves but set the record straight: "What Nietzsche really said gets lost in a maze of falsehoods, misinterpretations, and exaggerations" including, I might add on their behalf, scholarly slurs such as that of George Lichtheim in his *Europe in the Twentieth Century* (London: Weidenfeld and Nicolson, 1972): "It is not too much to say that but for Nietzsche the SS—Hitler's shock troops and the core of the whole movement—would have lacked the inspiration to carry out their programme of mass murder in Eastern Europe." It is, in fact, more than too much to say, and in a more honorable time might have provoked a duel.

David Krell, who translated the two volumes of Heidegger's *Nietzsche* (1961), and who therefore ought to know, says, at the beginning of his own slim volume, *Postponements: Women, Sensuality, and Death in Nietzsche* (1986), that "Big books are big sins, but big books about Nietzsche are a far more pernicious affair: they are breaches of good taste." Authors with axes to grind, agendas to push, or slants to slide on are as numerous as stars—at least as many as one can see most nights. Biographies such as Ivo Frenzel's brief *Friedrich Nietzsche* (1967), Alexander Nehamas's *Nietzsche: Life as Literature* (1985), Ronald Hayman's *Nietzsche: A Critical Life* (1980), or Rüdiger Safranski's *Nietzsche: A Philosophical Biography* (2001) dutifully march by, but not in this review.

Curtis Cate tells us, in the introduction to his new life of Nietzsche (2002), that he is writing it, not for the professional philosopher, but for the intelligent layman, for those who may not have read a word by this notorious blasphemer, in order to

> clear away some of the stereotypic prejudices that have, like barnacles, incrusted themselves around his name—like the naive notion that he was viscerally antireligious—and because the existential problems he boldly tackled—how can Man find spiritual and intellectual solace in an increasingly godless age? How can the desire to be free, and not least of all, a "free-thinker," be reconciled with the notion and practice of Authority needed to save society from collective anarchy; how can the egalitarian virus endemic in the very nature of Democracy be prevented from degrading what remains of "culture," and ultimately of civility. . . .

There is no concluding question mark, but these are carefully chosen flags of warning. Nietzsche has told us, and his own practice has offered evidence, that the conclusion of an argument—a belief as briefly put as a shout in the street—is almost as empty of meaning as the nearest social gesture, unless it is accompanied by the reasons that are supposed to support it, because leaving Vietnam, for instance, might have been a good idea if we believed it was an unjust war, but an equally sound recommendation if we thought we were not going to be allowed to bomb the place back into the Stone Age. *Collective anarchy* and *egalitarian virus* can be give-away phrases—if anyone wants to accept them.

Cate continues, a few pages farther on, to pose his questions.

It is easy to reproach Nietzsche for having, in his anathemas against pulpit preachers, contributed to the deluge by weakening the flood-gates of traditional morality. But the troubling question remains: what will happen to the Western world if the present drift cannot be halted, and to what sordid depths of pornographically publicized vulgarity will our shamelessly "transparent" culture, or what remains of it, continue to descend, while those who care about such matters look on in impotent dismay?

It is the mounting anger here that is interesting, although the idea that Nietzsche has flooded us with traditional morality has a certain perverse attraction: is Curtis Cate going to claim that Nietzsche is really a Republican?

In the literature about our subject, it is true that all the angles are argued, and the philosopher who preached of multiple perspectives must now suffer each passing point of view, as saints are supposed to have suffered their thorns, spears, arrows, and swords in the side. In this respect, writing a life of Nietzsche is far simpler and more straightforward than giving an account of his opinions, because, except for Nietzsche's worship of Wagner, there is little hyperbolic about the course of Nietzsche's friendships, studies, classes, travels, ailments, forest walks, or mountain hikes—well, perhaps the latter undergo some of awe's inflation—because he simply writes or he composes; because he's deep in a round of visits; he talks or teaches; he reads or rides from Naumburg to Basel in ice-cold railcars; he practices the piano; because, though he falls ill often, it is not from any height at which health may have held him; he's nervous, frail despite appearances, and easily discombobulated by bad news, by disappointment, and even if a series of precocious successes has marked his professional progress, Nietzsche nevertheless feels that an opposition to his person or his aims is everywhere active and nefarious; consequently, he is pestered by low enrollments and other academic issues, poor reviews, inadequate salary—routines of little drama and states of mind for which there is small public; and finally because what really matters to Nietzsche is what we started this list by citing—music, or better yet writing: they constitute the fiery center of his life, especially when paper is pierced by the pen . . . for in that place he may smite his enemies . . . yes, smiting his enemies is his profoundest pleasure . . . and he always sits down to do that.

Cate very capably carries us through Nietzsche's early life, although he does not dwell on the wholly feminized environment in which the boy was brought up after his father (a Protestant vicar whom Nietzsche in retrospect decided to adore) died of "softening of the brain" when his son was four. Quite a few pages later he does say that Nietzsche had chosen to study classical philology "as a kind of pis aller in order to free himself from the coils of theology, with which his devout mother and his pious aunts and uncles had sought to trap and tame his intellectual energies." Cate insists that Nietzsche's rejection of religion was a purely intellectual matter, but it is hard to imagine any of this philosopher's views not fueled by emotion, and by feelings very individually formed. Nietzsche was a lover of life but a hater of most of us who live it because we did not—do not—live it properly, fully, with appropriate abandon, with delight and with mastery, the way a dancer may leap and spin and even look askance, exulting in her total control of eyelash and limb.

Cate quotes Nietzsche's own response to his father's funeral—a memory made of tolling bells, organ music, and intoned words—but in a book distracted by data he does not dwell for a sentence's length upon the father's eleven-month illness, and the cries of pain that penetrated to the street. Soon after, Cate says, Nietzsche dreamed that a white shrouded figure rose from his father's grave, and, to tolling bells, after visiting a church, returned to the earth bearing something in its arms. "Soon after," however, was six months. Soon after this dream—namely the next day—Nietzsche's previously healthy two-year-old brother suffered seizures and died of his convulsions.

The early years of life were ones of constraint for Nietzsche, both because of the pious arms that held him and the regimen of schooling that the times and its institutions required. He found it easy to employ the effort needed to excel, so eager was he to break out into a wider world through any avenue of interest that offered itself. "It may have been a drawback," Nietzsche wrote,

> that . . . my entire development was never supervised by a masculine eye, but that curiosity, perhaps even a thirst for learning, made me acquire the most diverse educational materials in such chaotic form as to confuse a young mind barely out of the family nest, and to jeopardize the foundations for solid knowledge. Thus, this whole period from my ninth to my fifteenth year is characterized by a veritable passion for "universal knowledge," as I called it; on the other hand, childhood games were not neglected, but pursued with an almost fanatic zeal, so that, for instance, I wrote little books about most of them and submitted them to my friends. Roused by extraordinary chance in my ninth year, I passionately turned to music and even immediately began composing—if one can apply this term to the efforts of an agitated child to set down on paper simultaneous and successive tones and to sing Biblical texts to a fantastic accompaniment on the piano. Similarly, I wrote terrible poems, but with great diligence. Indeed, I even drew and painted. (quoted by Frenzel, *Friedrich Nietzsche*)

Though sectarian struggles were not absent from the wider world, Nietzsche's immediate environment was one of complaisant Christian certitude. His father, who immediately became a mythological figure, was a Protestant preacher, and the boy's family and friends would naturally have nudged him in the direction of a righteous neighborhood, and filled his mind with their beliefs and their values without, at first, feeling any need to indoctrinate, only to be as they comfortably were. Moreover, the schools they chose for him would naturally reinforce, in the normal course of instruction and discipline, the same ideals: that is to say, the principal questions had been answered. You did not live your life *in search of,* but *according to.* Nevertheless, Nietzsche's trapped intelligence found a way out to freedom through the classics: pagan texts that were supposed to teach Greek, not what Greeks thought; to make available their poetry and their theater without trying to answer Socrates' searching questions or swallowing the sweet poison of Plato. They were certainly not expected to encourage the salacious disrespect prevalent in the satyr plays or recommend Aristophanes' bawdy breaches of decorum. As for Latin, it was, of course, the language of the Church, but also that of the Roman gods; it was the tongue of Catullus as well as the halo of Aquinas. So if a profession was demanded of him when freedom was what he wanted, Nietzsche could choose the door marked "classical philology." Beyond it, the one God would become many gods, quite a few of them lustful, some drunk.

In this way Nietzsche escaped the first circle of constraint: the family. The family was at the heart of hell. But having reached the next level, this inverted Virgil found himself inside the educational system. What would it make of the mind? A tame mediocrity. There would be mentors, not mothers, now; there would be pathways to power, obstacles one hurdled by practicing the right form and accepting the right help, but the struggle at stake was of the sort in which the waistcoat could claim victory by undoing the vest. At the boarding school where the young scholar began to learn the ways of the ruler and the switch, there was one mentor who set such a bad example Nietzsche was compelled to admire him. His name was Ernst Ortlepp, a sixty-year-old translator of Shakespeare and Byron; someone who borrowed the robes of a priest, adopting a sermonizing tone without any sanction, and who testified to his fondness for Nietzsche, the prodigy sometimes in his care, by writing in his pupil's poetry notebook: "Never did I think that I would ever love again." (Quoted by Joachim Kohler in *Nietzsche & Wagner: A Lesson in Subjugation,* trans. from the German by Ronald Taylor, 1998.) Ortlepp was a figure out of Erasmus's *Praise of Folly.* He sang blasphemous tavern songs, he recited Byron, and he drank like a medieval monk, often wandering from his saloon onto the weedy side of the road, which led to his incarceration once as a public nuisance. Ortlepp improvised improper tunes on the piano to entertain his flock, composed fiery defenses of the habitually put-upon Poles, and had met, consorted with, and favorably reviewed Richard Wagner.

> It was in this figure of Ortlepp, the bibulous poet, that Nietzsche first encountered the two-faced Dionysus, god of sensual pleasure but also of the fear of death. In 1864, the year Nietzsche graduated from Schulpforta, Ortlepp fell into a ditch in a drunken stupor and broke his neck. Nietzsche described him as "a friend who sent bolts of lightning into the dark recesses of my youth." But for as long as he lived he did not breathe a word about the nature of their relationship. (Kohler)

Cate doesn't breathe a word about it either.

In academic halls, one writes for one's peers, and to satisfy their expectations—to win friends, to keep sponsors. Articles come first, small projects, research, translation—delicate nibbles at the hand that feeds. But an article is not an essay. Articles lie about the lay of their land. An article pretends to be clear about its objective and then must pretend to reach it. That objective will be minuscule though recondite. Moreover, the article does not halt at any point along the way to confess that its author is lost, or that its exposition has grown confused, or that there are attractive alternatives here and there, that its conclusions are uncertain or unimportant, that the author has lost interest; rather, the article insists on its proofs; it will hammer home even a bent nail; however, it does not end on a howl of triumph but on a note of humility, as if being right about something was a quite customary state of affairs. Polite applause will be the proper response. And a promotion.

Philosophy was the path out of philology, and Schopenhauer was a Hermes whose hand Nietzsche could hold on the way out. But philosophy was also another stage for the performance of academic follies. Competing schools demanded the loyalty of their members, blocked any advancement by their opponents, attacked one another in their journals, and attached themselves to outside interests—loyalists to this or that religious tenet, racial group, aim of state—whose attractive aspects could be used to their advantage. Of course, they were also wrong, wrong about everything; even Nietzsche's intellectual hero proved to be clay to his boot tops, and, as Cate observes, his devotees would blame the persuasive power of Schopenhauer's rhetoric for misleading them.

In the meantime, though, Nietzsche would share his enthusiasm for *The World as Will and Representation* with Richard Wagner, who lived nearby in Tribschen and who extended the young professor an invitation to visit him, an invitation Nietzsche was eager to accept, since he had already examined a few of Wagner's scores, and had been overwhelmed by the music, some of which he was able to play on the piano. Nietzsche quickly fell under the spell of the master of the house, but also under that of the great one's charming and demanding paramour, Liszt's daughter Cosima, the errant wife of the conductor von Bülow, who had brought her children to live with Wagner in Switzerland, and who took up Nietzsche with almost the same alacrity as her husband had. If the gods of the Greeks were supposed to be Apollonian, those of the *Nibelungenlied* were Dionysian from drum to trumpet, and Wagner was their realization. Nietzsche became a warm admirer and witty companion with whom Wagner could share his grand plans for German music and celebrate his numerous dislikes. In addition, Nietzsche not only composed music and then played it; he dared to do so in the presence of the master, who at first tolerated his disciple's efforts but later wearied of these vanities, for, after all, he had so many of his own.

Nietzsche's response to music, not only to the romantic masters, but to his own improvisations, was often ecstatic. He became transported, intoxicated, even visionary. Consequently, he might naturally see the same storms of feelings to be customary for the Greeks. Indeed Aristotle testifies to it, and Plato complains. Though Nietzsche is certainly aware of music's formal component—its abstract, even mathematical nature—he does not weigh it as he should. It is the primitive and, one might say, vulgar component of music, a vulgarity Wagner makes an art of, that earns it the highest accolade, and the name *Dionysian*. But to be swept away is just a prelude to the dustbin.

Having given his heart to Wagner, Nietzsche found it easy to add the new German state to his small list of beloveds, for Wagner had made the identification of himself with the new Germany easy. Both men had bemoaned the decline of its music, now in the hands of Jews like Mendelssohn, sentimentalists like Schumann, or that imitative newcomer, Brahms, as if Wagner himself were not sufficient cause for celebration. Words like *degenerate* and *purity* surfaced like corpses in the flow of their diatribes. *Cleansing* was invoked, but only its necessity. In 1870, Germany had attacked France, and patriotism was a party favor. Though Nietzsche was a pro forma citizen of Switzerland, where he taught, he could not resist the lure of the fife and drum. He was not of a temperament to remain neutral. Cate obviously enjoys expressing Nietzsche's distaste for what was seen then as the liberal (and neutral) point of view: ". . . a tepid philosophy for tepid souls devoid of any deep-rooted, personal convictions, ever ready to compromise, to swim with the prevailing current, to dilute whatever remained of their beliefs in a bouillon of tasteless 'moderation.'"

In his youth, because the acceptable strength of a soldier's glasses was enlarged to increase enlistments, Nietzsche had a brief obligatory stint as conscript in the Mounted Field Artillery; and he quickly became one of his troop's best horsemen, only to be brought down so hard upon the pommel of his saddle by an unruly mount that his sternum broke. For this second enlistment—because of his eyes, his past experience, and his present citizenship—Nietzsche was forced to join a medical unit, even though he knew nothing about tending the sick beyond the attentions he had given himself. Immediately, there was much to do. Behind the army, as it rapidly advanced, the wounded were left like dirty and divested clothing. Disease was also sweeping through the ranks. Rain fell and men fell; mud and maladies slowed the march. Nietzsche had to tend the sick and wounded in a drafty cattle car kept closed on account of the persistent rain, so that the consequences of dysentery, diphtheria, and festering wounds could be fully inhaled. Nietzsche soon came down with his patients' infections, but coming down with an illness was something he had practiced until he was nearly perfect at it. Discomfort was a companion that would never leave his side, and one he would never renounce. But the glamour of war and pride in the new German state were now only mud, stench, and sickness.

He suffered from hemorrhoids and gastric spasms for much of his life, as well as prolonged spells of insomnia, but even more debilitating were the migraine attacks that appeared after stress or in the midst of travel, especially when the carriages were cold and the iron wheels noisy. In addition, there was the effect of light upon his aching eyes, which were steadily worsening despite drawn curtains, dark glasses, and soothing compresses. Nietzsche undertook numerous consultations with doctors, who unfortunately saw solutions and prescribed remedies that defied the motto "Do no harm." Leeches were encouraged to feed on the lobes of his ears. He was often under his mother's care, and he was frequently so sick he had to summon his sister to his side, though she was not at the time nearby. Ulcers were recurrent, his nerves made him nauseous, but stress came and went, while his eyes were always on the blink. Too shortsighted to find one suitcase in a crowd of strangers, Nietzsche would lose a valuable traveling bag at a station. Drivers failed to find his hotel and dropped him in front of a tavern or a boarded shop. He would call his subsequent outrage "colic" and retire to bed . . . when he reached it. If Nietzsche tried traveling by boat, he became seasick, and again failed to locate his luggage when he landed. No wonder he would, like Tiresias—to compensate, and in self-defense—become a seer. Only Wagner could buck up Nietzsche's spirits with a bedside visit and his hearty manner.

When one is in pain, its bearer grows restless. Perhaps my hip, my catarrh, my fever will feel better in another room, downtown, in the mountains, at the beach. And Nietzsche needed woodland shade to walk in, good air, quiet circumstances, abstemious quarters in expensive resorts. Thunderstorms unnerved him. Lightning made him seek his covers. Heat was the worst, unless it was the cold. He was always seeking solace somewhere else, though travel itself seemed to bring on migraines and seizures. The seizures were unexplained but serious and frequent. Sometimes, instead of a fit, he'd faint.

"During the past year," he wrote to his sister as 1879 drew to a dreary close, "I had *118 serious* nervous-attack days. Lovely statistic!" (Cate, 296)

Diets would do the trick, Nietzsche was told, and they nearly did him in. *Mann ist was er isst,* the saying goes, but a man is also his illnesses. When he vomited blood, quinine was prescribed. He had "chronic stomach catarrh," specialists decided, so his rectum was flushed every morning with cold water. He ate nothing but small helpings of meat accompanied by Carlsbad fruit salts, and at evening a glass of wine while the leeches were drinking. This folly went on until another physician altered the menu. It was impossible for Nietzsche to read for any unbroken length of time, and equally hard for him to have an extended thought. Tramping through the woods, or hiking up hills, was supposed to be good for you, and I imagine Nietzsche's increasingly epigrammatic style appealed to the trudging mind, while his habit of hyperbole suited the mountain views. While reading him, I think we have to remember his steadily worsening physical condition, and understand how longing for a life of healthy and happy exertion might furnish his philosophical notions with their favorite imagery. His style reflected the fact that he scribbled on scraps, or dictated to friends. He wore optimism like a fur coat against the cold, and, in his search for a satisfactory communal life, grew increasingly solitary.

Although Nietzsche's first essays and meditations were written in better health and circumstances, his later ones were done in defiance of his doctors' ultimate orders to avoid reading, writing, and "every form of extreme physical and intellectual exertion." But for this patient, writing was breathing and had to be done, no matter the pain and damage.

Nietzsche's first major work, *The Birth of Tragedy* (1872), was a shrewd mix of philology, philosophy, and literary criticism. Although it would be less obviously about its author than most of the work to follow, Nietzsche begins being Nietzsche here. German intellectuals had been infatuated with Greece since the 1760s, when Johann Winckelmann published his first adorations. This strange man's idolatry was fed by the fact that he never visited Greece himself, but saw Athens only from the ruins of Rome, and it was encouraged by the profitability of his relationship with a fellow to whom history assigns the name Cavaceppi, a notorious "reconcoctor" of antique statues. The art world's subsequent romance is investigated by E.M. Butler in her definitive study *The Tyranny of Greece over Germany* (1935). What the Germans believed they adored were chalk white statues of ideally formed men and women who stood on their pedestals and pretended to be gods, each serene as a frozen lake, each perfected figure formed by a Greek master. What they also claimed to admire were the Greek philosophers and the Classical world of reason, harmony, and proportion, as reverentially depicted by the Renaissance painters: clusters of toga'd gentlemen reclining on stones or standing on white steps, conversing among pale columns in view of regimented groves, debating the nature of the right life. However, what they were actually admiring—Nietzsche included— were mostly marble Roman copies of Greek bronzes; copies, moreover, made by the imagination, since the originals had long since been smashed to bits or melted down to rescue the metal. When it was rumored that the sculptor Myron had done a discus thrower . . . lo! a discus thrower appeared.

But when Nietzsche studied the Greek tragedies (for, after all, they *were* originals, even though a great number of these plays were also missing), what he saw were satyrs and bacchantes, furious women and horny men engaged in usurpation, revenge, and adultery; and what he read in those Greek texts was of a world that included drunken revels and much frenzy, pleasure taken in prowess of every kind, pain from the malicious blows of fate, constant conflicts of interest, not lives of rational detachment but lives of passionate commitment.

It hardly mattered whether Greek tragedy had grown from the antics of a goat god or not; the categories Nietzsche used to explain its origins were going to be in Nietzsche's permanent employ, and shape his later, more developed view of life. There is, in culture itself, a persistent tendency to replace the natural world with a human one, and thus to downplay the animal in man, that part of him he shares with beets, beasts, stones, and stars. The Greek soul had been traditionally divided into three parts, two of which linked men with the plant and animal kingdoms, and these parts were regarded as lower than reason, often demeaning, sordid, and troublesome. Nietzsche cherished his own myth about animals. Because they had no memories of the past or expectations for the future, they lived fully and richly in the present, connected with all that went on in and around them, fulfilled by their instinctive functions, feeding on others, yes, but without malice and basically at peace with their own species as well as all others.

Human beings have to get drunk to recapture this basic state— that's how bad off they are—or go to soccer matches, where they can lose their minds in beer and contribute to the madness of the crowd, or, perhaps, preferably, listen to music so intensely they become the undulation of the notes, rising and falling, filling and diminishing with them, even moving their limbs to the flow like weeds at the bottom of a stream. "Consider the cattle, grazing as they pass you by; they do not know what is meant by yesterday or today, they leap about, eat, rest, digest, leap about again, and so from morn till night and from day to day, fettered to the moment and its pleasure or displeasure, and thus neither melancholy nor bored." "On the Uses and Disadvantages of History for Life," in *Untimely Meditations,* translated by R. J. Hollingdale (1983).

Yet only a small fraction of a napping cat is asleep, the antelope are on high alert as they graze, the buffalo stands still to listen, the horse lifts its head to catch a scent, the wildebeest remember to be cautious approaching the watering hole, or be scarce at evening when the lions hunt; and they become a flash of fleeing limbs when smoke is smelled, or when a white hunter has sullied the air with his odor and dragged his ass, gun, and gear through the brush for a better shot. The community swimming pool is full of snakes and crocs. Every bird worries the whereabouts of its next meal, and pecks the dirt, bark, berry bush, or buggy air for protein. Alaskan flies can bite the flanks of a moose till it runs amok. Constant grooming is required to combat ticks, mites, lice, and fleas. Parasites luxuriate in the damp warm gloom of the guts. The glorious happiness of a mindless browse in the gentle sun is never to be enjoyed by these creatures; the peaceable kingdom is a world at war, at hunting and being hunted, at alarm and incursion, at lessons learned through pain and maiming, or death is else.

Nietzsche calls the immersed life of the beast Dionysian, while the Apollonian represents the specifically human, self-conscious, and hence detached mind of man. Even our digestion is supervised and medicated as if it were a colicky baby. Apollonian self-regard separates us from the world, which becomes pure appearance. It dams our urges until they form a lake, and then releases spurts as it deems reasonable. The Dionysian values identity, the Apollonian difference. The Apollonian likes the solitude and honor of the mountaintop, where his thought can see so far and delve so deep that those depths, when seen, see him; whereas the Dionysian prefers the passions of the crowd, the openness of alcohol, the bestirring of a martial air, the camaraderie of song.

Greek tragedies, if generalizations so vast can be made, are more obviously built on the quite real conflict between tribal loyalties (the model on which feudalism is also based) and the more rational communities asked for by the city-state. If civil societies were to prosper, blood kinships had to be put aside, family ties loosened, roots uprooted, and habits of revenge relinquished. Between ties of blood and rules of law, there could be no compromise. That was the tragedy. The hero was torn apart (as Orpheus, Osiris, and Dionysius literally were) because the future could no longer contain the past, because justice had been removed from private hands, because shame stained only the slapped cheek, and birth could not assign your rank. Nietzsche is a man afloat, who fears the reef but seeks the harbor. In him, our contemporary conflicts are writ large, and their intractable contradictions are our tragic destination. The Apollonian ideal has no better representative than Immanuel Kant, whose dream of reason was of a kingdom made by individuals so rational and so morally secure they legislated exclusively for themselves, but did this only after determining what could consistently serve as a rule for all: anarchy as it was meant to be, the achievement of the autonomous individual. This ideal is exactly where the pagan arrow lands after its long flight from Socrates' hand—at the feet of the ultimate self.

Nietzsche's insistence that the math of the classical world contained irrational numbers received small applause from his professional colleagues, and *The Birth of Tragedy* was bitterly attacked. Nietzsche, however, thrived on combat; he needed adversaries; it was necessary to his work that it be a way through a forest of ignorance; he was happy to let his enemies define him. Their protests energized him, proved him right. At the same time, Nietzsche reacted angrily to every caution he was asked to observe, to every mark of legitimacy he was expected to sport, to every kowtow he was required to perform. Because he had lost his father so early in his life, Nietzsche was especially vulnerable to mentors and too passionate in his choice of them; however, they were never going to be around long. Hegel's world-historical individuals, Carlyle's heroes, and Emerson's self-reliant pioneers were everywhere hoped for, worshiped, yet, with relish, after a time of glorious regency, overthrown. It would be Schopenhauer's fate, and Wagner's also. Nietzsche would eventually overthrow himself.

Cate carefully details the remarkable career of Lou Salomé (a nimble, bright, strong-willed, yet surprisingly frail young woman, who was also escaping her past), naturally highlighting Nietzsche's "courtship" by omitting none of the affair's inept convolutions (an intellectual *ménage à trois*) as Lou slips between the closing paws of Paul Rée (her positivist admirer, subsequently a suicide) and Friedrich Nietzsche (her other tutor—*le tiers*—and unhappy suitor) into the arms of a similarly futile and gifted swain (Friedrich Carl Andreas, her pathetic though scholarly husband, who threatened suicide if she didn't wed him), then briefly allowing Rainer Maria Rilke (her spoiled boy poet) to climb into her bed before bounding on to Gerhart Hauptmann (the playwright for whom she was the "other woman," and who orders a character in one of his dramas to kill himself, perhaps so the playwright wouldn't have to), until finally—skipping a few beaux because she hid them better—she reaches Victor Tausk (fellow psychoanalytic student, soon, too, a suicide), and comes to rest in the company of Sigmund Freud (her teacher, colleague, and comforter), who, though ill of cancer, is charmed, wise, paternal . . . and appropriately famous.

This courtship, carried on at the level of eloquent adolescence by the principals involved—the beloved, her two suitors, fussy outraged mothers, nosy friends, a venomous sister—ends in misunderstanding, rumor, and scandal, with tankards of bitterness all around, although, as a consequence, Nietzsche is set free of Rée, Salomé, sister, and a score of illusions about his life, which would henceforth be increasingly solitary and unfettered, except for the constant company of all those passive emotions that he rejected as often and as publicly as possible, though they privately clouded his every hour and darkened every memory. "My distrust is now so great: from everything I hear I feel a contempt for me" (Cate, 390).

With *Thus Spake Zarathustra* (1883–85) he would deny his demons. Emerson, one of the few of Nietzsche's heroes whose clay feet aren't eventually noticed, might have called Nietzsche's books *compensatory*. The reader certainly bears a license from the philosopher to interpret his work in terms of his life, to inspect the perimeters of that single perspective with suspicious dogs, to confront the man instead of his ideas, and to employ the most outrageous rhetoric he can command in order to critique them. In the books of maxims and aphorisms that preceded *Zarathrustra,* as well as in those that would follow, Nietzsche used the same strategies in designing his attacks as you would for a war, because his was a philosophy of condemnation and exposure that defined its goals mainly by means of its oppositions. It did not tackle a problem; it assaulted solutions, and it did so principally by calling the solver's character into question. Logicians call this fallacy, appropriately, the ad hominem—i.e., against the man instead of the argument.

Moreover, the weakness of any idea and moral practice lay in its origins. Like Marx and Freud, Nietzsche looked to see in what hovel the bad had been born; in what expensive college the good had got its education; what were the "real"—that is, original—sources of some term's meaning, the reasons for this or that preference, this or that injunction, this or that exercise of power. As it had been, it still was. Logicians call this fallacy, appropriately, the genetic.

As if a crime had been committed (and Christian culture was a moral crime), the sleuth sought a motive: in the profits of the Church, the powers of the clergy, the persecution of heretics, the defense of dogma. If I tithed I was buying my way into heaven. If I was charitable, I sought favor or wanted to feel good about myself. If I turned the other cheek it was only for those above me and because I had to, while those below me I glad-handed and then struck with impunity. This maneuver is called the fallacy of the single cause. It also accompanies the fallacy of the fatal flaw as customarily as bread does butter, and not just because a flaw in the infallible dims the diamond, but because, when many considerations support a conclusion, a weakness in one may not be critical, whereas, after the reasons have been reduced to a single straw, a little kink is sufficient.

Nietzsche made an emotional machine of the syllogism. For instance, if he dislikes the consequence of some argument, he will allow his dislike to falsify the premises and make them merely an allegation. Evangelicals deal with Darwin that way. Nietzsche's use of language is almost entirely political: he sharpens his points by shouting, which inhibits a sober response, and repeats them insistently, as if he were running for office. He maligns the opposition, impugns its past, and adopts a prophetic tone as an excuse for vagueness.

To demonstrate the inhumanity of man to man, and therefore the corruptness of any human institution, I could cite data drawn from every column of the encyclopedia, but my evidence would not support the necessity of our malfeasances, just their prevalence. Similarly, cultural relativism relies on the testimony of a thousand quarreling tribes and ubiquitous differences of opinion. Yet from what generally is, one may infer only what will generally continue to be, never what ought to be. This mistake is sometimes called the naturalistic fallacy. The step from fact to value is so popular one might think it was a step that could be taken. Saint Paul, whom Nietzsche despised, used several of these sophistical arguments to incriminate the whole of humanity—"in Adam's fall we sinned all"— since every disobedience earns the punishment due the first. Nor should I be inclined to welcome the bearers of the rack and screw into my company simply because, as Nietzsche suggests, bloodletting leaders are needed from time to time to stir things up, and disturb the repose of the mind (a version of the view that suffering can be a tonic), for I can imagine a hundred kinder ways to rise to an occasion, and find challenges that might need my mettle yet do not endanger freedom, limbs, or life. It is also true that a noble deed might be bad luck for an innocent bystander, and an evil undertaking bring bounty to another, but these outcomes should not dissuade us from good works, or excuse crime.

Nietzsche insisted that every philosophical position expressed a perspective—there were no absolute or especially preferable standpoints—however, Nietzsche was allowed to have several, the rest of us only one; moreover, he misused the word in the usual way, emphasizing a subjectivity that is not necessarily present, since a geometrical perspective can be precise, as can a microscopic view, or a measurement made by machine. Nietzsche accuses our angle of view of being narrow and skewed, so that he can reduce it—as the strategy intends—to "only" and "merely" ours, whereas his is clear and wide and deep and sound as a sage's should be, standing on a mountaintop, using telescopic eyes.

Epigrams aren't arguments. A forest of hyperbole resembles a forest of bamboo; outside one thinks only how to limit its growth, inside how one may cut a path through. Some ideas are like steroids, and Nietzsche prefers those that make us stronger. "God is dead" did that for him, but he meant that the belief, not the deity, was done for, since what has never been can never cease to be. Nor is the belief—any belief—really dead: druids still frequent the forests, witches stir their kettles, mumbos jumbo, gourds rattle. Beliefs are running wild. Faiths fall, only to reappear as green and fresh as leaves. The Garden of Good Opinions has its weeds. What Nietzsche meant, and might have said—did say, in effect—was: a belief in God is no longer tenable to an educated mind. But what can we say to those educated minds that still exercise their right to be wrong?

Nietzsche threw up his hands. He exclaimed with disgust and despair. What else is there to do?

A god who begets children on a mortal woman; a sage who calls upon us no longer to work, no longer to sit in judgment, but to heed the signs of the imminent end of the world; a justice which accepts an innocent man as a substitute sacrifice; someone who bids his disciples drink his blood; prayers for miraculous interventions; sin perpetrated against a god atoned for by a god; fear of a Beyond to which death is the gateway; the figure of the Cross as a symbol in an age which no longer knows the meaning and shame of the Cross— how gruesomely all this is wafted to us, as if out of the grave of a primeval past! Can one believe that things of this sort are still believed in? [*Human All Too Human*, trans. by R. J. Hollingdale, 1986]

One stands in awe before the need of man to be deceived. When there are no satisfactory reasons for some heart-held conviction, and when it persists in spite of every philosophical complaint and scientific exposure—when, in short, argument is futile—one must look—as Nietzsche and Marx and Freud did—among folly's causes for the most vulgar, easily grasped, immediately profitable, and sanitized factors. The latter condition should not surprise us, because popular beliefs of every kind are held in a haven of unexamined premises and unacknowledged consequences. Few ask what else they must embrace if they are to hold this or that item of religious dogma or political suasion; or what, if it were indeed true, must inevitably follow from such a fact, for what will follow will be surprise, contradiction, absurdity, and confusion. These beliefs are symptoms, not systems; they are ignorantly and narrowly held; they become treasured parts of the believer's sense of self; they are talismans to calm fears and promise hope; they tell believers they must be humble because their beliefs make them superior, and that all men are equal except the ones they are asked to shoot; they unite us as nothing else will, and reassure the mind, because there really cannot be millions of such virtuous and faithful people identically mad and mistaken.

Up against such intractability, Nietzsche sermonizes from his own stump. And he makes promises in terms his opposition will understand . . . from his perspective, mind you . . . but with certainty. Yet it is never clear, it seems to me, whether Nietzsche is angry with Christianity because it is absurd, or because it preaches passivity and encourages acceptance. Any metaphysics or theology that denies life (those are his words), that prefers the status quo, will receive his censure. But why should one be optimistic when there is so little evidence for it? . . . in Nietzsche's life as well as ours. Because, brought to bed by a burning of the eyes, aching stomach, and bands of pain across your brow, in a cold bare rented room, disheartened further by your journey to it, depending upon people you can no longer trust, yet with your head nevertheless about to burst with announcements that need posting, there is no other weapon against despair—forsaken by your own skepticism, seduced by visions of what might be, and betrayed by opportunity and your own soul—than one loud *ja-sagend* after another. But this is acceptance driven like a truck toward a checkpoint.

What is new in *Zarathustra* is Nietzsche's emphasis on process. Opinions are stationary. They should be no more than resting moments on a journey. So also customs, habits, values, hopes. We should continuously remake ourselves, because our species is the species that defies its definition, escapes its class, and evolves inside its own seed. Man must overcome man. This is not a recipe for our present practice of buying new beliefs like sporty cars and chic clothes when we can afford them, but resembles more precisely scientific refinements, progressive moral illumination, continuous learning. Everything can be comical. Let us frolic. Let us dance. Nothing is untouchable. Nothing is so serious it cannot provoke mirth. Nothing is sacred.

Back in the world of chronic pain, depressing news, and bad weather, Nietzsche is quarreling with former friends and future enemies, and grows closer in his own frayed mind to "the crucified one" than to his Zoroastrian namesake (he will soon sign letters *Der Gekreuzigte* or sometimes *Dionysos*); yet despite the insidious depredations of syphilis, which was probably the undiagnosed cause of many of his torments, he produces some of his most esteemed books, principally *Beyond Good and Evil* and *On the Genealogy of Morals*. Nietzsche's behavior grew more and more uninhibited, as if, with an irony too bitter to be borne, the frenzied god had taken his body hostage, so it pranced and sang, with unthinking fingers played wild riffs on the piano, embraced strangers, or compelled him to turn on those closest to him in unrestrained fury, howling, sobbing while subsiding with weariness, then displaying a hunger for food that had not even an animal's limits. He was placed in an asylum. Later a patron, Meta von Salis, purchased a vacant villa above Weimar where Nietzsche and his sister (now his nurse and guardian) could live. Elisabeth immediately made extensive improvements to the property, which she calmly charged to her absentee hostess, whose fury followed but whose kindness continued. Nietzsche was oblivious to the century's turn, now nearly a sofa'd corpse whom visitors were allowed to view a little, like Lenin would be laid out later, though Lenin would be immune from the flu that slipped into Nietzsche's lungs, where, immobile as he was, it was soon a pneumonia which prospered until a heart attack ensued.

At the funeral services, they played Brahms.

KAFKA: HALF A MAN, HALF A METAPHOR

I awoke one morning to find myself transformed. I had been a man, but a man who was treated by my parents and my sister like a bug. Perhaps I was not so much an insect at my office; perhaps I was something else there, a blotter or a trash basket. Perhaps, like a bum, I was warned not to loiter when I was out on the avenue, or, while traveling on the train, I became just another newspaper or another sample case. Perhaps, to my boss, I was a worm. At home, however, a bug was what I was, a bug in a bed, a bedbug, sperm of the kind you could find hidden in my name—Gregor Samsa—for doesn't *sam* mean seed, a descendant? And so one day I woke to find myself more than a metaphor, more than a figure of derision and indifference. I was a bug, big in my bed as my body was, with a body bigger than any ordinary bug's, bigger than a rat's, a dog's, though I was small, considering what my life meant to me. To others, however, I was huge, monstrous, horrifying, all I always wanted to be, all I always dreamed.

Of course, I was so much more than they imagined, for when people treat you within the habitual range of their emotions, they leave reality out. I was a bug to them, but not with a firm shell, not with thorny legs or with furry feelers, no, I was a man, a son, a day-old breadwinner, who was, despite being poorly outfitted for it, just a bug, indeterminate as to species, and I lived an unimportant mostly invisible life, and survived on leftovers, crumbs, windfalls, hand-me-downs, spills. I dwelled with my parents, of course, though they depended on my salary and should by rights have been the bugs. I had a small room with four doors and a view of the rain.

On the wall I had framed the photo of a dominatrix, you would say, a genital symbol, you would say, Sacher-Masoch's lady in furs, with one arm thrust suggestively into her furry muff, how much more obvious could you be, you might say, far above my station, too, I would guess from her furs, her gaze, but who would deny a lonely little man his dreams? To be what they've made me be. Yes, I've waked from one of them a bug because my bones are all on the outside like a screened porch and I squeak—my hinges are unfamiliar to me—when my legs wave. However, my transformation is not complete, because I am still complaining about my work, work I no longer have to do now that I am a bug for all intents, though I'm not used to that yet, so I have caught myself in the middle of my metamorphosis, halfway maybe on my journey to an active bug life, when I won't have to worry about my boss, my job, the fact I've missed my train, must endure the nagging of my parents and my sister, Grete—good life to her now, eh?—or long any more for my mistress from the magazine, my paper love to whom I press my face; or fret my chores, my filial duties—that I'm late for work—or fret the rain that tells me, when I hear it falling, that I hear much as I used to hear—my mother chiding me about the lateness of the hour—yes—I feel much as I used to feel, can complain as I am accustomed to complain—yes, yes, thank you, Mother, I am getting up now—and, though there is a noticcable chitter in the rear parts of my words, I am confident that I am still somewhere a man. After all, I may be a bug but I am man sized.

Did you know my father deals in muffs? Receives muffs from a manufacturer, sells those muffs—as well as carded buttons, lingerie, handbags, gloves—to retail stores? Did you know that in addition to my work as a sample salesman, taking orders here, there, and everywhere as always, I help out late in the day at my father's shop, and toil (yes, that is the right word) in a government agency that handles workmen's compensations and injury claims? You have to have visible wounds and a showy limp to earn my notice. So if I brought a complaint, a petition, even my own case to my attention, I would not award a krone to myself for all my pains, the burns I have received from my father's glares.

Before I became a bug I wasn't the son my parents wanted, and now that I am a bug, I am more than ever a disappointment. I am somewhat surprised by my own calmness about this sudden change. I wonder now whether I shouldn't have enjoyed it more. It is a good excuse for remaining in bed with a pillow and my plight protecting me from the noises of my daily duties. Do cockroaches cocoon? I lie here and ponder the problem, but mostly what occurs to me is to wonder how I shall make the next train. Being a bug is rather a bother—to get out of bed, to dress, to shave. What a relief to have a reason. I want to explain but only my feelers will wave.

First, through the closed door, my mother reminds me; then, on the closed door, my father pounds and shouts and chides me; finally, despite the closed door, my sister asks me if I need anything. If I opened the door (my traveler's habit is to lock it) they would see a bug and be horrified (as they will be when it happens), but the real me is not a bug; the real me is not the me they know either; the real me is an author, though as unassuming as a bug, and out of sight the way a roach hides, with no point of view to speak of, inhuman in that way, but alert as any small creature who needs to remain unnoticed, whose life depends upon its disappearance, except when I assume the body of a snake and slither into the next room to request a little peace and quiet. Yes. True. I am often other animals. As in Aesop. As in Swift. One of my most recent biographers mentions "learned dogs and voracious jackals, psychotic moles, worldly-wise apes, and vainglorious mice."

A bug's biographer. You might imagine it the other way: a flea that observes the amorous frolics of its host. They do follow one another rather continuously—come in crowds—these dutiful recorders. This particular life of me has scarcely reached the shores of Amerika when another vast bio appears in Germany. The present one is by Reiner Stach, who subtitled it "The Decisive Years." It is mostly about Franz's seesaw affair with his mail-order fiancé, Felice Bauer. I understand that it has been given a wonderfully supple translation by Shelley Frisch. The latest one, not yet at your shores, is by Peter-André Alt and subtitled *Der ewige Sohn* ("The Eternal Son"). Stach's is a splendid effort, and will be hard to surpass. I shall have had one short life, but many and long are the works that try to transcribe me. Consider your own life and imagine how you would feel if the way you ate were an issue, if every weakened purpose you took to work were written up, every deception documented, the interrogations you mimicked and mocked carried on into your afterlife ("Was Franz Kafka a real man?"), and every letter you ever wrote, even those you never sent, were to be prominently printed in a learned book. Unless, of course, you had already cut yourself like a coroner into three enigmatic egos—the overburdened and suffering son, called Dr. Kafka at the Workers' Accident Insurance Institute on account of his law degree; the episoler and unhappy lover who signs himself "Franz" and begs for an immediate reply; the sensitive artist, diarist, and tormented perfectionist who stays awake to fashion nightmares for a sleeping world—while planning very carefully (though not all that consciously) for the immortality of each of them.

(If we were three, Felice was four. Franz almost immediately parceled her out. The first was the girl he met at Max Brod's place in Prague, the second the one who wrote him letters from Berlin where she lived and worked, the third the woman with whom he strolled when he visited her apartment in Charlottenburg, and the fourth is the person who leads her own Berlin life, has friends he does not know, and visits places he has not been. What a surprising lot of folks for one romance.)

In my writerly guise my pages will be as shocking as my present prehistoric carapace. I want to publish principally to prove to my father I can be a success at something. But not in my role as a writer, rather in my role as a son. Perhaps I would prefer my scribblings to stay unseen and my bound and printed sheets to remain unread, even though I have carefully placed a copy of my first book on the nightstand next to my father's bed. I want his approval so I can scorn it. I want his approval though my need makes me ashamed. I depend upon his animosity, for it defines me, gives me edges just as the man who cuts out your silhouette from a sheet of black paper does; and, for the sum of loose change, gives you the profile of a piece of land. My movements are awkward, my body cumbersome, my desires mixed. I can debate the situation with my head but however it goes—approval or blame—I remain a failure.

Yes, I remember writing a fragment of fiction about just such a situation. I am safely . . . my character is safely in his own bed, but it threatens to become his bride's bed too, so my reluctant bridegroom imagines sending his properly decked-out body to the wedding while he remains at home, unable to venture beyond his blankets because—well—because he is a "large beetle, a stag beetle or a cockchafer, I think. . . . I would then act as though it was a matter of hibernation. . . ." My metaphor would marry and make love. I would not be required to attend.

Yes, I must be a different species. I dislike everything my family does. I cannot eat what they eat; I cannot abide their games; the noises of their life are like the scratch of chalk; and they move through my room to other rooms like trains through a station. I only come out at night, when the card game is conceded, the last door closed, my father's lungs cough, and the parental bedsprings sigh. I come out into the comforting emptiness of silence, where I may lead my counterclockwise life.

That is why, as a fiction, I define my room by doors: because I have so little privacy in daily life. Doors will dominate my correspondence too. "Dear Fräulein," Franz shall write to Felice Bauer, "My wretched letter had to suffer through so much before it was written. Now that the door between us appears to be beginning to budge, or at least we have taken hold of the handle, I surely can, or even must, say it. The moods I get into, Fräulein! A torrent of nervousness is constantly raining down on me. What I want one minute, I don't want the next." How cautious Franz is too. He says he must say . . . what? but he does not say . . . anything. The door appears . . . to be beginning . . . to op—. . . Well, perhaps we have only touched the handle . . . His caution is that of a cat who may be kicked . . . at any moment.

My problem, if I were to put it simply, is the family, the dynamics of the family, the reach of relations, the forced feeding of custom and belief, the close embrace of the tribe, the shrinking circle that begins the words *obey* and *obligation* and concludes every *no* that issues from my father's mouth to sum me up as a zero. The family is formed by a system of functions: the father's to rule and provide, direct and protect, beget and mold; the mother's to cherish and succor, to bear and care; the child's to obey and prepare, to mate and become mother or father in another such system, perpetuating the name, supplying the tribe with more tribesmen, adding to its coffers, filling with good repute each grave.

To love as one might like to love is impossible. Marriages are arranged. Sex is overseen by a rabbi (in my case) and directed by religious rules and with economic expectations. In fact, the law is what is loved. It is worshiped because it preserves the position of the father. Obey the powers that be and one day you shall be obeyed. What you suffer now, you shall cause others to suffer, so your early suffering shall not be in vain. I cannot swallow this. I cannot get it down. I cannot incorporate. When I was a man I could not eat the good red meat from the family table; now that I am a bug I cannot eat it either. I am thin because I manage only lettuce and old air. My eyes grow as large as a starveling's, and my voice lacks the loud assurance of my father's, although its softness is often admired as one might admire soft cloth. I dress expensively, however, projecting a dark ethereality that has its own charm. I am too tall. My doctor finds me not quite well—bad digestion, underweight, and nervous as a gnat. He sends me off to a nudist camp. Well, not quite—to a sanitarium where sexually separated guests sometimes forgo all clothes on behalf of nature's benevolent breezes, and enjoy a roll on the morning's damp, democratically naked grass. Sickness has its own attractions. I can be too weak to work, and take to my sofa, behind closed doors, where I pillow my head in a dream. Or I reread my diaries. They make me despair. Then with great energy I can pursue a wild idea, a nutty project, while allowing my assigned duties to lapse, like a sentry who leaves the main gate to guard the latrine. The guilt I feel may be worth it, because this behavior drives my father beyond the edge of dither. Dr. Kafka brings undesirables home to dinner, but even that does little to improve my appetite. In addition, I Fletcherize my food: I cut my vegetables into small squares. Then I chew each bit slowly and with great deliberation. With distaste. My father hides behind his paper, through which, I know, he stares.

I hesitate to approach them. Girls, I mean, not the ladies whom one can hire like a hansom. Horses, apes, insects—any species other than the human—are my imaginary companions. Well, they all eat; they all mate. And there are always repercussions. As a son I am asked to breathe fumes at an asbestos factory, sit all day in the din of hammered tacks as secretaries type and the family yaps. No silence. No privacy. Not a hint of anything higher than a rabbi's reach to obtain a scoop of sour cream to dab on his latkes. Now my supervisor is hammering on my door. I try to make excuses but they don't come out right. Sometimes I am nothing but feelers.

I hesitate to approach the opposite sex—opposite, don't you say?—because sometimes I am smitten with a suddenness that leaves me dazed. A young woman like Felice Bauer, for instance, who shows up at Max Brod's house with her face empty as a plate, nevertheless entices me; she makes the right responses—she loves Goethe—she says satisfactory things—she says she finds nothing more repulsive than people who are constantly eating—and in minutes we are planning a trip to Palestine together as if we were geographical Zionists, as full of zeal as a jar of jelly. I like her to the point of sighing.

My biographer will prepare you for the abrupt obsessive nature of my attractions. Let us stop a moment to watch how Reiner Stach goes so skillfully about his business. It offers the reader a pleasure all its own. My friend Max Brod and I are visiting Weimar in order to pay our respects to the great God Goethe, and to visit his home where "the beech tree that darkened his study" had once been seen by a genius and was to be seen again as if we had traded eyes. My diary surprises me with what I've written: "While we were still sitting down below on the stairs, she ran past us with her little sister." Goethe. A garden. A girl. They will coalesce and later enliven the images of Felice Bauer with precisely the awkwardness that shows up in a tampered photograph.

But this figure was Margarethe Kirchner, the daughter of the caretaker, a carefree sixteen in an era when innocence and naiveté were expected of girls. Perhaps it was the bloom of her being in this garden given over to the dead that ensnared me. Encouraged by Brod, who was in a jovial mood, I advanced on this lovely with my smitten eyes, surprised by the absence of my customary shyness. She was called Grete. Despite this fortuitous link with the sister at whose hand I would be fed a few scraps of garbage when I became a bug, or the Grete Bloch who would become a go-between for Felice and me, biographers have largely ignored this passing item in my life, though some have allowed her a few lines, as Peter-André Alt does in his 2005 history. But Reiner Stach stages the encounter like a dramatist, allowing the little details to loom large, but on their own account, by releasing them without fanfare at just the right time. I remember she was standing by a bush of roses.

I pursued her during the several days of our visit, and managed, with Brod's connivance, to get her alone long enough to arrange an assignation, but this was not easy, Brod was busy networking (as you say now); we had our tourist duties to attend to (Schiller, Liszt, Goethe's garden house); and Grete was elusive, though I lay in wait as ardently as any Casanova near her sewing school, "holding a box of chocolates with a chain and a little heart." There is a snapshot of the two of us taken on my twenty-ninth birthday.

Finally, just as we were about to leave, she consented to see me for an hour. Later, when we met, she wore that "Pink dress, my little heart." We drove through the park together and I stubbornly hung around into the evening, even though I knew we had nothing in common, that there was no real connection possible between us. Perhaps that was itself the attraction. When I said good-bye her eyes were swollen with tears, but it was because her partner for the ball that night had disappointed her. "A woman bringing roses disturbed even this little farewell." Yet those roses concluded the episode as if I had written it. As, in fact, I had. Moreover, I would employ her name, as I would use other "Gretes," for that of my poor bug's sister; and even though she would order my brittle carcass to be tossed into the trash, I'd allow her to complete the metamorphosis that I began, triumphantly fluttering away at the end, you may remember, a fully realized woman.

The biographer must interpret such facts as he has on hand only so far as they fit into the life that is being lived, and while he can speculate as often as his readers may also be invited to do, his history should be as clean of simple conjecture as wounds of infection. My story of anxiety and anguish I have strewn with helpful clues, and it unashamedly displays aesthetic elements of organization. I never felt that Reiner Stach was building imaginary bridges between gaps in the debris I left behind, but was reconstructing events from otherwise scattered facts the way the broken lines of a sketch invite the eye to complete their intended course and see a complete form or finished pattern where there is mostly implication.

From the same materials as Reiner Stach has, I must construct myself as I step back and forth from fact to fiction—half a man and half a metaphor. Let me give you another instance: my suicide threat. Think back: I am sore beset (for sins of absence and inattention) by problems at the asbestos plant, and my parents' subsequent nagging has rubbed me raw. I complain to my diary: "The day before yesterday was blamed because of the factory. Then one hour on the sofa thinking about jumping out the window." When I receive my censure I am Dr. Kafka. While I lie on the sofa I begin to see myself opening the window, leaning out. . . . I envision—don't I?—the family's consternation—don't I?—with some pleasure. This visit to a daydream passes, as the months do. The family pressure concerning the factory becomes intolerable. In a burst of fear, guile, hate, and guilt, in one night I write "The Judgment," a story in which a father accuses his son: you have betrayed your friend, your mother, and myself; consequently "I sentence you now to death by drowning." Thereupon the son, obedient as a dog, leaps over a rail of the Charles River bridge. He waits, hanging by his hands, for the passage of a bus to cover the sound of his splash. In that same way I also fall, a fiction, into tear-wet water. And what is my concluding line? "At that moment, over the bridge, there came and went a ceaseless stream of traffic"—"unendicher Verkehr." Another meaning would be: "unending intercourse." Shortly I am writing the following to Max Brod: "I realized clearly that there were only two options for me, either to jump out of the window after everybody had gone to bed or to go to the factory and my brother-in-law's office on a daily basis for the next fourteen days." Because I am now both a figure of speech and a notorious fact—"a dried-up well, water in unreachable depths and uncertain even there"—in the end I do not die of a killing routine nor of defenestration. Max Brod gets my mother to cover me and my absences with lies. In fact, everybody lies, and Father doesn't notice. Not noticing what has been noticed is a talent we Kafkas treasure.

I have only to consider my situation and immediately, expressed in a phrase, an image arises to excuse and explain me. I shall set this phrase loose in one of my literary lives. For instance, here I am writing to Felice about myself (is there another subject?): "My life consists, and has essentially always consisted, of attempts at writing, largely unsuccessful. But when I don't write, I wind up on the floor at once, fit for the dustbin." Of course, when I teach myself to be a bug, that is exactly where I shall end—dead in a charwoman's pan. Scooped away like the breath of a whistle. In the same letter I go on to brag of how thin I am, but I shall be thinner when I write "A Hunger Artist." Then I shall resemble a small pile of old clothes.

But if you need any further demonstration of the way my genius works (and the occasional necessary unfriendliness of my biographer), consider the October 1912 expulsion of the Turks from the Balkans. The Turks were taking a beating and there were stories of atrocities, with photographs disgracing the pages of the papers. Max Brod's diary reports: "Took a walk with Kafka; the misery of the Turks reminds him of his own." Brod, for his part, writes a piece of poetic doggerel in which the misery of the Turks "brings to mind the misery of everyone who ever lived." Stach's comment—"It is difficult to imagine a starker contrast to his friend's response to the war"—is cutting, I admit, but if the misery of the Turks causes Brod to consider the misery of mankind, and myself to complain of mine, Brod's result is a verse shallow as a spoon, while I make mine into a masterpiece deep as the darkness in man that frightens us all. War, and the revitalization of death—DEATH LIVES! that's how you'd put it on a poster—was as real right then as the smoke from my father's factory chimneys.

As for ordinary living, we shall have our servants do that for us, Villiers de L'Isle-Adam said. It is a problem most serious writers face, because society is not prepared to pay for the poet's trip on its tram, and is equally unwilling to play a nanny in the home life of some novelist. It is not an offer of *vissi d'arte,* or *vissi d'amore,* by itself; it is marriage, family, work, recognized worth in the world, versus art, idleness, subversive thought, pointless practice, useless effort, repeated failure; and even if success is found in some solitary achievement, its fruit is seedless and dry and secret. It sometimes seems to be a brutal choice between being a fool or a philistine. The philistine lives, but shamefully; the foolish artist endures, repeatedly, semi-imaginary deaths and real neglect. For me this common problem was exacerbated by the closing cultural fist I found myself caught in: there was the provincial city, Prague, inside Prague the community of Germans, inside them the network of the Jews, among the Jews the family Kafka, within that—Franz—its son and heir, within him—me—the writer, longing to get out of my given skin, to escape my relatives, my race, my religion, my responsibilities, this entire region of the world . . . though when Kafka went I would take along his language.

But instead of escaping into the wide world, Franz withdrew. I wrote in code stories he couldn't finish, stories he couldn't bear to publish, pages he locked away in drawers as much to keep them in as anyone out. On those sheets I set down his private fears, yearnings, angers, resentments, his guilt and his remorse, as indifferently as a range of hills. I wrote of rented rooms from which the furniture would be removed. I built castles without kings, imagined courts without judges, without jurors, without justice, presented matters of fact that made no sense, created a clarity that was obscure, inflicted torments upon my characters that had no cause no name no amelioration no resolution. In so doing I demonstrated the divinity that belongs to art. An art that belonged to me.

Here, in Reiner Stach's biography, are five years of my life—only five—all his pages based on all of mine; though he has promised to give me two more lifetimes in succeeding volumes. It will be a wonder that even I shall wonder at. Reiner Stach does not endeavor to pin me down; rather he tries to follow me through my transformations; and when he is perplexed, and his data is divided in its recommendations, he discusses his dilemma with the reader. I listen in, because I don't have any answers. That is the marvelous and exasperating mystery of it. I am, like the rest of us, ultimately unknowable. Yes, I remember what Socrates told the Athenians, but the self was itself a discovery in those days, so the philosopher could scarcely be aware of the quarreling bunch each one of us now represents. Neither the public official nor the reclusive author is the same Franz who signed "my" prodigious letters. Indeed, Franz is one of literature's supreme artists of the envelope and its hidden epistle—that private communication that is nevertheless meant to be heard by the whole world. On the other hand, I—monk and metaphor—find it difficult to finish anything, and have kept my novels and my stories short, enigmatic, impersonal. That other Franz wrote nonstop, at daunting length, to women, and kept a diary the way some Germans keep their dogs: they feed them, comb their coats, and take them for their daily walks.

Reiner Stach is convinced that Kafka would have been horrified by the idea that any other eye than that addressed, much less the world's eye, might become privy to his correspondence, and Stach halts the progression of his story for a fine essay on the nature of the letter and the epistolary culture of the time. During 1912 at least one hundred letters are written to Felice Bauer in Berlin, who must have felt the burden of response grow heavier by the week. Letters work upon the mind in the absence of the body, whose only presence can be felt in a personalized penmanship or perhaps through a fragrance captured in a kink of the envelope, or absorbed by the paper, now so intimate a thing, since it has been inscribed by a mind the way skin is sometimes caressed by a lover's fingers. Letters bring news, companionship, business, affection, but also pain. They are full of gossip, mischief, lies, flattery, and similar, though softer, misconstructions. They are not always meant to please, and confessions that wound their writer may wound their reader too. Remember the diabolically contrived machine of torture that I imagined for "In the Penal Colony"? how it inscribes the broken letter of the law upon the body of its guilty party, deeper and deeper digging its point into the transgressor until he expires? Letters routinely sent and received create still further, still more binding expectations. "I will not suffer if no letter comes," I reassure my postmark lover. Yet if there is but the briefest delay I beseech her like a baby—"Dearest, don't torment me like this!" Days or weeks can lie like lakes between send and receive. Perhaps a message has gone astray or fallen into the wrong hands. One day her ink may refuse to dry. Something like that has been expected. Perhaps her end of the correspondence has teetered to its demise. The totter will not rise.

Unlike conversations, replies are pondered and positioned as though they were chess pieces. And are read, reread, and assessed under varying circumstances, many moods. They become bundles. They can be wrapped in ribbon. They can crouch in an attic to leap upon a generation far away. But in the normal course of things, to receive one is to receive a sweet—to keep unopened in a pocket until a quiet unmolested moment is available, or to tear open with the urgency of lust opposed by buttons. Stach observes:

> This material, physical aspect of letters and their unceasing whiff of reality posed an irresistible temptation for Kafka. He began to hover over letters as never before. They became sexual fetishes. He spread them out in front of him, laid his face upon them, kissed them, inhaled their smell. On walks or short business trips, he took Felice's letters along with him, to fortify himself.

Letters may strive to seem natural, conversational, easy, off-the-cuff. They aren't. They are mostly contrived. The absence of another face, the foreclosure of immediate response—of interruptions, questions, objections—and the inability of smiles, frowns, gestures, exclamations to burst in upon the quiet calm of composition: these felicitous conditions permit the letter to become more apparently candid, more duplicitous, more sincere in appearance, more hypocritical at heart; and because they are "evidence," because they are "on the record," and because they can be intercepted, stolen, snooped, leaked, they can be exceedingly guarded, especially self-serving, ardently devoted to their future in an archive. And if these letters are by Keats or Flaubert or Rilke, they become art. As art they require that postal distance the letters can then complain of. Their words make love of the kind the mind makes when the mind fears its body may not measure up. What did I write to Felice? "If I had saved all the time I spent writing letters to you and used it for a trip to Berlin, I would have been with you long ago, and could now be gazing into your eyes."

When Franz's relationship with Felice was at an end, she saved his letters; he burned hers. Burning was what the insurance adjuster had in mind—sometimes—for my own letters too, as well as my diaries and many of my manuscripts, but his scribbled intentions, meant for Max Brod yet tossed in a drawer and by no means consistent, suggested a will that was hardly undivided and resolute, rather one familiar with all the strategies that pride and high opinion may employ, including humility, even abasement. On his way to Berlin, where he intends to meet with Felice and settle the question of their engagement (I break it off), Franz writes to his sister, Ottla (July 10, 1914): "I write differently from what I speak, I speak differently from what I think, I think differently from the way I ought to think, and so it all proceeds into deepest darkness." This sentence, however, proceeds like a parade. There is a P.S.: "Regards to all. You mustn't show my letter or let it lie around. You had best tear it up and throw the shreds from the *pawlatsche* [balcony] to the hens in the courtyard from whom I have no secrets."

During the brief period this biography covers, in which I managed to write most of my major works, I am so busy being Dr. Kafka during the day, and spend so much of my time and energy every night writing Franz's letters to this poor puzzled patient victim of my waffling, that even Reiner Stach's judicious treatment of their inception, making, and appearance is quite swamped by Franz's pathological self-absorption—preoccupations that quite cripple the state of mind a writer needs to succeed at any substantial project in prose, namely a calm and knowing control of the elements of his art, and the kind of focus common to laboratory lenses.

And how did I break it off? This pre-Internet love affair? I broke off my three engagements. I broke off my three books. They were engagements too. What finished them, in a sense, finished me. If you listen at the break point of *Der Verschollene* . . . (called *Amerika* by Max Brod, but now renamed *The Man Who Disappeared* by Reiner Stach's fine translator, Shelley Frisch, and by Michael Hofmann in his version for Penguin Classics [1996], or, as you might also say, *The Man Who Went Missing*) . . . if you listen you can hear notes struck that were struck at the conclusion of "The Judgment," for that story really contains most of my motifs and themes—the sound of water under a bridge while traffic passes over it; a two-way crossing above, a one-way fall below; marriage, finance, and fornication hidden like a gift in one fist, or death and oblivion in the empty palm of the other. In this case, my characters, and, of course, myself in the guise of one of them, are traveling by train into the mountains—in Hofmann's splendid rendering which retains the tumbling of the sentence—

> Blue-black formations of rock approached the train in sharp wedges, they leaned out of the window and tried in vain to see their peaks, narrow dark cloven valleys opened, with a finger they traced the direction in which they disappeared, broad mountain streams came rushing like great waves on their hilly courses, and, pushing thousands of little foaming wavelets ahead of them, they plunged under the bridges over which the train passed, so close that the chill breath of them made their faces shudder.

The Trial, you remember, ends with a knife in my namesake's heart, while a sense of shame so strong that it will outlive him—for he is dying, as he says, "like a dog"—is the single pain he feels. At the frayed ends of *The Castle,* one version of the text, where it slowly dies away with the indecision of a river, refers to K as a man "going to the dogs." And I—I confess, it is I—I write to Max Brod, what my diaries confirm, that I have fantasies in which "I lie stretched out on the ground, sliced up like a roast, and with my hand I am slowly pushing a piece of this meat toward a dog in the corner." Whether it is the breath of death that comes to warn me and make my face shudder, or death itself that follows the blade as it twists into the heart, or the broken shell of a humiliated self that is shoveled up by the maid, I shall be already buried in the body of another creature when it dies, I am determined on it. There I shall live forever.

How did I break it off with Felice? I began by casting my ultimate refusal in the form of a proposal. All my letters testified to my dependency if not to my devotion. She knew I needed her. What would be the point of pressing a suit so continuously worn? So I simply listed all my shortcomings . . . again and again: "I am basically a cold, selfish, and insensitive person despite all my weakness, which tends to conceal rather than mitigate these qualities." It was an odd but calculated way of putting it, as if my weaknesses hid my strengths (that I was cold? selfish? insensitive? these were strengths?); because they *were* an artist's strengths: an artist must be ruthless, sacrificing self as well as lovers, family as well as friends, to the conditions of his calling. That is the romance we have woven about writing and the artist's life. The considerable competence of Dr. Kafka in his assessor's position (about which I have told Felice little) is a real weakness, because it keeps him in his cage. My devotion to Felice is a real weakness, because it draws me into a life of bourgeois responsibilities. My obsessions, my insecurities, my vacillations are strengths, because they excuse me from duty; they dissipate my ardor; they weaken my marital resolve. I am cruel to be kind. I am sparing my beloved the burden of my love.

Reiner Stach quite shrewdly sees what I did not see: that Felice, who says yes to this backhanded ill-meant proposal immediately—a response as astonishing as the question that provoked it—wants a husband who would keep her safe and well while she enjoys her own freedoms the way a young woman may protect herself with the companionship of a gay friend while traveling through macho-infested territories. Felice had her own family miseries—most everyone does, though she had not told me what they were: that her sister had secretly borne an illegitimate child, that her father was living with a woman not his wife, that her brother was a chiseler and a deadbeat—and the idea of being lifted out of such confines in an acceptable way must have seemed appealing. "I will get used to you," she wrote me . . . but I did not want to become acceptable. So I wrote to Felice's father about how unbearable I was. "I am taciturn, unsociable, glum, self-serving, a hypochondriac, and actually in poor health." Oh, yes, and "I lack any sense of family life." Felice intercepted this letter and prevented her father from reading it. We continued to play out our engagement in a landscape of fantasy, but it had become a barren courtyard shit upon by filthy flocks of words.

How did Franz break it off? He began writing to another girl—Grete—a friend of Felice. About Felice. About Felice at first. In precisely the same way that—at first—he wrote to Felice. Emboldened by his success with Grete, he proposed once more to Felice, who refused him quite firmly. But he persisted. Why did he persist? Because now he knew he would always be refused. And in a memorable moment, in a back room of a Berlin hotel, three women—Felice Bauer, her sister, Erna, and friend Grete, like the Fates—sat in judgment of me—well, of Franz, for I was scarcely there, though I felt the pain of their presumption, their disapproval, their disappointment. Still, I would not waver from my wavering. I had my own wounds to heal. My father had hurled apples at me. My father had sentenced me to death by drowning. Publication of *The Metamorphosis* had been delayed. I had begun my own *Trial,* a trial that would go well, because I would be judge as well as plaintiff, both court and accused, every worry expressed, woman present, or warder doing his duty taken straight from life. And now, in order to conclude this half decade of my biography, a war arrives. It will seem to bring peace while we wait for volume two.

Nevertheless, there was another yes. Despite misgivings, despite reproaches, despite all that has already befallen her, Felice arranges a private meeting between us in a border town. Well, not all of us. I don't think Dr. Kafka was present. Except as a sign of stability in Felice's mind. There, in Franz's hotel room—where Fraulein Bauer might have compromised her virtue in some eyes by presenting herself—I embraced her as I was meant to. . . . No. What did I do? in my nervous apprehensions, cornered like a rat, what did I do? I read to her from *The Trial.* Franz cowered behind the measured wall of my words. They were about a man who spends his life waiting at a gate for admittance. These were meanings as cruel as any transformation. I was shy, of course, embarrassed, awkward, and I tried to explain myself by giving to Felice a sample of a masterpiece, an excuse for all I had done or would do; here is a slice of me, take it and eat; but this was no communion, no act of heresy; it was "going to the dogs."

Still, through it all, I remained literature, as I had so often said. I clung steadfastly to that. Dr. Kafka had his job. In fact, he got another raise. Franz would write more letters as if he hadn't written any. He was their bundle of energy, their silk ribbon, their stamp, their swirls of ink. I was insufferable—yes—I climbed my walls— yet I was literature. These were fragments shored against my ruin. I could not be deprived of that. Or my monstrosity.

UNSTEADY AS SHE GOES:
MALCOLM LOWRY'S CINEMA INFERNO

Set the scene: in 1949 Malcolm Lowry with the collaboration of his wife, Margerie Bonner, begin a film script for F. Scott Fitzgerald's novel *Tender Is the Night*. Lowry has always been an avid moviegoer and is especially knowledgeable about the German silents. He pretends that he has done adaptations for a Hollywood studio in the past. He often dreams of seeing *Under the Volcano* on the screen. Some critics have perceived its cinematic qualities.

> The picture opens in dead silence with a tremendous shot of the night sky, the stars blazing. . . .
>
> Then we become aware that the silence is not complete, and of a faint yet steady rhythmic throbbing sound as of a ship's engine; perhaps its pulsation is that of a ship's engine, but the sound seems as it were set wordlessly and remotely to the rhythm and even the ghostly melody, in a deep bass sense, of the old canon *"Frère Jacques. . . ."*

Reset the scene: the screen fills with a page of the *Vancouver Sun* for August 1, 1947. It and some photographs run across four columns that are headed, WEALTHY SQUATTERS FIND RENT-FREE BEACH. One of the photos shows Malc about to take a dive from the rickety pier the couple had built at Dollarton. **Close-up** to show perilous but apparently effective crisscross pattern of its construction. **Cut to** Lowry's fuzzy barrel-shaped chest. **Linger. Lap dissolve** into this newsprint: "A successful novelist who could write a cheque for thousands, is 'king' of the beach squatters of Royal Row at Dollarton, ten miles east of Vancouver. Like hundreds of others in the Vancouver area, Malcolm Lowry occupies a tax-free house built on piling below the high-tide mark."

On the sound track, well in the background, children's voices can be heard taunting in unison. Lowry is careful to assign to any scene he is imagining at least one significant visual, auditory, or intertextual presence that serves as its symbolic name and is expected to follow the action in the role of reminder (about which more later): for instance, a highway sign, a properly jazzy tune—

". . . play a strange and melancholy piece on the piano, like the best kind of jazz, a thing of many twelfths in the left hand . . ."

—perhaps a few swooping seabirds, or even a nursery rhyme, such as (I might suggest):

This is the shack that Malc built. . . . This is the sack that sat in the shack that Malc built. . . . This is the malt that lay in the sack that sat in the shack that Malc built. . . . This is the fault that fermented the malt that lay in the sack that sat in the shack that Malc built. . . .

Note: The Lowrys have lived here, off and on, since 1941, in a crude cabin that had been jerry-built by unemployed lumber mill workers in the 1930s. The present one is their third, and they designed and nailed it together themselves. Although the site furnishes them with nearly as many miseries as joys, joy in their bottle-to-mouth life is especially prized, and Malc thinks of it as paradise. Why not? Here he can stay sober for a month at a time. Eat and drink cheap. Swim in cool to cold to icy water. Work in furious manic bursts. Walk in wet woods. And here *Under the Volcano* has been licked into its final shape. Nevertheless, when they receive this unpleasant notice in the press, they are about to leave on a rather extended trip through the Panama Canal. Margerie is bored with poverty's paradise. She wants to experience for herself some of her husband's sudden notoriety and enjoy their first decent financial footing. They intend to visit countries like France and Italy that have warmly welcomed *Under the Volcano.* Moreover, she has recently published her own book and needs to taste a bit of triumph. Luckily, the *Brest* is going to dock briefly in L.A., a city where she has friends, where she met Malc on a blind date, and where she had a fleeting career in film. Lowry is persuaded to go along, though not without trepidations. He was familiar with trepidations. They were like the shakes, only mental. Now success rather than failure was to expel him from his Eden.

Flash forward. Another opening. Similar but contrasting scene. Do you remember any of those negligible movies in which we are shown a forlorn pregnant girl (maybe it is Bette Davis) sitting in a Pullman carriage while the train leaves the station with its wheels rasping a continuous refrain—Chi ca go . . . Chi ca go? The play of a similar card opens one of modernist literature's more extraordinary novellas, *Through the Panama,* which readers will once again have available to astonish (and probably bore) them, thanks to this anthology of leftover, mostly ignored, and out-of-print pieces of literary wonderment we might say were shards from the working life of Malcohol Lowry (as Conrad Aiken called him). This time, though, the chant is made by a mongrel American-built Liberty ship with a French registry and Breton crew that's headed for Holland, so its music is mongrel too.

> Frère Jacques
> Frère Jacques
> Dormez-vous?
> Dormez-vous?
> Sonnez les matines!
> Sonnez les matines!
> Ding dang dong
> Ding dang dong . . .

The next sentence (in Lowry's caps) is reminiscent of my parody (above) of a childhood exercise in rounds:

THIS IS THE SHIP'S ENDLESS SONG.

This is the engine of the *Diderot:* the canon repeated endlessly . . .

Stay loyal to the descriptive notes while filming the scene that follows immediately—

Everything wet, dark, slippery. Dock building huge, dimly lit by tiny yellow bulbs at far intervals. Black geometry angled against dark sky. Cluster lamps glowing—they are loading cardboard cartons labeled, PRODUCT OF CANADA

—except replace the name of the ship (a charming change) with *Di der ot Di der ot Di der ot.* Malc's joke, of course, but musically better than *Brest.*

Background note, do not try to film. *Through the Panama* is largely written in sentence fragments because it is supposed to be the journal of Sigbjørn Wilderness, Lowry's stand-in; because drunkenness is full of discontinuities; because such a style suits Lowry's cinematic imagination; and because it is actually based on the journals that Margerie and Malcolm Lowry kept on an exactly similar pilgrimage.

Their logs were a record that Malcolm dressed up and made presentable as if for a date: indeed, the very November 7, 1947, that Sigbjørn and his Primrose (the wretchedly named couple of the story) begin their voyage bound for Rotterdam from Vancouver, British Columbia, leaving behind just those shacks over which the credits scrolled. I spell out these details not only because the story does, but because Lowry's notes for all his journeys are full of names like these, of places little and large, of advertising signs and other come-ons—Burma-Shaves for one—map points which he will invest with prophetic or talismanic powers, lists of families found on graves, wisps of music, duly recorded snatches of overheard conversation, especially bits of local lingo, the more vacuous the better—"You like egg?" "*Si. Oui.*" "Whose egg will you have?"—scraps of a bye-the-bye life he can then repeat like a mantra until they achieve that status, or by such use wear paths that the past may employ to gallop to the present with warnings about what's coming; meanwhile inserting—to serve as a perception that will rivet the reader—images of exacting beauty. Who is getting off the boat at Port-au-Prince? ". . . ambassadors from a neighboring state, and medals like the inside of fantastic watches." The "just jotted down" style not only disarms complaint, but encourages the dignitaries—who are wearing those medals that look like watch works—to walk the plank.

These notes and journal entries, these unfinished gestures and false starts—versions of short stories, hunks of novels, poems too, an intended play—were to be allowed to grow to their full size, and then, like ingredients tossed into a stew, mingled together, so that, after some time luxuriating in the author's mind, they could finally be presented to the world as a *pièce de résistance* called *The Voyage That Never Ends*. It is an appropriate title, too, for this judicious new assemblage that Michael Hofmann has made. (Sherrill Grace also borrowed this name for her 1982 study of the fiction.) Lowry's voyage, though, was a dream undreamt and a promise unkept. At one level the writer's conscience must have known that the confident outline of this gargantuan project (of three, five, seven, or on occasion eleven volumes) could only momentarily ward off the worries of lovers and friends, and weaken the skepticism of editors, while the work that had to enjoy a sustaining wind if it was to reach shore would remain becalmed in a sea of Seagram's, garnished by a guilty self.

If this volume manages to be a bit more than "an anthology held together by earnestness" (the fatal phrase with which Jacques Barzun condemned *Under the Volcano* when he reviewed it in *Harper's Magazine*), it will be because the collection contains more than one masterpiece, several of the more remarkable letters ever to confound the genre, and is unified by the sin-sore, hungover self-consciousness of Malcolm Lowry at the helm, unsteady as she goes.

Future flashbacks. The reader will not immediately know that certain months of the year, as well as specific days in those months, were celebrated by Marge and Malc the way betrothals, birthdays, or other anniversaries are by ordinary folk, or were felt to be full of menace and bad luck like November 2, the Day of the Dead in Mexico, or, more privately for Malcolm Lowry, November 15, the date his Cambridge college friend Paul Fitte confessed that he owed money, was a homosexual, and had syphilis in dreadful addition. Lowry so sympathized with his friend's plight that he helped Fitte wad his windows and a door with newspapers to assist the gas, and, when he saw the need for more gin, said, "Now do it," as he left. Fitte did asphyxiate in his bed as advised, but what Lowry chooses to commemorate is the day of the body's discovery, not the night before, when alcohol had helped them both erase reason, dull conscience, and seal a room.

One could include June 7, 1944, when a fire destroyed the couple's beach house and consumed the manuscript for a novel, *In Ballast to the White Sea,* revisions for another called *Lunar Caustic,* most of their clothes, all of their furniture, a swatch of skin from Lowry's back, and immeasurable amounts of recent optimism.

All-sins days also had significance for the Lowrys because of their importance in the lives of Lowry's characters, with whom their author often became enmeshed, forgetting he was not the Consul of *Under the Volcano,* or Sigbjørn Wilderness of *Through the Panama.* He had drawn so intimately upon his own doubts and addictions to create them that he sometimes became confused and acted in the real world the way he might have imagined his surrogate behaving in his fictive one. But these were only the simplest of the mix-ups. In *Through the Panama,* Lowry's protagonist is said to be writing a novel whose principle character, Martin Trumbaugh, is also (what a coincidence) the author of a manuscript called *Dark as the Grave Wherein My Friend Is Laid,* so that sooner or later the reader will encounter a sentence that will have been enacted in Malcolm Lowry's life, and in the life he writes for Wilderness as well as in the life Wilderness is said to have written for Trumbaugh, such as, "where did I put my shoe, did I have a shoe? I did, and the lost one seemed in the right place, but then where are the cigarettes, and where am I?" Indeed, where are we? For our first wonder should be about Lowry himself: did he mislay his shoe or did he borrow the loss of it from two stories and a few stupors away?

The Basilisk, remember, dies from the look in his own eye when he peers for the first time into a mirror. Here, the mirror is customarily behind a bar, or sometimes it is the window of a bus, or the glassy surface of a still sea. In one case, it is a photograph of Margerie holding up a mirror in which Malcolm can be seen taking the picture. *Through the Panama* is one of the earlier and more significant self-reflective texts (the champions in this genre are Flann O'Brien and Paul Valéry, an odd pair, though Lowry is thinking of people like Pirandello), and demonstrates, over and over again, how "realistic" the maneuver and the mix-up are.

Note to department of special effects, who will have to superimpose images of these several selves like closed—and then fanned—hands of cards. The rationale is as follows:

We are constantly inventing additional versions of ourselves, either to unsettle our friends by making surprisingly dissimilar responses to familiar situations, or to meet changes in circumstances with an equally changed self, and sometimes to prepare ourselves for surprising eventualities—as we often do in sexual daydreams. We populate our lives with the lives we need to live them—dreaming ourselves into the selves we fear we are, or desperately want to be; and if we retell our little fictions often enough they pass from wishing 'twere, to seeming such, then to being so. Reiteration is a prominent feature of reality. And Malcolm Lowry is a master of reiteration. Then sometimes our voices, our values, and our presentation of self shift abruptly, in unforeseen ways, so that our bowling persona arrives in time to hear the Sunday sermon, or we wink at the wrong coworker at an unpropitious moment. Come on, we say to the preacher, let's have a drink.

(A quite subordinate note: the principal problem with John Huston's film of *Under the Volcano* is that Albert Finney's performance treats the Consul as little more than a fall down drunk, and forgets that Geoffrey Firmin is also a stand up Malcolm Lowry.)

Technically challenging shot (about which warning was given above) **of five Albert Finneys in El Farolito.** (Camera should not miss the seven Coca Cola signs that enliven its bland façade.) Alcohol makes you garrulous even when talking to yourself, have you noticed? You are sitting two abreast on both sides of the bar—you pour, you drink, you talk, you listen, you nod—how easily bought is agreement—you have several yards of fellow feeling between you and the next stool, where you sit in communion with that pleasant other guy who will finally fill you with remorse and loathing, anger and resentment, because a perfectly comfortable evening has turned ugly—why had the bartender so contemptuously splashed into your glass? And the mirror blinds your eye when only a moment before it had shown you sitting with a smile meant for a girl—why is someone tugging at your arm—a friend, lover, wife—a wife become whore, become enemy?—and it makes you want to fling things, angry now with the people you've hurt because their wounds still bleed, angry about the way they ruin a moment you were enjoying with your inner self, when peace between the five of you had seemed to have been established, but now only war . . . only war appears possible.

Cast of characters. Yes, the bartender (provider of the good, yet with the evil offer of the apple), the imbiber (the nursing babe and parasite), the mariner (and teller of tales, thief of texts, confessor, bearer of guilt), the wedding guest (who now should know better than to lend an ear, also a witness for the prosecution), the angel of assent (the weak will's weak adviser, liquor's toady, chief in charge of excuses and the hero's only friend), hail fellows all, well met, each uneasy parts of a seated self who might readily be given a starring role in a forthcoming fiction, are enjoying a pleasantly shaded early evening in one another's company until . . . until the albatross (or some similar emblem) is shot and the bird hung about the imbiber's neck, consequently—alas—bottles become empties because drink is immediately siphoned off by the gods, the bar closes, or provisions are exhausted, as when at sea, far from supplies, rationing is required; and then the tale cannot be concluded, the tongue is sundried, your companions leave you to seek success elsewhere; so the check—alas—will not be paid, no cheek—alas—will receive your tears when you weep, no sympathetic ear will hear you gagging in the john, and all your intentions will be snickered at, because the only wish you have left is for the next drink, which will steady you, reform your purpose, alert your listeners, and entice you, the bartender, to ask if you, the sot, will have another.

A cinematic issue. Although a writer of fragments (and a movie script is as prefragmented as a jigsaw), everything that Malcolm Lowry does has to pass through Malcolm Lowry, is digested and assimilated and relieved by him from breath to bowels, so that inter- as well as intratextuality has to become a major method. He sees a shore, swallows a glass of wine, reads a bit of news, absorbs a few frames of a silent film, is moved by a bit of your book or mine, writes a drunken line, says hello or stumbles in the street: it all becomes his, is owned by his consciousness, and that passing shore or reflecting glass or bit of news—the film, the panorama, or the greeting—if he feels he's paid his price for it, we may only rent.

The novels of B. Traven, Nordahl Grieg, and Conrad Aiken, for example, were adopted, and became his, even to the edge of plagiarism. All the books of boozers, like Fitzgerald, become his property. In particular, *Under the Volcano* is tethered to him. He does not release his books to have an independent life, because they are his present not just his past, and form his future. Henry James closes the covers of one novel in order to start another, but Malcolm Lowry tried to have his other texts, enlarged by further work, swallow like a whale his only triumph. *Under the Volcano*'s protagonist, Geoffrey Firmin, does not die with a dog down in a ravine. He is up and about in the next book, just a ghost under an assumed name.

Of course, when writers record such internal tussles between our multiple selves; when they treat art, other texts, ideas and dreams, with the same seriousness and importance to consciousness as acts, emotions, sights, and scenes; when they drop concert programs, official forms, or clippings onto their pages as if spilling a purse, they are deemed difficult, artificial, self-referential, arcane, cold, unreal, indifferent to their audiences, who apparently want their reality as customized as their cars, quiet as death, as equipped with the same lies as their lives, and providing a ride over even the bumpiest pavement so smooth and easy that they'll need to stir the cream in their coffee simply to create a spiral.

Through the Panama reenacts a pilgrimage, and that requires a journey. Whether Lowry is going by boat, bus, plane, or train, he is usually performing a penance, and seeking to be thus shriven for a mess he has made in someone's bathroom, or worse, because he has put hands to the throat or fist to the eye of a lady he has got drunk and who will be easier to kill than himself. It is significant, I think, that a particularly ugly April night, when he choked, beat, and kicked a girl he protested he loved nearly to her demise, does not receive a mention in Lowry's calendar of those days that are so threatening, drear, and heavy with guilt, he has to hide from them at home or flee by road or rail to any obscure destination.

However, this nearly murderous episode adds significance to the ad depicting "a murderer's hands laced with blood" that ominously appears and reappears in *Under the Volcano: Las Manos de Orlac: con Peter Lorre.*

Reset scene. Our principals, Primrose and Sigbjørn, are bunking in the chief gunner's cabin. Wilderness approves of the ship, and they like the good grub. Martin, however, has been given a little shack on the beach, about which he has nightmares full of fires and flooding waters. Here is a technically superb passage in which the three selves merge. Each thinks the first two sentences, though they are attributed to Martin.

[M, S, L] Martin thought of the misty winter sunrise through the windows of their little cabin: the sun, a tiny little sun, framed in one of the windowpanes like a miniature, unreal, white, with three trees in it, though no other trees were to be seen, and reflected in the inlet, in a high calm icy tide. Fear something will happen to house in our absence. [S, L] Novel is to be called *Dark as the Grave Wherein My Friend Is Laid*. Keep quiet about house or will spoil voyage for Primrose. [L] Intolerable behavior: remember Fielding with dropsy, being hauled on board in a basket on voyage to Portugal. Gentlemen and sense of humor. Had himself tapped for water every now and then. [L, S, M] Hm.

"Hm" is a sign that this reference will be pondered and gain depth, for Henry Fielding is another of Lowry's imaginary drinking companions—a rake whose indiscretions are said by friends to have contributed to his jaundice, his asthma, and his gout, but who protests that these ailments are due to daily work and his devoted service to his country. Fielding describes his journey to Lisbon, seeking a warmer climate than either London or Bath can offer, in a journal that will be published bearing that forthright title. Moreover, the journal invokes epic parallels and constructs an allegorical struggle, as Fielding's biographer, Ronald Paulson, observes, "between the captain and the wind, and, with the wind, allusions to Aeneas, Aeolus, and Neptune's *Quos Ego*." As Fielding, felled by gout, is carried aboard ship, he feels as if he is running a "gauntlope (so I think I may justly call it) through rows of sailors and watermen, few of whom failed of paying their compliments to me by all manner of insults and jests on my misery."

More evidence of the importance of this text to *Through the Panama* is furnished by Fielding's opening entry ("Wednesday, June 26, 1754. On this day the most melancholy sun I had ever beheld arose, and found me awake at my house at Fordhook.") This is the selfsame wintry sun that appeared for Martin just a moment ago, because Lowry will always remain obedient to the principle that sentences of the same syntax, games with the same structure, symbols with the same subject, coincidences of all kinds, myths of the same form, stories with the same plot, journeys with the same aim, and all who thirst and suffer from guilt and perpetual dryness, girls of the same slimness, souls who need numbness, lives that play with death as if life were checkers played in a kitchen, each and all are the same girl, soul, sentence, game, myth, plot, song and cinema; they are victims of the same plight, have made the same messes, and have the same pain.

What would clinch these distant identities? Crimes of the same kind. Smollett had accused Fielding of stealing two of his characters from *Roderick Random;* Lowry had pleaded guilty with innocent intentions for his liberal borrowing from Aiken and Grieg; as for Coleridge . . . his thefts from the German philosophers were notorious. And related to addiction too. It was "the spectre that would haunt the rest of his career." You cannot call it "borrowing" because the plagiarist cannot return his thefts with a note of thanks.

The crew is chipping rust. Next they will be painting the ventilators.

A return to the movie. As our ship is about to stretch out along the long coast of Mexico, the weather grows warmer, the engines labor somewhere in that monotonous refrain like an insect thrashing in a web, the sea seems as sullen as the sky, and we switch cameras to follow the shadow of a plane falling south through the beautiful opening pages of *Dark as the Grave Wherein My Friend Is Laid* (handy to one's hand because it is only pages away in this collection). In contrast, the beginning of a story, "June the 30th, 1934," stresses engine noise by suppressing it: "Silently the train for Boulogne drew out of the Gare de l'Est. This was surprising. One had expected an excruciating din. . . ." However, the deep-sea freighters of "The Forest Path to the Spring" that arrive in the bay as quietly as mist, leave with their lumber and "a great list, tilted like wheelbarrows . . . their engines mumbling . . ."—guess what?

Brother Jack will show up in text after text, but sometimes, the way a bird's *teach-er, teach-er, teach-er* will, in the next moment, sound like *cheat-er, cheat-er* to the same ear, the engines will say,

"Please go on! Why not die!" in the plainest English, before reverting to *"Sonnez les matines"* in the clearest French.

This children's chant follows Lowry's words about like their threatening heartbeat. Frère Jacques is possibly a pilgrim on "the Way of Saint James," a monk who has been assigned the task of alerting others that it is time for matins (there are many conjectures), and who has failed this time to wake himself. It is the pulse for these texts, their ground bass, a memento mori, blood beating in the ear.

Special effects again. The special effects are planned by Lowry down to the last *whaa, whaa* of Bix Beiderbecke's horn playing "In a Mist," and he chooses each musical piece very carefully in order to achieve, for the sound track, another kind of commentary. There is, for instance, a song for a marimba. Then into the text of *Through the Panama,* because an albatross has been sighted, float marginal notes taken verbatim from "The Rime of the Ancient Mariner," and soon we are the reluctant guests at another performance of that poem, in unison with memories of *The Journal of a Voyage to Lisbon, Outward Bound, Moby Dick,* and several others. The passengers in Sutton Vane's play find themselves on a crewless ship bound for the afterlife.

Data. You can't film data, and there is a lot of data of the sort the ship's log will accumulate. The ship's positions, particularly, dotting down the map with the windblown ship of the mariner. Malc counting the shearwaters—those birds who know how to rest on a wave.

That's how it shall be rendered: a montage of mountains, seascapes, and red lines drawn on charts that fill the screen. Now the marginal notes are no longer the mariner's but Lowry's, paralleling his pages of mislabeled fiction with columns of colorless info and chatty book talk. While the main body is bemoaning "the fact that having been unable to buy a bottle of Martell from the steward," Lowry, that is Wilderness, that is Trumbaugh, had become dependent "upon an invitation from the skipper for a drink which had never seemed more necessary"; the margin is recounting how "William Paterson, founder of the great bank of England . . . began life by walking backwards through England, with a pedlar's pack on his back."

The marginal notes squeeze the text until the canal is completely traversed. But the mariner's thirst continues to Curaçao, where a case of rum is purchased, calming the surface of the soul, although, for the ship, there are rising winds. The camera continues its relentless movement, the ship its song, the storm its threat. Malc, his wife, and his motley crew of phantoms are spectators to the world. What makes moving pictures moving pictures is not the fact that things and people, trees and water, move, but that the camera leaves one scene for another, leaves one set of circumstances for another, rests like the shearwater on a wave, but must soon fly off to feed upon the changing light—drive off, steam off to the comfort of another name, the interest of another place, to the chant of change: *ding dang dong* . . . until the picture fades to black. Dissolves.

Perhaps we should leave it to the Ancient Mariner's master to say what our experience should be, if not what it often is. "The reader should be carried forward, not merely or chiefly by the mechanical impulse of curiosity, or by a restless desire to arrive at the final solution, but by the pleasurable activity of mind excited by the attractions of the journey itself."

Hofmann's collection includes a generous sampling from Lowry's letters. Letters were a strength and a necessity for someone customarily cast as an alien, out of luck and far away from friends, posting and picking up his mail in Cuernavaca or Curaçao, and even borrowing the letter form for one of his most impressive stories (here included) "Strange Comfort Afforded by the Profession." Of course, he risks being a bore about his work, constantly worrying about it, explaining it, defending it, pleading or conniving for it. It is also clear that part of him has never outgrown his schoolboy years. He is both ink and blotter—wholly self-absorbed. But he is a jolly tavern buddy too, mellow and amusing, garrulous to a fault, with letters longer than patience and often linked together daily like barges behind a tow. Lowry customarily ricochets from one current bit of reading to the next, associates not freely but compulsively, and propels himself from explanation to complaint with the same remarkable energy he repeatedly displays in his literary work, sometimes catching his own train of thought barely before it leaves the station.

Some of Lowry's poems are here as well. They have the advantage of bluntness. The rhymes go *mirror, horror, terror, error, collar,* $ as the poem travels to Dollarton. "This ticking is most terrible of all— / You hear the sound I mean on ships and trains, / You hear it everywhere for it is doom . . ." In the prose, too, Captain Hook and his crocodile are regularly invoked, as well as the devoured arm and its abominable watch. "How like to Man is this man and his fate, / Still drunk and stumbling through the rusty trees / to breakfast on stale rum sardines and peas."

Sidelong shots: If movies move and music moves, Lowry's favorite locales move too—the buses boats planes taxis trains—a restless mind, a roving eye—but the persistent reflexivity of the texts (*Up the Panama* or "Down the Forest Path" would make more sense), the piling on of parallels (though two could count as tracks and disappear into the distance), the array of aggressive symbols like buttons on a tunic, shards of scenes and bits of thought, perceptions briefer than butterflies, clips and tears and tatters taken from reality, the writer's command to ponder each one, fondle it even—a swatch of idle speech, a shadow that has wandered away from its figure— these combine to bring any narrative to a halt, the ship lies becalmed in the heat, and we are staring straight ahead in a bar, at a naked babe above the bar, at bottles in front of the bar, at our own smeared face, looking for something in flicks of light that will console us, that will go behind reality and find a better appearance, hence the help sought in the kabbalah, in Yeats's *A Vision,* in the Ouija board, in premonition; but if we examine Lowry's capture of *Tender Is the Night* and watch him not only alter it into a sort of sea voyage of his own, including the heroic drowning of Dick Diver (to redeem him in the eyes of his love, redeem Fitzgerald too, another pretty party boy, save Malc, Sigbjørn, Martin) at the movie's close, instead of

Diver's gradual, almost dusty disappearance into the small towns of upper New York in Fitzgerald's version; indeed going so far as to turn the *Brest,* once renamed *Diderot,* into a vessel now christened *Aristotle—*

> Lap dissolve to the *Aristotle* steaming outward bound—as the overlapping echoes of the siren die we are aware of the ship's engine, like a bass accompaniment to the rhythm and tune, very faintly at first, of Frère Jacques.

—a ship that will sail straight into a dreadful storm resembling the one that concludes *Through the Panama,* breaking to pieces in the process, unlike Malc's craft, which survives a loss of steerage to struggle through to safety. Meanwhile Martin (Sigbjørn, Malcolm) like the mariner, has made promises to the sea gods he won't keep past two smooth days, but who, perhaps as a punishment for being so remiss, will be compelled to tell his tale to anyone who will listen.

It's a wrap. The camera floats across a gradually subsiding sea to glide up a beach in a long slow undulation (stay with the water as its depth shallows until we can see sand shifting slightly with the current), and then lifts its attention to the walls and towers of the town Dick Diver knew as Antibes before panning to the star-filled sky, in a shot just this corny and unconvincing.

THE BUSH OF BELIEF

Henry James's short story "The Tree of Knowledge" might have been more literally and less sacredly titled "The Bush of Belief." At the center of the pleasant little paradise, which seems to be sculptor Morgan Mallow's life, stands that artist's complacent certainty about his genius, a confidence that he has faithfully sustained through a productive although unheralded life. Mallow's entourage is as small as his fame is restricted, and consists of a wife so devoted she receives no other name than Missus, their only offspring, Lancelot, and finally this son's godfather, Peter Brench, a literary figure we have learned to call "the friend of the family," and a man who counts among his numerous discretions (including a prolonged though muted adoration of Mrs. Mallow) his refusal to publish his own literary endeavors.

These players form a box—the boundaries of a garden, if you like—of the most traditional kind: husband, wife, son, friend of the family. The dynamics of their relationships are determined by a diagonal that triangulates the box so that sometimes we are dealing solely with the family trio, while at other times with the romantic triangle of friend, wife, husband. The tale is itself of the simplest. Each individual, in ignorance of the true convictions of the others, is endeavoring to maintain the group's belief in the genius of its center—its grand master—and therefore each member's reason for being. A comedy of errors ensues and epiphanies abound.

The story is told from Peter Brench's point of view, and therefore is in the service of this careful man's proudly held convictions, some of which are stated early and openly, while others emerge with some shyness: (first) that he has managed to maintain his friendship with Morgan Mallow while never for a moment compromising the principles of his taste by lying or deception, not easy since (second) Brench considers Mallow to be a charming man but, as an artist, a shallow pretentious hack; (third) that Mrs. Mallow's allegiance to Morgan Mallow's genius is the basis of her love for him; (fourth) therefore that Brench can be loyal to his love for Mrs. Mallow only by protecting her opinion of her husband as well as he has hidden his own; (fifth) that the son shares her idolatry and her error; (further, sixth) that Lancelot, despite the hopes the Mallows have for him as a painter, has no more talent than his father, if as much; (seventh) that Peter's reluctance to publish maintains "the purity of his taste by establishing still more firmly the right relation of fame to feebleness"—that, in sum, although Peter Brench has "the misfortune to be omniscient, . . . it is ignorance that is bliss." And therefore it is folly to be wise.

The Mallows put on Italian airs as if they were tunes on a phonograph, and James takes obvious delight in describing the pretensions which furnish their Eden; however, its serenity is threatened by another misconception: that Lancelot Mallow (such a disastrous name) has been born to the brush rather than to his father's chisel. The Mallows embrace the difference because Morgan had always been a bit disappointed he'd rounded and smoothed so many stones rather than coloring and brightening canvas, and his son's success in this line would do much to right that hereditary wrong.

Peter Brench does what he can to prevent it (he throws money in the young man's path—a common enough gesture in James), because he fears that the Paris experience (for that is where Lancelot is headed), by educating his eye, will reveal his father's achievement to be as banal as his own talent is manifestly *manqué*. Before Lancelot spurs his horse toward the center of the painter's world, Peter and Mrs. Mallow have this delicious exchange:

> "Don't you believe in it?" asked Mrs. Mallow, who still, at more than forty, had her violet velvet eyes, her creamy satin skin and her silken chestnut hair.
>
> "Believe in what?"
>
> "Why, in Lance's passion."
>
> "I don't know what you mean by 'believing in it.' I've never been unaware, certainly, of his disposition, from his earliest time, to daub and draw; but I confess I've hoped it would burn out."
>
> "But why should it," she sweetly smiled, "with his wonderful heredity? Passion is passion—though of course indeed *you*, dear Peter, know nothing of that. Has the Master's ever burned out?"

Peter Brench smothers all honest response to ask whether Mrs. Mallow thinks her son is going to be another Master? and receives an armload of rationalization in reply.

> She seemed scarce prepared to go that length, yet she had on the whole a marvellous trust. "I know what you mean by that. [She does not know, of course.] Will it be a career to incur the jealousies and provoke the machinations that have been at times almost too much for his father? Well—say it may be, since nothing but clap-trap, in these dreadful days, *can*, it would seem, make its way, and since, with the curse of refinement and distinction, one may easily find one's self begging one's bread. Put it at the worst—say he *has* the misfortune to wing his flight further than the vulgar taste of his stupid countrymen can follow. Think, all the same, of the happiness—the same the Master has had. He'll *know*."
>
> Peter looked rueful. "Ah but *what* will he know."
>
> "Quiet joy!" cried Mrs. Mallow, quite impatient and turning away.

The Bush of Belief

Henry James, as if he had been tutored by his brother, makes his entire story turn on the distinction between belief and knowledge (truth and opinion); and then upon the differences among (a) knowing a fact, (b) understanding what someone means, (c) exercising a skill, (d) affirming a faith, and (e) having an experience—for each of which the word *know* will sometimes serve.

Lancelot learns that indeed he is a dauber, a muff. "But I'm not such a muff as the Master!" For, as Peter Brench is more than disconcerted to discover, the son saw through his father as sun through clear glass early on. And, as Brench's beliefs continue to come to grief, he learns that Lancelot's mother, the silken and satiny Mrs. Mallow, whom his love has lived to protect . . . that she has also known all along. Each member of this saintly trio has conspired to keep from the others the downcasting truth lest it remove *cher maître* like a title from the Master, and shatter the blessed ignorance which holds the little group together.

So it not unexpectedly turns out that Peter Brench, the omniscient one, has not known, has only believed; and in caring for Mrs. Mallow as Mrs. Mallow cares for the Master, he has mirrored her love without receiving, as she has, any in return. His errors, in fact, have been many, because he wrongly supposed Mrs. Mallow loved, in the Master, the genius that the genius believed he had, when it was not the artist but the man; it was not the quality of the result, but the passion in the process, that drew her to Morgan Mallow and held her there.

Peter Brench had a horror of error; he did not wish to risk making a fool of himself; hence his own general silence: no protestation of love, no public productions. And in the end, he knew none of the kinds of knowledge aforementioned: not Morgan Mallow's faith in his talent or his joy in creation, not Lancelot's recognitions, not Mrs. Mallow's passion for passion. To keep his intelligence unsmudged, he cleaned the implement but failed to use it.

James's satirical intent in this piece is clearly evident and broadly stated. The names of the characters are signal enough. Morgan Mallow cannot possibly be anything more than a soft bog; Mrs. Mallow has lost sight of her own self, hence has no name of her own; and "Lancelot Mallow" is a ludicrous combination. What might have been a shrewdly observant "Peter Bench" is wrenched just enough to spell out confusion, so that when this gentlemen says he has "judged himself once for all," his name belies the accuracy of that boast.

Critics have been no kinder to this story than the art world has been to Morgan Mallow. One dismissed it as "a bore." Most writers on James ignore it altogether. Summaries of it in volumes pretending to be inclusive are curt and unflattering. "The usual narrator is given an external appearance which might have served to clothe a minor character in a better tale."

The kind of knowledge that gives James his epistemological misgivings always concerns the nature of moral good and evil. Belief is grounded in gossip and depends upon the interpretation of social intentions. Its unreliable nature leads invariably to ambiguous conclusions, and guilt is spread over everyone like grease over toast. The screw that can be given one more turn is a regular feature. If Peter Brench is mistaken about Mrs. Mallow and her son, and they, in turn, are wrong about him as well as one another, might not Morgan Mallow be in no doubt really about his own deficiencies, and be keeping up the charade of his purity and ambition for everybody else's sake, for how can he disabuse the faithful of their belief in him? The story does not turn this far, but it gives us the mechanism for its movement.

Moreover, what gives Morgan Mallow his dignity, despite his hollow pretensions, is that fact that his passion for art appears to be genuine if none of its products is.

There is, nonetheless, the suggestion that both Mallows might more readily succumb to mammon's temptations than their ideals should approve, if ever they were offered the opportunity; and James has great fun with the wealthy Canadian couple who wish to commission Mallow to do a tomb for their three children. Here, the word *moral* is deployed like a skirmish line in front of an absent army.

The Bush of Belief

Such was naturally the moral of Mrs. Mallow's question: if their wealth was to be assumed, it was clear, from the nature of their admiration, as well as from mysterious hints thrown out . . . as to other possibilities of the same mortuary sort, that [*sic*, what?] their further patronage might be; and not less evident that should the Master become at all known in those climes nothing would be more inevitable than a run of Canadian custom.

The reader should be ready to believe that the arty ideal the Mallow clan embraces, they embrace because no prettier mate has made itself available. They have gone to bed with what they must.

James leaves us in a quagmire of doubt. Peter Brench believes that Mrs. Mallow believes that Mr. Mallow believes in his genius, although later he is led to believe that she has never believed in him any more than Peter Brench has. So it is not only possible that Morgan Mallow knows his failings too, as his wife knows, as his son knows, as the family friend knows, as the world, in its treatment of his work, seems to know; but that the Master's purity from profit is also a pose, though as genuine as circumstances demand, and that were the world to come to his door with wealth and glory to confer, he would not turn the world away as he might a salesman with only encyclopedias to sell; rather he would graciously accept the proffered laurels, and sharpen his chisel, and endeavor to keep up with this welcome run of intercontinental custom.

Mrs. Mallow believes that her husband has a passion for art, if he hasn't the genius we suppose he supposes he has, but she believes that Peter Brench hasn't such devotion, and cannot have known "quiet joy." Although joy has been denied him, we know that Peter has his passion and has been more faithful to it than most husbands. He knows quietness, and if his passion has been sterile, at least it has not peopled parlors with a "little staring white population" of mis-scaled statuary.

If the suspicions the story stirs in us are sustained during still

133

another turn, we may wonder if Morgan Mallow's commitment to art isn't more a matter of necessity than devotion. Then Mrs. Mallow would be wrong about the pure part of her husband's nature. A plot that has turned itself to the point of Peter Brench's epiphany and disillusionment might be turned almost interminably.

To eat of the fruit of the true tree of knowledge might not be, in our secular world, such a bad thing. Just beware of the berries on the bush of belief.

We readers don't know—can't know—why, when, what, or whether. We can only believe what we believe. And understand how well we've been warned.

HENRY JAMES'S CURRICULUM VITAE

The Intricately Constructed Phallus

As I opened the first volume of Sheldon Novick's biography of Henry James (*Henry James: The Young Master*. New York: Random House, 1996), I had to stifle a cry of "Oh, dear, are we going play palsy-walsy?" when I read . . . "please allow me, after this brief preface, to direct your attention to Henry James, with whom I would like you to become better acquainted." My designated leader then began the tour of his author's life by drawing a curtain, like Parson Weems on a naughty Washington, to reveal that his man "is sitting comfortably at a sidewalk table on a broad crowded boulevard. Perhaps he is in Paris. . . ." How do you do, sir? . . . is that what I say? Then I rather impulsively asked myself whether I remembered Henry James being this chummy with anyone, although, after a thoughtful moment, I had to admit he must have been so with his nanny. Still, I wasn't sure I wanted to sit at a cafe table in a town I couldn't safely call by name, next door to a man palpably enjoying "his usual pink grenadine glacée, with two straws, on the white tablecloth beside him" while "watching the passersby with grave eyes." In less time than it takes to read a line, they would be "striking gray eyes," and the object of our scrutiny would assume a Napoleonic posture that, "despite [its] dignity . . . seemed to invite confidences." Ah. confidences, of course. "A young man stops to talk, and then sits down with him."

Oh, dear. So my guide is going to take that tack. The paragraph, and the preface, conclude: "A couple in evening dress stop. Soon there is a circle of young people around him, and they remain until long after midnight, talking." So this is the Henry James we are to meet—a man about town and a magnet for youth? Well, midnight is a bit past my bedtime, I'm afraid.

I had heard the gossip. The gossip was that a number of industrious scholars had recently discovered a "hurray-he's-a-gay-guy" to put alongside Proust and Wittgenstein in the alternative pantheon, since countless previously unread, suppressed, or unpublished letters showed that the suspicion of gayness, before only briefly caught sight of, had to be changed to a conviction, because this new information replaced all prior hypotheses and removed their protections. These prior excuses for Henry James's apparent chastity were: (1) he had never had much of an active sex life on account of a lackluster libido; (2) there had occurred a mysterious injury to his back that had unmanned him elsewhere; (3) the women he loved tended to meet tragic ends—Minny Temple's death from TB had made him mourn, Constance Fenimore Woolson's suicide had made him angry—so he became as skittish as a wary cat; (4) his vital juices were so thoroughly absorbed by his writing and his delicate social studies that the impulses of ordinary men only acted on him indirectly, the way an initiated carom slowly reaches its culmination by nicking the one remaining ball into a corner pocket; (5) his psychology was such that physical desires were allowed to manifest themselves only through an inordinate interest in the marriages of others, a trait odd for a confirmed bachelor, even though, in his circle, marriages were mostly matters of money and hierarchy, not love and passion; or (6) that ultimately James sought aesthetic transcendence, even saintliness, and was ascetic because heaving and grunting were simply not something a person of his excessive refinement should ever sink to, nor would he wish us to picture him doing anything that partook of common coarseness—eating kidneys ill lodged in a publican's pie, for instance, or visiting the loo and enjoying his relief like Leopold Bloom.

Henry James's Curriculum Vitae

Though the evidence was supposed to stare everybody in the face, it was also deemed scandalous and detrimental, so that otherwise admiring eyes were turned away, and mum was the word, or at least some form of discreet dismissal would be expected. Certainly, this has not been an uncommon reaction of biographers to bad news. They ignored Edith Wharton's adulterous affair with Morton Fullerton (gay himself Monday through Friday); and devoted followers of Wittgenstein wore zipped lips for some time with regard to Wittgenstein's homosexuality, as well as his "mysterical" leanings, to mention but two from a posse of precedent. For positivists the second failing was by far the worse. Although Fred Kaplan's *Henry James: The Imagination of Genius: A Biography* (New York: Morrow, 1992) had spoken of Henry James's homosexual tendencies plainly enough, Sheldon Novick (a lawyer by trade) apparently felt that there was still a case to be made, and in his first volume he argues his position as if he were before a jury.

The biography, which concludes with the second volume, called *Henry James: The Mature Master,* just published (New York: Random House, 2007), begins with another forward flash. The ill and aging James has had to leave his home in Rye and take up lodgings in London once again, and there we find him, entering his seventies, his typewriter on his desk and his literary secretary, Theodora Bosanquet hard at it, transferring his voice to the page "through her strong, boyish fingers." But our guide has only begun beating his drum. "It is curious to think of James striding about the Chelsea flat evoking for her powerfully sensuous images, and at the last, when he was close to death, dictating *The Ivory Tower,* an intricately constructed phallus around which he set his characters dancing to Miss Bosanquet's music." If "boyish fingers" is sly innuendo, what must the ivory phallus be?

The Effeminate Old Donkey

What are the data that determine any person's life? Of the things we desire, do, see, think or feel, what ones should be discarded like spoiled paper, and what should be retained? How shall the residue be weighed? How shall these elements be joined to one another? And why should we really bother putting the puzzle together at all, at such expense of time and cogitation? because our own aims— our worship and our animus—certainly direct the construction— the gathering, the sorting—of even the least scraps of information. What is important to the genius of our author? Shall we watch, if we are able, while the poet washes his hands in the lavatory basin? Or follow our subject's fingers slipping through her lingerie drawer? Study her dance card? Or count the clapping in his last ovation? Are we simply in need of matters of greasy fact, and desire to proceed directly to essentials as on a fast train, or are we altogether in love, and value like a sheared curl every wisp caught by a collar, every lip mark on a glass, any footprint made by our darling descending from a carriage, and regard the shriveled core of our hero's gnawed apple as a religious relic? Perhaps our prizes are to be those two straws lying on a café cloth, or are the ones we cherish peeking out the neck of an abandoned soda bottle?

Although we know she launched a thousand ships, we do not know the color of Helen's eyes. To look into Medusa's was to suffer consequences, but what of Henry James's gray gaze? Was what he saw sucked up and carried off into a narrative he was engaged in making, or has he saved a trait for use in creating a lady of quality? Was it filed next to more looks like it—perhaps of apology or reproach—behind the master's imperious brow? Not long ago, biographers read Freud first, then made their subject a patient. It was an important but tiresome development, as most are. Other biographers buried their victim under mounds of data, a democracy of detail that admitted of no hierarchy and held out no hope. Still others loved backgrounds so much their portraits were like those avant garde Turners that depict figures, castles, passes, peaks, disappearing in a smoke of color.

Novick is a novelistic biographer. By that I mean that a great deal of what he includes in his life of James is decoration. It is not necessary for the reader to know that "For a small fee, a stout red-faced woman carried off his dirty linen once each week and returned it heavily starched and pressed," but to learn these trivial daily tasks makes us feel at home. Still, unless the linen was metaphorically unclean, Lytton Strachey would not have given any notice to it. Of course, Strachey was not above pulling facts from their contexts as if they were aching teeth. Novick provides rich social and intellectual backgrounds for the actions he depicts. He is aware of his subject's psyche but he does not psychoanalyze. *Honorable Justice,* his fine book on Oliver Wendell Holmes, has prepared him for the necessity of historical and geographical surroundings, and he supplies them: hills, dales, barns, and towns; wars, riots, scandals, labor movements, acts of Parliament; but he is acutely aware that although James was an ordinary guy when nature required him to be—our bowels do more to make us equal than the revolver—it is Henry James's head that bends when he enters a taxi, and that not even a spot of tar on the street is safe from his scrutiny.

Novick is also attracted by the lonely little item that might enliven the page and brighten its story. Some are irresistible. When James's aunt Kate dies she leaves a rather hefty estate. Among the lesser spoils is a shawl to which Alice James is given a "life interest," and which, to an amusement that barely covers her annoyance, she understands must be returned to the estate when she herself is through with it—a restoration only her ghost can carry out.

The hazard for our text is James's sexual orientation. It becomes an idée fixe, the life warped by this single somewhat suppressed inclination, and the reader begins to feel roughed up by its insistence, as if he were having to endure a repetitive ad whose message will follow him home like a stray, regardless of his dislike, his shouts and shoos, or his internal resistance. Sometimes loudly, sometimes in a whisper, the point is made. Often the issue in question is simply presumed. "His only indisputable love letters were written to men."

When we open volume two of this life we do not find ourselves curbside in perhaps Paris, but in the upstairs study of Lamb House, Henry James's home in Rye, smothered in atmosphere, a sea-coal fire flickering in the corner grate. He is correcting the morning's dictation. One can almost see the camera approaching for a shot, say, of a manuscript page of *The Golden Bowl.* James's achievement matches his figure now: stout, massive, stately. Out of the dim short days of winter, the persistent theme emerges like a figure in a trench coat. James is said to be traveling in "vaguely defined circles that a later generation—not entirely accurately or fairly—would call aristocratic and homosexual and that the middle-class press satirized as 'aesthetic.'" Yet even if not quite "fair," Sheldon Novick will mention it. Twice, in the next two pages, London's winters will be called "masculine," because they aren't the stylish Easter season of balls and banquets or the vacation flight of the family to a cooling seashore cottage. "Painters' studios . . . were masculine salons where artists and writers . . . formed intimate friendships." Friends, too, will receive this honor: "Arthur was a slender, reserved, manly, and serious young man. . . ." A character, Hyacinth Robinson of *The Princess Casamassima,* when he decides not to commit the murder his anarchist organization has assigned to him, is said to have made a "manly choice."

The other sidelong word is *intimate,* and these two are scattered like peekaboos about the text. When quizzed by his family about his London plans, James replies that "he is too good a bachelor to spoil by marriage." Novick gratuitously adds, "Of the intimate friendships that he has formed, he says nothing." As if he should confess to having taken up sodomy. A young, handsome (we must have these adjectives) Scandinavian sculptor, Hendrik Andersen, Novick's choice for leading man in this heart's play, is introduced with the warning that he will "be a most intimate friend." Is an intimacy measure available? Yes, it seems there is. Upon learning of the death from tuberculosis of Andersen's brother, James writes a letter whose babbling gush makes one cringe. Can its recipient really believe in the genuineness of the emotions so sloppily represented? Andersen is addressed with two "dears" like a flight of stairs leading to a "dearest." James's heart is aching, bleeding, breaking. He is in torment. Having shown that he is in even greater pain than the griever, James invites Hendrik to Lamb House in Rye, where James is now living, so that he may "take consoling, soothing, infinitely close & tender & affectionately-healing possession of you . . . to put my arm around you & make you lean on me as on a brother & a lover, & keep you on & on, slowly comforted or at least relieved of the first bitterness of pain . . ." Hendrick has lost a brother but he has gained a lover who will be—wow—another brother. So James's offer is not as erotic as it might immediately seem. While "panting" to see Arthur Benson, a new friend, the next day, James sends a note apologizing for not having written sooner, but says that, instead, he is looking forward to "answering you with impassioned lips." True—this is rather an exaggeration if taken for "hello, dear chap."

The evidence, such as it is, is in the letters, and somewhere in the 10,423 of those which we possess, some explicit revelations may emerge, but what we have now are missives full of emotional hyperbole, effusive flattery, and infantile cajoling that become less convincing as the verbs of desire and the adjectives of adoration accumulate. "I love you" may carry some small weight, but "I love love love love love you" less.

Sometimes hostile witnesses can be useful to your case. Frank Harris and Harold Frederic are called to the stand. According to the counsel for the defense James had finally reached such eminence as to attract attackers to him like mosquitoes drawn to CO_2, and one such was the new editor of *The Fortnightly Review*, Frank Harris, who "privately accused [James] of effeminacy, of being part of a shadowy conspiracy of homosexuals," and wrote in his autobiography that James's "well-formed, rather Jewish nose was the true index of his character." Unfortunately, for this testimony, Harris's opinions were not expressed in print until 1926, when they were privately issued in Paris nearly a decade after the object of their malice had died. A better example is furnished by the novelist Harold Frederic, who was allowed to say in a letter to *The New York Times* (to my surprise) that "Henry James is an effeminate old donkey who lives with a herd of donkeys around him and insists on being treated as if he were the Pope. . . ."

Oscar Wilde's plays aren't James's sort of thing, nor does their success improve his judgment of them, but James nominates Wilde for membership in one of his clubs, and supports him during his scandalous trial, although the scandal, for James, is often worse than the crime. James is not the kind of homosexual who feels he must always stick up for his sex. Novick, however, sometimes seems surprised. "In *The Tragic Muse* he gave what now seems an all-but-explicit and negative portrayal of an openly gay man. This latter is particularly puzzling, because James's own loves were, so far as is known, exclusively male."

James was unquestionably attracted to young mostly gay men, and for a variety of reasons. There appears to be enough sexual longing in him to serve a dozen, but in addition the young men flatter him, confirm his views and feelings; their own effeminate ways not only match his, but precisely because of the "feminine element" in their composition, they have more tact, sensitivity, cultural polish, and manners than bluff sailor sorts or other types of tough guy. James's androgynous character is one of his great strengths as an artist, and he knows that the feminine in men does not merely mean the loss of a rough edge, but is often the best, the most civilized part of them. *Manly* is not his word of worship. *Civilization* is.

The Bachelor

If you are a bachelor who is going to be a bachelor because your career must not be compromised by more family obligations than you already bear, you will naturally seek out the company of like minded single souls of both sexes, but particularly of your own; so that to be often seen with men will not be worth a comment, nor will your frequenting of places where husbands are gratefully severed from their wives and children—of which an English private club is a perfect social instrument—be understood as anything less than necessary in order to enjoy, even if in visit-bits-and-pieces, what its members once, as bachelors, uninterruptedly took pleasure in: a quiet read, a nice port, reposeful dinner, good cigar, a leather-bound snooze. The club can be both your living and your dining room, or your library where you can borrow a book, peruse a periodical or the daily papers, rub the better shoulders.

To that end, Henry James became a member of the Reform Club, the Rabelais Club, the Savile Club, the Omar Khayyam Club, and the the Athenaeum, whose library was especially alluring. "On the other side of the room sits Herbert Spencer, asleep in a chair (he always is, when I come here) and a little way off is the portly Archbishop of York with his nose in a little book." Later, in Rye, he joins the golf club, though he only goes there for tea after a long walk. To learn more of his chosen town he also frequents the local pub. James eventually has a bed-sit at the Reform Club, and works there when beset by solitude's drearies at Lamb House, his place in Rye. His steno, then Mary Weld, arrives discreetly through a side door to breach this manly bastion.

At the same time, as a bachelor you can attach yourself to the fluttering edges of various sorts of interesting or useful families by your availability for dinner, your help in small emergencies, your avuncular warmth, and, of course, because you are a person who may carry the cachet of significant guest and important friend from one place at table to another as if you were a slice of something from the roast. In addition to being agreeable, these relationships will be of great value to you when the materials that most stir your muse are the ins and outs of social commerce, the hypocrisies that support manners and put a roof on good behavior. Social life will not

seem frivolous even when it is supremely so, and if you have cultivated the observant, ambitious, and witty, you will have anecdotes
aplenty—ore worthy of being relieved of its roughness and rounded
into impressive rings.

You will be a winner with brats of every kind, producing in them
just enough fear and strangeness to induce attention and the relief of
obedience. After all, the bachelor does not have to suffer the embarrassment of their education or the humiliations their maturation will
inflict. In effect, you can play grandparent without the necessity of
years. It is sometimes difficult for a father to put himself back in his
own strident youth when he is the brunt of his child's complaint,
but for the bachelor it is easy. He is already there; in a critical sense
he has obtained every family's prized position—that of the only
child.

The Busy Body

James spends an unaccountable amount of time socializing at
his various clubs and otherwise dining out ("Dear Mrs. Bell, I am
engaged to go to 4 different places this afternoon between 5 & 6:30,
& to do, besides, 17 other different things"); when in London, which
is often, he keeps rather regular attendance at the theater, usually to
see plays he will review; there are of course the customary weekend
junkets to the sumptuously appointed country estates of the rich
and titled—teas and shoots, stiff chairs and parlor pianos; as if evenings were not full enough, he has his own little dinners for six to
preside over; then space in the day must be found in which to tend
to the needs of his sister, the frequently bedridden Alice James, as
well as other visits to the sick, and such Good Samaritan assign-
ments as his tenderness insists on, for if you have many friends, you
will have many bedsides. Sunday calls of courtesy are de rigueur, of
course. One's calling card must get about even when its owner does
not. More important burdens—the consequence of diligence and
honesty—are overseeing the settlement of estates (Alice James's for

instance) or acting as a literary executor, or arranging, over considerable distance, the burial of Constance Fenimore Woolson after her suicide in Rome.

None of the day's drudgeries disappear just because you are busy elsewhere, so you must hunt for lodgings, hire servants, dispose of and acquire furniture, move from a pension in Paris to a room in Rome or a villa in Venice, because London is impossible in high season, Rye lonely in winter, Italy always enticing. During his frequent periods of depression James is driven to seek a sunnier disposition in sunnier, lazier climes.

Visits to America were infrequent and irregular, but they required a major commitment. Often illness or death was the occasion for a crossing. He stayed in Cambridge when he had to, enjoyed New York when he could, and took a year off to travel the lecture circuit as far as Florida, the Midwest, and California, with intermittent halts to have some teeth pulled. At all points James was industriously absorbing scenes, gathering anecdotes, obtaining suggestions for plots and themes, learning about issues he might attach to his singular interests, and allowing his impressions to be absorbed by his ravenous artistic unconscious like a stockpot that is cooking its way toward cassoulet.

Then he must discover a moment for dashing off letters of a business sort or those required to retain his good standing in society (thanks for this socialite's party, that author's book, a weekend's pleasure). What cannot be dashed are publishing problems, theatrical issues, political causes. Naturally he must stay in postal range of his many, mostly intimate pals. Novick writes that while away from the city, James "kept in touch with his London friends by patiently writing letters in the evenings after dinner, often writing until the early hours of the morning." He saved his worn-out wrist and hand for these chores, and began dictating to a typist his articles and books, but his work as well as his social life was frequently hampered by various other physical ills: chronic backache and constipation, jaundice which seized him in Venice, those periodic depressions, attacks of gout which made him goose-step when he had to walk, and, as he aged, a case of shingles that sent him to bed, bouts of angina announcing the end, many of the latter accompanied by fears that he was bereft of friends and alone in his misery.

Meanwhile, James managed to compose new plays, or adapt some of his stories for the stage, and oversee their production; choose, edit, revise, and preface texts for the New York Edition; supply magazines with stories, articles, profiles, travel pieces, and reviews; furnish publishers with triple-decker novels, serialized romances, and singular masterpieces.

The Family Man

James's ties to his extended family were strong, yet he lived apart for most of his life, and his brothers fled the nest as if they had just burst from an egg. Speaking of eggs, women of James's class were slaves of their wombs and spent large portions of their adult lives pregnant, since families were commonly large, in a condition closer to an illness than a blessing, and one that often ended, not just shortened, their lives. Henry's mother managed to have five children in seven years, and although they were healthy kids, Alice, William, and Henry suffered from severe bouts of depression, William and Henry had inherited their father's bad back; both lives would be threatened by a congestive heart, while, like a consumptive who catches cold, Henry would be a victim of his father's stammer. "James had twenty-one first cousins on his father's side alone. . . ." Henry's sense for the family bordered on the feudal, and that meant hierarchy, discipline, duty, property, and privilege. His immediate family had a dash of ordinary in it, but father, daughter, and two of the four sons were extraordinary individuals. James himself remained uneasy about his roots until he acquired Lamb House, where he was finally firmly affixed to a place that would gather and hold history as he hoped it would hold him.

Full of envy for his sibling's success, William James does not come off very well in Novick's account. He is often in Europe for extended periods, alone; he issues invitations and then is absent when the guest arrives; he offers advice that is most always bad; he complains about the stipulations in his relatives' wills. William especially had to envy Henry's freedom from family routines, emotional demands, and daily tasks. At the same time he disapproves of his brother's swirling social rounds, since they cut into the time set aside for work. The family's complex relationships are handled deftly, and Novick uses amusing little details to enliven his account, which is often fuller than Edel's earlier, five-volume, businesslike approach.

As William begins to enjoy his own success and the brothers begin to share ailments like two old soldiers their war stories, they grow easy in each other's company and more confident about their responses. The pair share an intense trust in the senses; they are fascinated by the phenomenon of consciousness; both value the individual above all else and bring a moral passion to all they do; but how other and inherently at odds they also are: William the Scientist and a seeker of acceptable means, and Henry the Aesthete, who values the intrinsic and the solemn worth of things in themselves: the Doer and the Viewer, one always going somewhere, the other always already there.

The Old Pro

Writing was once a genteel occupation, which meant it was meanly paid, and casually esteemed. England, in particular, was a nation that cherished its amateurs. Philosophers did their thinking on their days off; writers wrote through the stillness of the night as their genius required and their obsessions demanded. Poets alertly awaited the call of their muse because she never rang twice. On the continent, where rationalism flourished, scholars and philosophers had become professors, and what they professed was a discipline. They policed themselves, and standards were watchfully upheld.

Professors formed organizations like guilds and enjoyed positions in universities and status in society. Professors were trained and professors were paid. Naturally they were rationalists, because it was important that their subject seem serious and appropriately strenuous. Empiricism was more easily espoused, and the English took to it as if the strain of thinking deep thoughts was simply bad manners. In America Emerson, and later Josiah Royce, tried to elevate the level of thinking to German standards, but with little lasting success. Finally, the First World War destroyed most influence that remained. Who needed *Wahrheit* when impressions would serve?

Nevertheless, because the novel was such a popular form of entertainment, at no definite time but gradually as twilight, it became a profession too, even though it was not taught in academies like painting or music. James becomes a hired scribe. So he writes what he needs to write to make a living, to get ahead, to please and increase his audience, and therefore to respond to demands of taste and form and subject. James is aware of the sort of compromises he is obliged to make if he wants to write for the lady mags and for the stage. "Oh, how it must not be too good & how very bad it must be." James knew his audience, and had his order of battle, because a piece could appear first as a serial in a magazine ($), then in a nicely printed three-volume set as a novel of substance ($$), and finally in a cheap one-volume reprint for the arbor, the bedroom, or the train ($$$). If you are a realist, as James preferred to think of himself, he must research his books, and research always rolls the author toward the edge of journalism. To save time and increase income, a story may be puffed to the size of a novella, or modified to become a play, or taken apart to appear as vignettes. Travel has its pleasures but not their descriptions. Nonetheless, they pay the way. The loquacious master tries but he can't write concisely (be, like Wilde, cynically witty) or baldly enough to achieve success in the theater.

James suffers the pains of haste, laboring to realize a deadline, canceling all the other occupations of life but for this one, a load of obligation that grows heavier as he waits for the moment when he can coldly push the installment out of the house ahead of its perfecting, onto a public whose indifference to perfection is not consoling. His wrist, hand, and arm begin to rebel against their years of labor. Eventually he will have to resort to dictation. It will be difficult for him to grant works like *The Spoils of Poynton* their due, because they underwent too many metamorphoses and would seem cobbled together, or because they were written in a rush only to light the flame under his dinner pot. Some of the disdain he felt for his readers was his shame at having written to their level. "If that's what the idiots want, I can give them their bellyful." More and more he resents the "monctary world" of the professional writer. Still, as he enters his major phase, he is sending out a prospectus for *The Ambassadors,* arranging for the publication of a volume of stories, setting aside *The Wings of the Dove,* whose plot had not impressed the publishers—in business up to the gaze of his great gray eyes.

James did not sum up the year's work each December 31 the way another pro, Arnold Bennett did, noting in his journal that "This year (1928) I have written 304,000 words; 1 play, 2 films, 1 small book on religion, and about 80 or 82 articles"; but his year's receipts enabled him to lease his house in Rye. Bennett settled for a steam yacht. Neither of these wordmillers could complain about their output. As Novick says of James at the end of his late period: "In five years he had written a massive biography, a volume of short stories, and three of the greatest novels in the English language, all the while maintaining a busy social life, managing his own business affairs and a complex household."

The Great Masticator

In his own notebooks, James often talks to himself, tries to buck up his sagging spirits, encourage his muse to greater exertions, and remind himself of his duties to perfection. He is also not above threats. "I must make some great efforts during the next few years . . . if I wish not to have been on the whole a failure. I shall be a failure unless I do something *great!*" He gave public utterance to these standards in a lecture prepared for presentation during his travels in America, "The Lesson of Balzac." ". . . the lesson [is] that there is no convincing art that is not ruinously expensive. . . . Nothing counts but the excellent; nothing exists . . . but the superlative." Of course, this is the lesson of Flaubert, not of Balzac, who bit off more than he could Fletcherize.

Overweight and feeling ill from the burdens of work, James resorted to the dietary methods of Horace Fletcher, the so-called "Great Masticator," whose food fads were widely followed during the Victorian period. To recover his health, he begins to eat as he writes, cutting his food into very small bites, and then chewing those thoroughly (thirty-two times was recommended)—ruminatively, as the cow the cud—biting even liquids (good wines *are* chewable), swallowing slowly, savoring every flavor. You will write, read, eat less if this method is your model, and your bowel movements will be "no more offensive than moist clay, and have no more odor than a hot biscuit." A diet low in protein is also recommended. James's health does improve and he becomes a partisan of the procedure, even visiting Fletcher's palazzo in Venice. But James so ardently ground his food into gruel during his last years that he began to loathe food, if not his late style, and his doctors ordered him to cease.

James's novels were, after all, spoken into the ear and hence to the consciousness of a stenographer, who then repeated their character like orders to a set of ready fingers, fingers that spelled out what James had mulled over in order that they might be formed into an utterance in the first place; it was a slow process, like rekneading risen bread; so that now, as these words appeared on the typewriter's paper, they did so to their own reassuring music—the metronomic clack of the keys—and James's deliberate, clear, and careful dictation.

All fine writing should be speakable even if it is not actually spoken; it must be mouthed, for that is how we first learn language, how we make in the world our earliest contacts. Although the childish hug that James often promised his friends is more intimate, it has a compressed range of meanings, whereas we learn to say *love* as we learn to feel it, even if we later spell it *luv*. To our earliest sounds cling our most ancient memories, and a word that is never said—*hendecasyllabic*—is dead. As James argued in his last American lecture at Bryn Mawr, it is "the medium through which we communicate with each other. These relations are made possible, are registered, are verily constituted by our speech, and are successful . . . in proportion as our speech is worthy of its great human and social function: is developed, delicate, flexible, rich—an adequate accomplished fact. The more it suggests and expresses the more we live by it—the more it promotes and enhances life." James could not have envisioned the avid text messaging that now holds so many lines of vapidity open, as a window to a foul smell, or the thumb punching that has replaced the typist's skills, or the intoxicating space of ignorance and indifference that it promises to provide through its absence of voice, its lack of face to face, its refusal of touch.

His style is a kind of Fletcherizing, too, the cutting of his chosen experience into very small parts and the mashing of that until the original shape of the thought or feeling disappears and is replaced by a kind of cogitation that moves like a molten liquid through one thing then another until it finds its own form. Others may think that his stammer is a better metaphor, but *stammer* implies inability, whereas, when we properly digest our encounters, they dissolve into new uses and join the body of our being. The following example, that Novick more fully quotes (except that he ends the sentence early, with a period after *carriages*), may help to illustrate what James is doing. When Strether, in *The Ambassadors,* is standing on the balcony of his Paris apartment, inhaling the night air, and sensing the palpable presence of his lost youth, the passage concludes (I have lightly diagrammed the sentence to show its rhetorical structure and phrasing):

> It was   in the outside air
>   as well
>   as within;
> it was   in the   long watch,
>   from   the   balcony,
>   in the   summer night,
>   of the   wide late
>   life
>   of   Paris,
>   the   unceasing
>   soft quick rumble,
>   below,
>   of the   little
>   lighted carriages
>   that,
>   in the press,
>   always suggested
>   the   gamblers
>   he had seen
>   of   old
>   at Monte-Carlo
>   pushing up
>   to the tables.

Mastication, as a metaphor, will perhaps serve the analytic side of James's style, but it leaves out the corresponding synthesis: how this sense of past possibilities left unfulfilled, and now beyond recovery, returns to Strether, as, so differently reconstructed, James returns it to us—through a waft of warm air, a few moving lights, and the sudden commonplace sound of a turning wheel on the carriages that will carry so many alternative lives away. Here, as always in his work, not only is every word naturally a sign ("soft quick rumble"), but everything referred to by these signs is a part of the language of the world (carriage wheel) and the consequential understanding of the self (gambling tables). In this exquisite form, this perfect pace, in this small music, this crowd of meaning—here is our Henry; this is our man.

AN INTRODUCTION TO JOHN GARDNER'S
NICKEL MOUNTAIN

It was late in the day on September 14, 1982. The voice at the other end of the line identified itself as representing the *Los Angeles Times*. Its quality resembled the self-important sort that does documentaries. The voice wondered whether I would be interested, since I had been John Gardner's most vocal opponent during his life, in writing his obituary—they might call it a closing debate—for the paper. Close what? John is dead? Why is that? I foolishly stammered. He had been killed in a motorcycle accident. The voice confessed to knowing little more. They would naturally need the obit promptly. The notice needn't be long. Its length would be left to my discretion.

The shock of this news, so callously conveyed, had addled my wits; otherwise I would have been angry immediately instead of angry later. Isn't it a bit odd, I finally managed, to ask an alleged adversary to perform such a function? The voice said that odd was the interest. It would be (the word used wasn't *edgy*) edgy. Well, I am a friend of John Gardner's, I said, replacing my *odd* with outrage, and I wouldn't be edgy. Then I was edgy, and hung up.

I don't believe I was ever more than John's rhetorical opponent, stationed at one side of the platform at a public debate or standing at the other end of a kitchen table, late at night, full of Scotch and happy disagreement; still, he might think it strange to find me holding the door for readers as they enter this early novel of his, a novel

An Introduction to John Gardner's Nickel Mountain

that came into view only gradually and much later than its composition, as *The Sunlight Dialogues* also had, and a novel that probably had its origin in an assignment for Jarvis Thurston's writing class at Washington University in St. Louis, whose philosophy faculty I later joined, a city John's first wife, Joan, grew up in, and where her family still resided.

In one sense I shouldn't have been surprised that John had died in a motorcycle accident. It was a wonder that he hadn't provoked such a calamity earlier. He was inclined to drive very fast while drunk. He tended to get drunk rather regularly. In various vehicles he had hit things before and had passed out at the scene as if composing the first draft of his demise. He mostly whacked his own head and broke his own bones, either skiing (he told me) or galloping on horseback through a woods, by falling down in driveways, or while attempting to reach his hotel room by climbing the façade of the building. He was reckless with everything: his life, his love affairs, the fidelity of his friends, his family, his academic career, his debts, his views, his writing. I was the careful one. You are like a lady who has seen a mouse, he would tell me; you climb no more than a chair.

In another way, it was impossible to imagine John other than alive. Everyone who knew him was astonished and confounded by his energy, his enthusiasm, his rapid grasp of circumstances, his generosity and good nature. He would teach all day, party much of the evening, write all night, and was readier to meet the world when it rose than I was after a proper rest. He could work in silence; he could work in hurly-burly. His typewriter clattered to catch up with his mind. He had Falstaff's capacity for drink, for talk, for revelry. He was a drop-in guy who loved drop-in people, yet he longed for quiet and preferred living in the country. Once back on the farm, where wheat and grain said not a word, he would lodge a rock band in his barn. He was so often onstage, playing a part in an opera that had two sunny acts and a dark one, that I guessed his energies were theatrical too—not less real, but somehow untouched and thus not worn down by the rough rub of ordinary things.

Before *Nickel Mountain* was a mountain it was a series of hills.

Lots of early novels start this way, especially if you enroll in a writing class. Its first assignment will ask for a short story, because a short story is more quickly written and more easily discussed. John's was set in real time—winter 1954. Which meant its author was twenty-one. The story survived the corrections of the class to find publication in the student literary magazine. John was then an undergraduate. Several stories also set near Batavia, New York, followed, mostly written at Iowa, whose famous workshop he attended as a graduate student, though he was to obtain a degree in medieval studies. Bit by bit a volume of linked pieces that could be sent off to his agent was amassed. The agent predictably responded that collections of stories are difficult to market. So the manuscript was parked like a second car while new models were made to run past it. The old jalopy soon had fewer miles on it than the spiffy current model.

Not a good situation. John had begun writing in what is called "the realist tradition," a manner naturally appealing to his rural upbringing and its evangelical flavor, but as he encountered the temper of the times he found it advantageous to put his academic interests to use, and adopt the trendier tendency called, as if it were a new perfume, "fabulism." These folks were said to treat literature as a game, to display their style as if it were the latest fashion, and to be so disenchanted they were impervious to spells, and could not be morphed into croaking frogs or—bewitched—become snarly hairy beasts or put with a charm into beauty sleep. If a fairy tale were to be approached by any such, it would be, like Coover or Nabokov, with a killing jar and a net. In an interview at the time, John unwisely said:

> I have nothing to say, except that I think words are beautiful. I'm a stylist; for me, everything is rhythm and rhyme. There are a handful of other stylists, like Gass, Elkin, Barthelme, Barth, and Ralph Ellison, who have nothing to say either. We just write. I guess Samuel Beckett is the model for all of us, which is ironic, since he descends from Joyce, who still thought he could save the world with literature.

An Introduction to John Gardner's Nickel Mountain

Playing the devil to our own Faust, we often persuade ourselves to be true, things we feel clear to our feet are false. Still, at least partly under the banner of the enemy, John published *Grendel,* which was a big hit, and *Jason and Medeia,* which wasn't. Fables, parodies followed, texts that swallowed texts, texts that played the very games his postmod opponents were accused of. Meanwhile, *Nickel Mountain* was sitting quietly back at the ranch, no longer written in the style his public expected to see. Or so it seemed to John at the time. He had tinkered with the text now for more than fifteen years, knitting the sections together, connecting the dots. But was the book still his? He suggested to his agent that he publish it under another name. However, he still valued the novel and did not wish to cast it from him like a disgraced daughter. So, while it might seem a troubled relation, he would acknowledge it and take it in. When he published the manuscript at last in 1973 it became his third bestseller. In our world, irony is inescapable.

Now it wore a subtitle: a pastoral novel. *Pastoral* is the label for a popular genre, that of an archaic reflective poem that initially pretended to provide bored shepherds with lyrics for the tunes they piped, the songs they improvised. These songs generally celebrated the herdsman's simple life (sans wolves and rustlers), and depicted nature in a peaceful and cooperative mood. Classical forms merged with Christian easily enough because Jesus, at least metaphorically, was said to be our shepherd and we his docile flock. At first the pastoral was a purely poetic form, but soon novelized versions, still in verse, appeared, one by Boccaccio, for instance, another by Edmund Spenser, as well as *The Countess of Pembroke's Arcadia* of Sir Philip Sidney, who made his of prose and let it darken in the direction of elegy. Soon there were as many pastorals posted over Europe as sheep. Its voyage to America was inevitable, since America was the New World, where those who fled Europe would enjoy rebirth— become free, pure, and self-reliant. Emerson was not the first to say so.

There is more evidence for the existence of dragons than for the noble savage or the simple plowman who lives in innocent and happy harmony with the earth; but the New England farmer did satisfy his needs by snaring rabbits, shooting squirrels, picking berries, milking cows, and tilling the soil. He did clear his land of rocks and trees, build his house, cut his firewood, feed his stock, weave his own cloth, and churn his cheese. He did enjoy the unmediated relation of his work to its products and, in turn, their treasured satisfaction of his necessities. Moreover, the pioneer (for that is where we are now in the story) could not hope to survive without the assistance of the community which assembled to help him raise his barn, harvest the crops, repel Indians, teach his kids, fiddle up a dance, worship God. Trade was mainly barter; your word was your bond; your property became yours by the sweat of your brow. Such a life had values that should be very reluctantly lost.

You had much to fear, most of it inexplicable: fire could consume the forests, drought turn topsoil to dust, hail beat wheat to the ground; winds too, might blow away your buildings or lightning strike them, rain that overran streams and flooded rivers could also drown the crops. Moreover, given time, peaceful villages grew to the size of more stressful towns. It was true that cities were still far off, but even their distance was a lure. They were all Sodoms, and would be as bad as Gomorrah tomorrow.

Into this fragile Eden the devil sent the tractor to replace the horse, the ox, the plow. It made unnatural noise, spewed smelly smoke, ran on fuels found and refined in faraway reaches of the planet, required trained mechanics to repair, was a trouble to house, lured little boys by its growling song to desire a place on the driver's seat, and mangled John Gardner's brother one day when John was at its helm, leaving him with an unrepayable debt of guilt. The powerful nostalgia that determined a good deal of John's preferred way of life held out the promise of a farm without farming, a garden without the machine, a cloister of retreat and contemplation, where the writer, like craftsmen of old, worked his words till they bore their fruit.

An Introduction to John Gardner's Nickel Mountain

It also inclined John to imitate, in mostly unfortunate ways, his father's defining habits: these included riding a Harley, a contraption which appears to have become a kind of motorized pen and penis for the both of them—the devil in another one of his disguises. His father worked late into the night and so would John. His father was a womanizer. John would womanize too. His father preached to his neighbors, ditto John, who would advise, hector, extol. After that it was easy to be just as earnest with his students, and then with the wide world. A direct causal connection between parent and child, as these parallels suggest, should not be drawn, but the set of such an example helped make certain convictions and courses of conduct comfortable. The traditional Protestant values of ambition, hard work, and the need for self-improvement, when allowed to prosper in a very bright multigifted person (in music and drawing, for instance) paradoxically propelled John into the academy, another Arcadia, but one of sophistication, complexity, and competition, of indirection and distance, of irreverence, license, and worldliness. Although writing classes are the least scholarly of institutions, the ivory tower could not be mistaken for a barn, and the two worlds these structures represent never found a comfortable fit.

During the great age of the novel—that of Dickens and Thackeray, of Tolstoy and Dostoyevsky—the relation of the writer to his readers was widespread, intense, and warm. Authors were intellectual and moral leaders; they were honored and attended to, often persecuted in consequence, but always significant. Their novels reached out to their audience the way many movies do now, and regulated the beat of their hearts. Fiction's imaginary characters seemed more real to its readers than the grocer down the block; their human sympathies were wrung by the plight of poor Copperfield; they laughed when Trollope skewered hypocrites like Mr. Slope; and they nodded with understanding at George Eliot's revelations. I think John Gardner wanted this relation to remain, or to be restored if it had really disappeared. A great novel could actually create a community among its readers, a place where their spirits if not their bodies might live, laugh, and love with some sort of security. Balzac and Dickens did it as no others could, and as the great epics of the past had. When, with great excitement, John showed me the drawings that were to illustrate *Nickel Mountain,* or spoke of the design for *October Light;* when he affixed to his books wonderfully chosen epigraphs or gave his chapters fulsome titles, as the old style had been, what he revealed he wanted, it seemed to me, was not parody, as some critics said, but parity.

And sometimes John did what he dreamed to do. He caused to rise up like an enveloping vision a fictional world that would help us live better in the real one. Not such a bad ambition. The reader will feel some of that absorption here. But the time was not in tune with such conservative ambitions. It was all right for I. B. Singer to write nineteenth-century novels in the twentieth, but even Singer's Yiddish was as old as the past it represented. Gardner was Now and he should be depicting Nowness. But Now was a dismal, complicated, mean, deceptive, derivative mess. While in his academy mode, he could escape into the medieval by translating Anglo-Saxon (brilliantly, by the way) or writing *Grendel* (quite as dazzling) and by finding allegorical relevance in his tale, if he wished, to our contemporary plight like that plum once plucked from a pudding; however, an Eden of everyday decency was not very readily available, though, like D. H. Lawrence he did bear, as protectively as a newborn, utopian hopes even through the center of Sodom—a city that offered a lecture circuit that could be completed on a motorcycle, consequently giving him the opportunity to make converts, to spread his inspired word; but it also granted him an income, adulation, women, and whiskey. John was torn by ambitious ideals and indulgent temptations like a losing ticket at the track.

In this book, the conflict, as American as any Indian, is like that between bow and bowstring—its result is full of aim and energy. Characters rise from the page as John wished them to, and stride into their story. Consider the paragraph that opens the section called "The Devil," and introduces Simon Bale, who "was a Jehovah's Witness." A long deliciously rich sentence follows, with Gardner as good as Faulkner:

> He would appear one Sunday morning in the dead of winter, early, standing on your porch, smiling foolishly and breathing out steam, his head tipped and drawn back a little, like a cowardly dog's, even his knees slightly bent, his Bible carefully out of sight inside his ragged winter coat, and his son Bradley would be standing behind him, as timid as his father but subtly different from his father—not so perfectly hiding his readiness to shift from fawning to the kind of unholy fury that was going to be his whole character later—and neither Simon Bale nor his son would seem a particularly serious threat—especially on a bright December morning with a smell of January thaw in the wind and churchbells ringing far in the distance, the blue-white mountains falling away like Time. All it took to get rid of the two was the closing of a door.

You can't win an argument with writing like this. Nor are you likely to close the door, especially now that you have two copies of this piece of prose, like father and son, friendly suppliants in search of your soul. It is an honor to hold the cover open for you . . . and for them.

KATHERINE ANNE PORTER'S
FICTIONAL SELF

Katherine Anne Porter's reported life was made of myths, most of them planted there by Porter herself, and many meant to improve her humble beginnings, refigure the course of her early years, and conceal the existence of her numerous marriages or frequent affairs. Of people fleeing their origins, some are inclined to brag about them afterward, proud of the distance they've come, while a few are so indifferent to the past that they manage to recall only whatever is routinely demanded by official documents. That leaves those who are still ashamed or hateful about their history, desperate to deny it, and prepared to rub it out if they can. There is something feudal about this embarrassment, because it gives credence to the claim blue bloods make for their superiority. The "nobility" can not only strut and preen, they can command, since others seem driven to grovel before those of elevated status, and appear to envy any member of the upper crust who got there, whether through birth, inheritance, marriage, or by old-fashioned hook or crook.

You have to remember the past rather clearly if you are going to lie your way out of its existence, but you also have to be able to enter your new history so completely that it replaces the truth even in your own mind. Katherine Anne Porter had no actual memories of her mother or of life in tiny Indian Creek, Texas, where she had been born, so she imagined some, and then discovered them again when she searched her past, like finding gold ore shining in the water of the stream where it's been planted.

Moreover, when you falsify your own life, you can later be open and generous in your account of it, draw upon it for any fiction you may write, confident that your real self's safety will be assured. You can even second Madame Du Berry's challenging brag, as Porter did: "My life has been incredible. I don't believe a word of it." Eventually, however, the curious, and any others who care, will grow skeptical, believe only the worst because they assume only the worst would be concealed, and—the unfortunate consequence often is—they will not mind, after so much misleading, if they mistake a truth for a lie the next time, or even every time.

Through photographs and other evidence, Joan Givner, Katherine Anne Porter's 1982 biographer, demonstrates that most of the settings for Porter's reenactment of her life's rites of passage in "The Old Order" were actually supplied by memories of a sojourn in Bermuda (when Porter was thirty-nine), despite the author's claim that they were captured from her childhood. *How it ought to have been* quietly overtook *how it was.* Thomas F. Walsh, in his essay "The Making of 'Flowering Judas,'" unweaves the many threads that have gone into this masterful story's composition, disproving Porter's claim that "my fiction is reportage, only I do something to it; I arrange it and it is fiction, but it happened." Normally, what happens in the composition of fiction is that scenes, characters, and settings for the story are lifted from different places and times in the experience of the author to create a new cast and an altered environment; but it is not, I think, customary for the writer to maintain that all of them were derived, in the order lived, from one place and one time in one life. We have to keep in mind, too, how many of the events that matter most to a young writer take place in books, those vessels of imagination that have so often rescued us from every day's disappointments, and give us pages which, never settled, sift through our unconscious still.

So, though Katherine Anne Porter's fiction is notably lucid, her life history is a biographer's nightmare, full of false connections and alleged events, and blank about substantial passages of time, as if they had happened during intermission and were never a part of the play.

After her mother's death, Porter was raised by weak men and many women in the household of her fraternal grandmother, whom everyone called Cat, not because of any special grace or caution but because it shortened "Catharine" by two-thirds and cauterized its odd spelling. She was a dominating figure, by her granddaughter's account, and ruled her household with a Calvinist's morally severe self-righteous hand. In 1892 it was more than a brief toddle from Indian Creek to Cat's farm near the Texas town of Kyle, one hundred miles away, but in terms of a child's escape from the short street that a small town can seem to be, the move widened the world by at least two roads.

The five hundred people there, with their close local Protestant ways, were Katherine Anne Porter's first teachers, and supported a school where she received, from age six to twelve, the little formal education her circumstances allowed. Townsfolk went about their business in full view of her wide eyes. They also regularly read from the Good Book, where one could be warned of serious threats to the safety of one's soul, enjoy instructive allegorical stories, and encounter great prose. School primers taught virtue and obedience; nearly every page gleamed with moral varnish, while figures like Joan of Arc and Cotton Mather provided stirring examples of the prowess possible for a woman, and the merciless hatred some men had for them. From her grandmother she learned manners and had the fear of God "systematically ground into her tender bones." Loose family ties and impoverishment compelled Cat to offer room and board, in the guise of governesses, to a Miss Babb and Miss Mudd, from whom Katherine learned spanking and calisthenics.

According to Darlene Harbour Unrue's 2005 biography, *Katherine Anne Porter: The Life of an Artist* (Jackson, Miss.: University Press

of Mississippi, 2005), grandmother and her dependents provided
Porter with a loving, watchful, closely guarded yet colorful environment, stocked with what would later prove to be a useful cast of
characters: a former slave, Masella Daney, who remained a household helper; Daney's husband (an ironically named Squire Bunton),
who lived near and rode by regularly on a mule named Aunt Fanny;
as well as a couple of hired hands, one of whom was a morphine
addict, while the other (Old Man Ronk) became the model for Olaf
Helton in *Noon Wine* (a destiny no doubt unfelt). Cat finally completed this list with

> a long procession of dreadful old women, of a most awful gen-
> tility, who consented to act as a sort of upper house keeper and
> companion and general nuisance, who merely took it out by
> gritting their teeth at us and wishing, in low voices when no
> one else was by, that they could blister our skins for being such
> bad children.

Young ears must have been captivated by the ubiquitous voices of
Southern storytellers, leaning back in stiff chairs against the hardware store's porch wall, shaded, certainly, from the sun, a length of
straw caught like a savory cliché between tongue and teeth, droning
on of Bull Run or Lee at this ford or that railhead, Jackson charg-
ing through a stand of trees, repeating the feats and foibles of relatives whose odd mien and strange ways were usually instructive and
always engrossing. These figures were connected by a verbal chain
of recollection that reached at least to the moment when some fabulous ancestor's feet had first hit the turf in the New World.

To sustain interest in its story, every family had to have an ancestral secret that was kept as zealously as a shrine for Mother Mary;
and we should add, to all the customary local wash, the buckets
of bravado and romance that kept white the Southern dream, each
tale's tallness teaching how the laws that govern the truth might
be repealed. Typically, these were the sort of stories that Porter's
grandmother maneuvered with considerable style through occa-

sions of former opulence and ease—gowns and balls and beaux and canapés—that made Porter "hunger for fine clothes and other comforts of wealth." In 1962, after *Ship of Fools* became a best seller, she bought herself a "huge square-cut emerald set all around with diamonds," a ring larger than the one she had invented for La Condessa to wear in the novel and an imprudent purchase at twenty thousand bucks. It is Givner's opinion that "It was the idea of the ring, rather than the actual object, that she cherished; it became the symbol of her success and the subject of numerous anecdotes."

It has always seemed to me that the storyteller's social assignment, which furnished the origins and directed the development of narrative, was to glorify the past and its daring deeds, protect the family tree, justify male ownership of land, women, and personal property, direct and legitimize the passing of power from father to rightful heir, one generation to the next. Oral histories helped unite communities, extol their chiefs, and define the various rites and ceremonies pertaining. No wonder their tales tended to be about male gods and their heroic human counterparts. Nowadays this history is a weakening string of memories, but at one time the bard's recital was the main conduit of authority, making sense of the past, fostering acceptance, and focusing pride—whether true or false or fabled mattered only to outsiders. Old anecdotes gave present circumstances heft, scope, interest, and instruction. In so many ways you were your forebears, and the storyteller taught you whom to hate or emulate, what to aspire to, and, like the Bible, what to believe, how to behave.

Every society, every religion, every nation-state and ethnic enclave appears eager to employ such historical myths, or first fictions, in their manipulation of the masses. Certainly narratives need not take the novel's form to be effective. In fact, serious novels now seem more likely to undermine them.

For many Southern writers these romantic sagas were acceptable, and they were eager to protect the honor, habits, and basic creeds of their culture, although a lacquer of criticism contributed to the glow of objectivity. Katherine Anne Porter was sawn in two, and not by a magician. She despised the actual family system and its methods of operation: its smugly narrow stupid views with which it infected its children; its monarchy of men, their posturing and pomposity; its stifling so-called moral grip; its hypocrisy concerning women— courting them like queens, breeding them like sows. If a man were not the ruler of a kingdom, even not the owner of all he could survey, at least he was the master of his own household, made the main decisions, chastised deviation, doled out the dough, did the deep thinking, got all the mail. Katherine Anne Porter knew this system was based on a lot of poisonous pish tosh: she had seen how weak her father was; how his mother ran the house; yet all the essential perks were still his. Daughters were to be taught householdry and well married if possible; if not, as old maids they could sew in a corner and care for the sick.

Porter passed much of her adolescent years in a series of convent schools that were so eager to snatch a young Protestant from Luther's hands they would waive tuition, a generosity that her father found irresistible. Such schooling also made her more acceptable to a nineteen-year-old suitor with wealthy parents named John Koontz, whose Catholicism could not dampen his desire for drink or lessen his pleasure in abuse. Porter's marriage to this stalwart lasted nine invisible years, most of them miserable, though it removed her from her relatives, gave her a noticeable social upgrade, and took her to a somewhat larger, mildly industrial town named Lufkin. This new location often allowed her to ride on the family's ranch nearby and feel how it was to have a mighty force between her knees.

According to Darlene Harbour Unrue, the couple's eventual divorce yielded this deposition from the husband: "Nine years after the wedding he admitted that from the beginning of their union he was frequently guilty of adultery, extreme intoxication, vile name-calling, and physical attacks that resulted in Katherine Anne Porter's broken bones and lacerations." The charges may have been rather starved for substance, but Porter enjoyed a harvest of grievances all the same. The pair moved often but packed their problems with their pajamas. On one occasion, husband threw wife down a flight of stairs, "breaking her right ankle and severely injuring her knee." On another, he beat her unconscious with a hairbrush. The view one has of men and marriage from the foot of such a fall, or from an instrument that in another hand should pursue only fashion or caresses, tends to be as permanent as Adam's; nevertheless, Porter tried to save her marriage by converting to Catholicism, a move I find mystifying, though I was never consulted. Largely, what it meant was a redirection in her reading habits and the discovery of new authors—always a plus—while the Church's rituals encouraged her to ponder the impact of belief upon behavior and appreciate the role of symbols in the imagination. She also learned, as she began to write, how things grow more real when they are put into words, because without storytelling the past would pale beyond even the pale of paper. The fattest, most familiar story of all is the one we tell ourselves about ourselves, repeatedly, as if before bed, as a daily comfort or admonition, throughout our lives.

When Joan Givner wrote her *Katherine Anne Porter: A Life* in 1982, her subject had four husbands (Porter customarily claimed there were three), but when the editor of the Library of America collection (*Collected Stories and Other Writings*), Darlene Harbour Unrue, published her *Katherine Anne Porter: The Life of an Artist* in 2005, the marriage list had swollen to five, none of them one of Givner's early candidates, Ernest Stock, the handsome former member of the British Royal Flying Corps, with whom—it turns out—Porter had only "a relationship." I suspect that, for appearances, affairs might have been called marriages sometimes, and, for convenience, marriages said to be affairs, until who knew what the situation was, and who would any longer care?

Unrue discovered that after Porter's marriage to Koontz ended in 1915 she wed H. Otto Taskett, a handsome Englishman who lasted the length of a sentence, though, as a fiction, he received many more in *Ship of Fools,* as did all of her husbands. Despite appearances she did not marry Stock in 1926, simply spent a summer with him in a rented house. Now and then a year would have more than one summer. After this one Porter had gonorrhea. Subsequently, in 1917, someone named Carl von Pless blew through Porter's life like a prairie wind. Then, from 1933 to 1938, following a lengthy and rocky liaison, she was married to someone as short as she was. This was Eugene Pressly, a young fellow from the Institute of Current World Affairs in Mexico City and later of the U.S. Foreign Office. He was her devoted companion on the sea voyage from Veracruz to Bremen that became the setting for *Ship of Fools,* and he would travel with her, over the next seven years, to Berlin, Paris, and New York before disappearing over the horizon en route to Venezuela.

Porter's final bet for wedded bless was Albert Erskine, a young graduate student who had followed Robert Penn Warren from Memphis to Louisiana State University's English department. He was another "handsome young man," this time of twenty-seven, who was bewitched by her beauty, sophistication, and charm, with a background in literature that enabled him to appreciate fully the corresponding charm, sophistication, and beauty of her work. As the brief life of this marriage wore on, the charm was perhaps the first to go. Porter's sophistication was admitted to be forty-eight years of maturity instead, and her beauty quite a bad habit. To get rid of her husband, and as a favor, since he was eager to marry another woman, she established a residence in Reno.

The trouble with the men Porter married was that they were still men. She was beautiful, had fabulous legs suitors would insist she be proud of, the voice of a seductress, a figure that drew looks, so that men, their private part plump, would fawn and favor her and, what was more important, inadvertently make possible a fuller, freer realization of her talents and her dreams; but you often had to marry them to take the next step up, to enjoy the security their money and station could confer, or enjoy the acceptance society gave to such arrangements; except that when tread upon these "partners" grew sullen and unruly, wanted the pleasures of her body without giving any pleasure in exchange, so that, when refused, their passions grew petulant, their entreaties tiresome, their presence wearying.

Beauty did not make Porter proud; it made her vain; and these repeated romantic misadventures sapped her emotional energy. Perhaps they were the reason she was a frequent procrastinator and stingy with her work. Daily life can be taxing; running around on the road can give any head and heart the dizzies, and the dizzies can cause you to sink onto strange sofas. Inconsistencies are bad investments and Porter had her share: she was at once cold and promiscuous, romantic and calculating; she sought both solitude and society, thus the emotional space necessary for composition, and the excuses to avoid it. Though very aware of pregnancy's dangers to her health, to her way of life as well as the prospective child's, Porter longed to be a mother. In consequence, she suffered miscarriages, required abortions, and "lost children in all the ways one could."

Porter knew what it was to be poor, but she nevertheless regularly lived beyond her means. She flirted with religion but was too intelligent to commit. She deplored her humble origins, said she disliked the South, yet she longed to put down roots, and was fascinated by the myths that glorified her region. In spite of that she fled every place that offered itself in order to live like a Gypsy. In her day Marxists were the most relentless of the political bores, and I feel it is to her considerable credit that no -ism, -ist, or -ology could tempt her, no fashionable jargon lead her into obfuscation, or fad of intellect seduce. Porter supported liberal causes, both in print and on the street, and was vigorous in her denunciation of fascism while demonstrating a mistrust of minorities that was thoroughly Southern and deeper than a streak.

F. O. Matthiessen observed, as early as 1945, that Miss Porter (as she was then addressed) had a "high reputation among nearly all schools of critics" and was regarded as "a writer's writer," which he assumed meant that other authors could learn much from her consummate craftsmanship. Although Porter was thirty-two when she published her first story, "Maria Concepción," her signature style was in place and more assured in its use than she had come to be in her life. Her sensuous yet hard-eyed prose would never need improvement and would be flexible enough in tone (ranging from the famous impersonality of "Maria" to the witty sarcasm of "The Wooden Umbrella" or the revulsion of "The Leaning Tower") to accomplish whatever effect she required.

Matthiessen feared such praise might mean to readers that her work was arty and esoteric. (I would add to those adjectives the words *fancy* and *frilly, mannered* and *difficult.*) When reviewers take the trouble to compliment a writer on her style, it is usually because she has made it easy for them to slide from one sentence to another like an otter down a slope, since they are presumably eager to find out what happens next or what fresh disclosure will yield surprise. So they are happily immersed in the account, lose all touch with mere words, and feel as if they were present when D'Arcy does this or Miranda that, or when the mangy dog chases the cat. Porter herself, who sometimes knew better, compliments Hardy on his ability to put her in his chosen place and let her "see." She should have said "and let her read."

In the same year and season that Matthiessen published his little piece in *Accent,* Gertrude Buckman wrote this about "The Leaning Tower" for the *Partisan Review:* "It has for a long time been apparent that Katherine Anne Porter consistently writes a luminous prose, of an exactness of choice and suggestiveness of phrasing, which is altogether extraordinary. Miss Porter's work has probably been subjected to the kind of scrutiny that most writers hardly dare to hope for, rarely achieve, and can almost never withstand. That Miss Porter can bear such careful reading proves her much more than simply an excellent stylist." This praise is well meant but it is also withdrawn as quickly as it is offered. For most critics, the presence of "style" requires assurance that there is also "substance." Style is wrapping paper and ribbon, scented tag and loving inscription. If you are careful, the tissue can be reused for a birthday or another Christmas. My aunt ironed such paper as she fancied, and stored it like linen napkins in folded flat stacks beneath her bed.

Style, I should like to protest, is the result of that "exactness of choice" that Porter exhibits. Whether unconsciously or by intent, as Poe was purported to, the writer chooses subjects, adopts a tone, considers an order for the release of meaning, arrives at the rhythm, selects a series of appropriate sounds, determines the diction and measures the pace, turns the referents of certain words into symbols, establishes connections with companionable paragraphs, sizes up each sentence's intended significance, and, if granted good fortune, because each decision might have been otherwise, achieves not just this or that bit of luminosity or suggestiveness, but her own unique lines of language, lines that produce the desired restitution of the self.

You cannot miss the rhetorical beat of passages such as this one from "The Leaning Tower" of 1941 that buries the reader under shovelfuls of scorn. Charles Upton, the principal character, is taking a walk, looking for a lodging, on his sixth day as a newcomer to Berlin.

> He would wander on, and the thicker the crowd in which he found himself, the more alien he felt himself to be. He had watched a group of middle-aged men and women who were gathered in silence before two adjoining windows, gazing silently at displays of toy pigs and sugar pigs. These persons were all strangely of a kind, and strangely the most prevalent type. The streets were full of them—enormous waddling women with short legs and ill-humored faces and round-headed men with great rolls of fat across the backs of their necks, who seemed to support their swollen bellies with an effort that drew their shoulders forward.

It might seem sad enough to be so described, but the feeling is still, though dismayed, detached. The next paragraph plays rough. These depicted people are window-shopping but the windows are both mocking and reflecting them.

> In one window there were sausages, hams, bacon, small pink chops, all pig, real pig, fresh, smoked, salted, baked, roasted,

pickled, spiced, and jellied. In the other were dainty artificial pigs, almond paste pigs, pink sugar chops, chocolate sausages, tiny hams and bacons of melting cream streaked and colored to the very life. Among the tinsel and lace paper, at the back were still other kinds of pigs: plush pigs, black velvet pigs, spotted cotton pigs, metal and wooden mechanical pigs, all with frolicsome curled tails and appealing infant faces.

The expelling puffs required to cross the page over all those disgusting *ps*, the alternation among the vowels the *ps* accompany, the word *pig* itself, made of *piss* and *gag*, the feel of the tongue against the teeth while performing the doubled *ts* of *spotted cotton*, the marvelous march of the metaphor as it moves from examples of the real thing through sugary still eatable samples to reproductions in plush, then wood, and finally metal, and the mingled reflection in and through the glass of pig parts, piglike imitations, and pig-acquired forms and faces: they play together to create her style in this passage and prove her worth.

Any resonance beyond rhetoric to this passage? You bet. It takes the toil of butchers, bakers, gimcrack makers to provide the fare, shopkeepers' time and money to acquire and arrange the space, an entire culture—for this is Nazi Germany—to collect the crowd, and Porter to imagine a lonely American looking for his lodging in this coarse and gluttonous community. The scene is a construction, as all literary descriptions are, because an actual eye would sweep its subject in one look, then send attention here and there in a flick or three. Instead, we are given a summary in the guise of a moment, a habit in an instance, and a judgment meant for forever.

The sight of fat people apparently sharpened her pen. These two sentences from "Noon Wine" are famous: "He wasn't exactly a fat man. He was more like a man who had been fat recently."

A moment ago I wrote: "to create her style and prove her worth" as if I were sure that proving her worth was at least one function for perfection to perform. I suspect Porter's art had to be a form of salvation for her, but perhaps I am allowing my own attitudes to intrude the way my pack ratty aunt scuffled into this text seven paragraphs ago. In the careful practice of the arts of prose, Porter could avoid mistakes, when, in life, she was invariably putting the wrong ring on the wrong finger. On the page she could wait until she and her skills were a match. In time she would learn her art from the kind of reading that teaches writing, and choose according to her lights, picking her mentors wisely—internationals such as Henry James and Virginia Woolf, because Southern writers were treacherous guides and might lead you to the most dangerous monster of all: Faulkner's all-swallowing world. The perfection of the work would hide the imperfections of the life. Then she could look at the past without either shame or guilt. There she would discover problems worthy of her and conquer them. Her life's journey was in the company of a load of fools as well as the freight of friends, but she would board no friends and embark the fools to Bremen from Veracruz.

Although its author might have been characterized, at one time, as a loose baseborn woman, her much admired style bore every mark of the aristocracy, and had taken her to the White House of John F. Kennedy, where she had dined more than once. That style was neither very inventive nor exploratory, but it was precise about perception, adept at dialogue and scrupulous about dialect, rich in recollection, careful with abstractions, sensuous and frank while never coarse, otherwise always high-toned, never casual or breathless as if her vowels had been running.

Porter relaxed her standards somewhat when writing essays or doing reviews (which occupy a good half of her Library of America volume), but Katherine Anne in an apron is still a wonderful cook. Her pieces on Edith Sitwell, Eudora Welty, Virginia Woolf, and Katherine Mansfield are observant and generous pleasures; she roughs up a pompous T. S. Eliot in defense of Thomas Hardy, takes Lady Chatterley for a thoroughly deserved walk in the woods, and in "The Wooden Umbrella," one of three pieces on Gertrude Stein, vents her spleen with wit and accuracy. Who but Gertrude and Alice wouldn't

enjoy the following characterization? "Considering her tepid, sluggish nature, really sluggish like something eating its way through
a leaf, Miss Stein could grow quite animated on the subject of her
early family life, and some of her stories are as pretty and innocent
as lizards running over tombstones on a hot day in Maryland." Porter
attacks Stein with admirable wit and considerable understanding.
The essay is masterful. The difficulty for Porter is that her being
somewhat right about Stein simply doesn't matter. At the end, Gertrude sits amid the wreckage of her furniture like a Roman senator
undisturbed by his city's scrumbled marble.

Porter is a discriminating and passionate critic, but she deals
mostly with a work's general effects and does not venture to bore
her reader with the many small strokes which, when so many are
completed, create the ultimate result. Unless she is reminiscing
about an experience of her own. Then the lines are drawn like bow-
strings. For instance, when Eliot reads in front of Joyce (and Porter)
at Shakespeare and Company: "The poet before us had a face as
severe as Dante's, the eyes fiercely defensive, the mouth bitter, the
nose grander and much higher bridged than his photographs then
showed; the whole profile looked like a bird of prey of some sort. He
might have been alone, reading to himself aloud, not once did he
glance at his listeners."

Her own commentary can be eloquent—though executed with a
bit of the shapelessness she is prepared to risk in an essay—when
she remembers an anecdote about Tolstoy which alleges the old man
said, as mad as Lear, that he would tell the real story about women
only from his coffin and only when he felt the shovelfuls falling on
his face. "It's a marvelous picture. Tolstoy was merely roaring in the
frenzy roused in him in face of his wife's terrible, relentless adorations; her shameless fertility, her unbearable fidelity, the shocking
series of jealous revenges she took upon him for his hardness of
heart and wickedness to her, the whole mystery of her oppressive
femaleness. He did not know the truth about women, not even that
one who was the curse of his life. He did not know the truth about

himself. This is not surprising, for no one does know the truth, either about himself or about anyone else, and all recorded human acts and words are open testimony to our endless efforts to know each other, and our failure to do so."

Our ignorance is reassuring to Porter because the self she fears she has, she hopes will remain unknowable to others, while the self she wishes she were takes its public place. Yet the self she regretted and the self she desired are actually states of the populous nation a self is: cowgirl, coquette, cook, queen, artist, the disillusioned well-used lady, and the girl with a dream—a roaring, riotous, shrewd, and foolish community of loving and quarreling equals.

During a notable moment of scrutiny as she entered her thirty-eighth year, Katherine Anne Porter confessed, "When I was quite young I decided to set my limitations moderately. Maybe this was my mistake. For by setting my bounds, I find they are real things and have a way of closing upon me without my (conscious) consent." Although O'Connor, Welty, and Porter obliged us by writing novels, it's as short story writers they are generally remembered, where more polish for small surfaces is routinely expected, whereas writers like Tolstoy and Faulkner—well, they are moving mountains, and it doesn't matter if they leave a small mess here and there like great chefs in their kitchens. Does it?

KNUT HAMSUN

Once the only Knut Americans knew was Knute Rockne. Although the less-known Knut was born a generation before the celebrated one, and obtained a Nobel Prize in literature, our better-known Knute won a record number of football games for the University of Notre Dame. A Catholic God gave his team these victories in spite of their Lutheran leadership. The famous coach-to-be picked up the additional -e when he was only five and his family emigrated from Norway to Chicago. Only Ireland sent a greater proportion of its impoverished population to the United States, and these Norsemen naturally headed toward areas with familiar climates, similar ores. Michigan had iron, Minnesota lakes, North Dakota snow, but none had mountains. This absence had to be suffered.

In his youth Hamsun also spent some time in Chicago as a cable car conductor, but he never earned the concluding -e or achieved movie-star status either. Rockne was killed in an airplane crash at the age of forty-three, while Hamsun survived TB, success, disgrace, and confinement to die a very old man, though writing still, at ninety-two. After his trial, he grew even more obscure despite the runoff from his Nobel glory; because Knut Hamsun was the perfect Nordic Nazi, a self-made man who came out of the back-mountain farms of northern Norway seeking to be recognized and praised; who ruthlessly achieved his goals (his Nobel Prize book, *The Growth of the Soil,* was a perfect Blood and Struggle novel, admired by Germans generally but by Goebbels most significantly), yet a success who was fated to have most of the people he appreciably affected eager to forget him: a wish that was, until recently, largely realized in Allied countries. The English language, in particular, turned its back on him (as he did to it) even before the Norwegians did.

Now Norway has a museum devoted to Hamsun's work, not as a spiritual guide or patriot but as a writer of certain prudently selected books, beloved by schoolchildren and a credit to Norway. This shrine has been established in Hamarøy, a small town fastened above the Arctic Circle where Hamsun could be said to have "grown up," though it would be hard to find anyone more "on the go" than he. Both institutions will no doubt be careful to distinguish the honorable literary hero from the dishonorable Quisling, perhaps through the use of separate display cases and stern warning labels. A larger-than-life bronze statue was put in place at the same time to remind us of Hamsun's steadfast defense of his German loyalties and his resolute defiance of the war crimes court. No one will be able to display the gold medal the Nobel hung around the author's neck, because Hamsun disgraced the prize by regifting it to Joseph Goebbels, himself a great creator of fictions. Back in Oslo, meanwhile, the twenty-seven volumes of Hamsun's collected works are scheduled to appear, complete enough to smother any critical objections under a crowd of pages and a crush of words.

I read *The Growth of the Soil* in high school, as many other Americans did. I remember that it opened like a child's primer, and that I much preferred Ole Edvart Rølvaag's *Giants in the Earth.* I think I thought it less mannered, less "Me Tarzan, you Jane." Rølvaag was also born a Pedersen. Perhaps there were too many Pedersens among Norwegians in either native or adopted country, and the writers sought, as a defense against anonymity, a name that was less ubiquitous and of their own assignment. In any case, Hamsun believed one's name to be of great importance, especially his own;

consequently his authorial self suffered many revisions before he got it right. Upon a frosted windowpane he wrote his childhood name and then protected it from teasing erasure with snarls the way a dog might warn the household door. For his first publication he admitted to being Kn. Pedersen. Subsequently he altered the spelling of Knud Pedersen to Knut Pederson in order to shed some Danish tarnish. Next his signature was lengthened to Knut Pederson Hamsund, though the newcomer, let in like a cowbird to the nest, muscled Pedersen out for good. For a time he spelled himself, more Germanically, Knut Hamsunn. Because of a printer's error that pleased him, Hamsun let the n fade, and the dropped d rest.

During the portentous opening of *The Growth of the Soil* an initially nameless man appears on a wilderness path. The creature represents a semiprimal person who calls himself Isak. He will pry stones out of the earth, hoe the cleared land, take for himself a woman worthy of his hulk and education. We are immediately led to understand that this man, simple and crudely hewn as he is, shall persevere through every hardship; but what we may not immediately realize is that Isak is Man the way God should have made Adam: the way Nature wants him to be; moreover that, in another sense, Isak is Hamsun, who has also dug for his dinner, mostly by living in remote rooms and in a landscape of words. Hamsun also appears as God in the guise of a wanderer who pulls a few providential strings when required. It is Hamsun's favorite role, to observe his hill of ants as if they were a hill of ants. Among the many writers whose central subject is their image in the public glass, Hamsun is perhaps the most loyally devoted to his task. And when he confesses his faults, he is always coldly proud.

Knut Hamsun was born in poverty and raised in servitude. He was sent to work for an uncle who would pay for his keep, and whose palsy made the child's unexpectedly fine penmanship of considerable use. Hamsun saw much to read in the size, shape, and condition of hands, and his were frequently whacked for copying mistakes. His interest in the words themselves also arrived early, and he must have felt, in this sort of upper-class manual labor, both its similarity to the tailor's trade his father pursued, and its difference from the art that his hands were already itching to emulate. Hamsun would later sometimes falsely laud this unpretentious life—falsely because he knew he was utterly alien to it, was a slacker about his tasks, and dimly ashamed of his connection to them. As if he were avoiding recruitment, he attempted to run away, and attacked his own leg with an ax, not the best method if you intend to travel. Hamsun even romanced the idea of suicide. When he dreamed, he dreamed of stories written on the sky, of Hamsun's glory waving in the wind of the world's attention. His parents had no way of understanding such ambitions, and he would never be able to say, with any success, "Look, Mom and Dad, look at what I've done." So he would cut them out of his life, along with most of his siblings, one of whom he would sue much later for assuming Knut's adopted surname.

It is a habit of relatively unmodernized nations to allow their publics to be instructed by poets and writers. Citizens are proud of their "giants," often worship them immoderately, and are personally encouraged by their words to embrace cockamamie beliefs. The wreath of wisdom is not wasted on composers, who are said, instead, to have sublime or deep feelings; but it is thought to fit many a writer's furrowed brow and their highly developed sense of importance. In Europe's northern climes, the myth of the honest, simple peasant at his plow, suffering many a setback to be sure, but resolutely plodding on, was, in structure if not in participants, the same as a fable of Aesop or a Satire of Horace. We all know the latter's about the country mouse and the city mouse. Something like it was being enacted on literary stages all over Europe during the years preceding World War I. At first, Hamsun was that country mouse who rejected his poor and simple origins for the wine and women, the glory and connections of the city. In Horace, the city mouse complains of his friend's food, while the country mouse feels threatened by the city and scampers back to his farms and barns well before getting his tail nipped or his whiskers singed. But this was not to be Knut's fate.

Unlike the country mouse, he did not learn his lesson in one go; he would get repeatedly lured by the presence of publishers, fleshpots, and gambling casinos, and repeatedly spurned, burned, and sent home broke.

The society of the country mouse is manageably small, and its organization is advertised as simple; but the world is complex and this mouse's response to its challenges is naive. In country mouse's community everybody knows everybody, it is commonly said, as if that were desirable; however, all fall prey to the busybody whose nose is alert for scandal, and since scandal is essential to any kind of life, minutiae will do: you may be blamed for the cut of your hair, how late your lights shine, the name of your pony. The family is everything and everyone's social position; equally secure is the domination of religion, the rule of the patriarch, and the fisted grip of place: little town, little crime—small town, small mind; there is considerable social cruelty to accompany custom's subjugations, since every whisper is a roar in a village.

Throughout our present world, tribalism has become a danger-ous and crippling handicap, like a harelip that refuses repair. In the small town that fiction loves to imagine, everyone's similarities of look, taste, and opinion will make them neighbors of the mind, comfortable about who is next door. But that's why the community's parochialism continues to grow, and its distrust of strangers deep-ens. There is the reliability of routines to be admired, and the tyr-anny of tradition to be feared. The country mouse, the boast is, lives in harmony with nature, yet his life is a war against harsh climates and their extremes, and in front of many problems he exhibits a pas-sive fatalism. Indeed, unlike the working city mouse, who is often merely a cog in a distant machine, he has a close relation to the soil, his implements, and all the celebrated fruits of his labors; however, he has little leisure, his nose has worn out its grindstone, and his eyes are as narrow as a needle's. The mice of haystack and barn-yard know what's what, what's right and what's wrong; however, they receive their moral clarity through dogmatism and bigotry. The self-sufficient tillers of the soil want desperately to be independent of the city's sort of world and end being merely indifferent to it, while their own community squelches freedom the way it juices fruit.

The country mouse can brag of the miles he has walked, the muscles he has made, the stoicism he shows toward pain, but he can heal only the skinned knees of childhood, not the calamities of adults; his frame is customarily thin and undernourished; of illness he has no solid information, no skilled assistance, no supportive institutions. But then, this animal fears, more than any avalanche or sudden freeze, not facts which he imagines are always in front of his face, but the onset, like an epidemic, of the new, the unexpected—scientific ideas and their invisible instruments.

Hamsun's own ambivalence was as regular and evenhanded as a metronome. Moved by a sense of his worth that was nevertheless wholly unearned, Hamsun would seek verification of his superiority from those elitist hedonists who had money, lived in the city, went to the theater, and worked in editorial offices. To get noticed he played the braggart and buffoon, but he would be followed, his entire life, by the curse of the self-taught: the embedded belief that he was inferior, a fake, an academic outsider, for there would be holes in his education (as good as it was, considering circumstances), and sometimes these holes were larger than the subject. This was the ground of his intense hatred for intellectuals; and even the Nobel Prize, which would seemingly buy him membership in any academy whose bell he wished to push, could not cover up the narrow spotty character of his tutelage or obscure his origin, since Hamsun was one of those plants whose roots tended to lie in full view as though they were voracious crawling vines.

For a period he might seem charming, even interesting, to the literati living it up in Oslo or in Copenhagen, but eventually he would be deemed a clown, a country bumpkin, a flashy parvenu, who waved money he had cadged from trusting publishers in front of the world's face, expecting it to feel the breeze; so that after each embarrassment an angry and chagrined Hamsun would gallop off to anyplace that didn't know him. He already had "a runaway's personality," and felt an alien from the moment he was first slapped on the behind—*ein Fremder unter Fremden,* as Rilke, another wanderer, put it—a stranger among strangers. Moreover, he was comparing his early awkward efforts to write with those of the local masters—Ibsen, Bjørnson, Lie—only to suffer shameful results. Still, Hamsun's humiliations were mostly those of personality, not character, since he possessed an arrogance whose engine was powered by public attention, and located in the rear of the machine.

As a stripling, Hamsun had already been a farm boy, store clerk, shoemaker's apprentice, sheriff's secretary, ditchdigger, peddler, salesman, and teacher. He felt he had been scorned in neighboring countries as well as in his own, and later that feeling would apply to every nation except Germany, where a generous publisher appears to have immediately welcomed him; where his sales would always be strong; and where its step and his temper were in time. His obligatory poor boy's voyage to America was too much like the job-to-job and hand-to-mouth existence he suffered at home, but he did find opportunities to represent Norwegian culture to American audiences. This more appropriate occupation led to a commission that brought him back to the United States two years later, and furnished him material for one of his earlier books, *On the Cultural Life of Modern America,* a sour diatribe, already typical in its antimaterialist sentiments and hatred of democracy. An earlier biographer of Hamsun, Robert Ferguson, remarks that: "America pleases him not. Not its politics, not its language, not its women, not its sensationalist press, not its crass materialism, not its analphabetism, not its literature, not its painting, nor yet its theatre." Economically, Hamsun uses one dislike to drum upon the head of another: "Instead of founding an intellectual élite, America has established a mulatto stud-farm."

Hamsun was more than a living encyclopedia of distasteful traits, for traits need be mentioned only once, like the length of a nose; whereas our principal biographers (Ingar Kolloen and Robert Ferguson) must bravely repeat the occasions when they are displayed. Hamsun, it seems, had pejorative names for every creature that he felt he outstripped, which was most of them—the native Lapps in particular. He grew quickly sick of old people, even when he became one; regarded tourists with disdain; mistrusted intellectuals of every mental elevation; was a practicing misogynist, detesting just those women he most desired. He hated whole nations, especially if they spoke English, or anybody who belonged to the urban working class, and held in contempt all forms of public life. Perhaps to support his irrational view of mankind, he made acting on whims a habit, however inconvenient his impulses were to others. He drank himself into a hospital and a state of shakes; lied right and left—to publishers particularly, to women he wanted to ride, to publishers he wanted to diddle. He squandered his first wife's fortune at the gaming tables but gambled less with his own money. He was treacherous with his literary rivals, and bad mouthed them whenever he had the public's ear. He shirked his family responsibilities, disappearing for long periods, especially if one of his wives was about to give birth, and frequently pulled up his and his family's stakes, moving them about against their will, but at his humor.

There was nothing funny or fictional about Hamsun's sufferings, his moments of miserable shame, his frequent disappointments: hadn't he starved, fruitlessly wandered, been denied his chances to advance in the cultural system, and even been told, by a medico in Minnesota, that he had a galloping case of tuberculosis and didn't have long to live? The blood he coughed up would prove to be caused by bronchitis, but he preferred to think he had outwrestled the devil.

Leo Lowenthal's prophetic thirties piece on Hamsun has a fair summary of his subject's inclinations, which include "the pagan awe of unlimited and unintelligible forces of nature, the mystique of blood and race, hatred of the working class and of clerks, the blind submission to authority, the abrogation of individual responsibility, anti-intellectualism, and spiteful distrust of urban middle-class life in general."

Hunger was not Hamsun's first work, yet it was youthful, full of the immediacy of its material, deliberately limited in its diction, shocking in its depictions, and surprisingly indecisive in its conclusion, as if the text were a length removed from a hose. It is made of a very simple prose, almost as if written by a child. The gait is a little awkward, so the child sometimes seems a toddler. Meanwhile the narrator reads the world the way a tracker reads a trail. The characters jump to conclusions. Moods come and go with the regularity of a toy train. A part is readily taken for a whole, but the whole is simply whatever it is, a noun with its adjective leaning quietly against it. That is: modifications are few and unrefined. Complexities are ignored. Complexities are a human invention, and despised. The basic things of life are prized out of necessity; consequently wisdom about them is seen as savvy. However, the touch of the author is sure when directed to rustic things, and many simple scenes are indelible. That is because objects, acts, ideas are surrounded by so much silence, so much space—like an argument between mutes, like a table that is all top—that their very presence is treated the way a rare visitor to your hut would be: you offer a biscuit; the biscuit is eaten; a few grunts of agreement are exchanged.

The hungry young fellow of the title, famished for food, yes—for sex—yes—but more than these, for recognition, loves to bait strangers with lies, outrageous stories they politely respond to with their own accommodating falsehoods, until both contestants are spiders contributing to a common web; then the knowledgeable instigator suddenly accuses his mark of making things up and forces him to leave in shame and rage; or he follows women, engages in stare-downs, asks them inapplicable questions aimed at puzzling their heads, and then interprets their responses as inviting or meaningful; or in a public place he suddenly exhibits a bizarre walk, emits strange sounds just to turn heads so he can accuse passersby of impolite staring at a poor jobless youth of hidden genius. The text acts in the same way its narrator does. Readers are also to be caught in this web of Hamsun's devising, and shown up along with everybody else. In that sense, Hamsun's prose is splendidly rigged for its work. Other similar routines establish the error that commenced this paragraph, because, though our narrator is young and hungry, he is no one's fellow.

Paul Valéry's well-known witticism, offered once to André Breton as you would a smoke, pretended that Valéry could not bring himself to write fiction because he might have to sign for sentences like "the marquis went out at five." His trepidation is repeatedly justified by Hamsun's first success—*Hunger*—a novel composed (down every paragraph, over every page) of prose possessing no literary interest whatever: such as "I took the blanket under my arm and went to 5 Stener Street." This sentence opens a scene (powerful in its context but banal in its construction) during which our penniless protagonist fails to sell his blanket, and thus concludes: "I took the blanket under my arm again and went home."

John Updike, with his customary acuity, picks a sentence from *The Wanderer* to comment upon that I have grown to prize above all the others, though it is hard to know what help the translators have given Hamsun to reach bathos in a tub no deeper than five phrases, no longer than one line: "Mrs. Falkenberg was standing in the yard: a human column, light in color, standing free in the spacious courtyard, without a hat." Updike notes that the lady later vanishes in "a haze of rhapsody," a phrase that is also accurate about most everything in *Pan*. In some later works, like the misnamed novel *The Last Joy*, Hamsun's pedestrian style slows to the halt that follows a hike.

Hamsun insists on banality because regularity is what recommends the simple life. There are no surprises: none when the leaves turn, none when the snow arrives or dew weighs the morning grass. To escape your consternations, you can always row your boat out to sea and sit upon the slowly rising tide. "Night comes and he does not go home, the next day comes and he does not go home; no, he follows the usual pattern, lets the boat drift, fishes for food, goes ashore, cooks, eats, sleeps. It is incomparable, this wonderful idleness and sloth."

Humans, alone, are unpredictable: suddenly a randy shepherdess will appear before your hut door, or a hunter from the village rest his gun against a rock you prize. Perhaps a tourist bus will surprise an empty inn, or a Lapp from even farther north materialize upon a mountain path. If you are a penniless wanderer, a fortuitous wad of money may be pressed upon you. The plot can count on what the plot needs to march it from A and B to Z because, in the wings, fortuitous interventions await their moment on the page.

The narrator of *Hunger* treats interior states with the same nominal objectivity and dispassion (even when weeping, throwing up, or cursing) as he does the exterior world, because, to this starveling, "in and out" sit on the same park bench, and even the narrator's glib falsehoods gain the status of realities in no time. This detachment, even in the middle of an outburst of emotion, and the rapid shifts of mood that torment Hamsun's narrator, struck reviewers in his time as revolutionary. Shortly, however, they withdrew the credit Hamsun thought his due by recalling the vacillations of Dostoyevsky's people, whom they had once accused of the same faults, but now praised for displaying real conflicts and rare glimpses of some of the deeper recesses of the psyche. Characters who stayed inside their descriptions were soon called wooden Indians and stereotypes, while those who were obedient to impulse were said to be truer to life.

So are we really like that? Must we be incomprehensible to be free? It seems to me it scarcely matters whether the writer believes or understands this or that, perceives acutely, or feels deeply, or imagines wonderfully; what matters is whether these qualities reach the page. If it is a disordered mind the novelist is portraying, it is not important that the picture meet the approval of a psychoanalyst (who will insist upon a cause), but whether it is convincing in the world established by the text.

The comparison with Dostoyevsky was strengthened in quite the wrong way by a story of Hamsun's called "Chance," whose scenes at the roulette table almost necessarily resembled those in the Russian's novella *The Gambler*. Both men had experience enough in that squanderous milieu. The German version of the tale drew a charge of plagiarism from one critic.

Neither Ingar Kolloen nor Robert Ferguson goes very far with this incident, which resolved itself mostly by evaporating, although Kolloen tells us that Hamsun, with his characteristic whirligig condition, was himself initially shocked by the resemblances to the point of trying to squelch the piece, yet he later offered "Chance," unchanged, to his German translator. If he thought that in German the similarities would not show or be seen, he was mistaken. German publishers, who had been clamoring for his work, fell silent and grew remote. Hamsun, according to Kolloen, believed "that one of his fellow Norwegian writers must have fed the critic"—his accuser—"false information." That is as far, in this severely reduced English edition, as Kolloen is prepared to go, whereas Ferguson is characteristically reflective and, I think, perspicacious: "This suspicion, that his contemporaries and brother writers, as well as the press, were dedicated to the aim of destroying him . . . gave him a fanatic strength, a determination to triumph over the imagined odds in the stratospheric sense, and by the exercise of his talent alone force the establishment to hail him as a great writer. . . ."

Hamsun worked from carefully gathered batches of notes to shape short sentences into brief paragraphs. These many small gulps of prose, numbered like chapters, form the procession of anecdotes that make up his books; and his present biographer follows that lead, beginning each section with a teasing headline the way TV's evening news tries to catch our attention, followed by a lead-in sentence, and the necessary paragraphs with their own entry and exit, then concluding with a dramatic summary that manages to be enigmatic too. Let one example stand for many. While the twenty-year-old Hamsun was trying to survive in the United States, he was kindly given a job by the pastor of a Unitarian Church in Minneapolis. The pastor's wife was sympathetic to his parlous state, which included being misdiagnosed as a victim of tuberculosis. Bedridden, the young man confides to her his fear that he shall die before ever having known a woman. Eventually, instead of the hired whore he hopes for, she offers herself. Kolloen's terseness imitates Hamsun's manner perfectly, and the one-two punch is powerfully delivered.

> He refused her.
>
> It was high summer and Hamsun asked Drude to pull open all the curtains. He demanded she light some lamps, many lamps. He could not fill the room with enough light. He loved the light, he told her.
>
> She no longer understood him. Everything was different between them now. She wondered if he had gone mad.
>
> One night he set fire to the curtains.

Did this action bring the fire department, consume the house, damage his relationship with the husband? We are never told. We aren't told Hamsun had bronchitis instead of TB either.

Unfortunately, Kolloen is infatuated with this rhetorical device. He employs it to render nearly every section of Hamsun's life as routinely as if he were slicing a loaf of rye. Eventually, its appearance becomes annoying: "A man walked in and sat at the neighboring table. . . . Hamsun had been a guest in his house on several occasions. . . . Now, they pretended not to see each other. . . . There was good reason for Hamsun to be unsettled by this chance encounter with Erhardt Frederik Winkel Horn. He had been having an affair with his wife."

The conviction Hamsun has that each man is a mystery (except for English tourists and other objects of his scorn—they are just the stupids we take them for) is rather delightfully played out in *Mysteries*, a surprisingly lighthearted little novel that unpacks like a box of puzzles the inner selves of its characters, yet leaves the puzzles puzzling even after we've found a place for all the pieces. I think the reader is supposed to feel that a mystery is what we each ought to strive to be. We are to run away and play hide-and-no-seek in our unconscious.

Three problems: (1) If Hamsun is always working out personal issues and settling scores in his books, how shall he manage to escape the egocentric predicament? Joyce's *mememoreme* seems to account for everything. (2) The psyche is a strange unfunny place; it tends, when unveiled, to be ugly, or silly, or dumb, or childish, or really evil. Where do the generosities lie concealed—those virtues too shy to be ordinarily seen? A few acts of benevolence in *Hunger* succeed brilliantly in undermining themselves; that is, they turn out to be not so nice after all. (3) In trying to render the random and the inexplicable, the text may exhibit the paradox of imitative form (Coleridge's famous caution to Wordsworth that he should not render a dull and garrulous discourser by being dull and garrulous). Hamsun's stories wander with apparent aimlessness. Why not call several *Wanderers*? He did so.

After *Hunger, Pan* is perhaps the most celebrated of Hamsun's novels. It also makes allegorical gestures, but its loyalty to its symbolic structure is a bit more devoted. In *Hunger,* the town through which our hero caroms is called Christina (an early name for Oslo), and the text will suggest, on more than one occasion, that its hero's suffering is Christlike; on the other hand he complains like Job and curses God and in the end simply leaves town. Making a holy mess and then leaving is Hamsun's principal fictional formula. It always seemed to work in his life.

The principal struggle that *Hunger* depicts is between the body and the ego's ambitions. Neither God nor his city is an agent of the ensuing suffering. In *Pan* the pain is self-inflicted, too (Pan shoots off his big toe, an old enlistment dodge), with pride and power, as well as the rifle, the punishing instruments. The mythological Pan is a goat god, a hunter of food and a hunter of women, who meets more than his match in a beautiful hard-to-figure out-of-town tease. A tiresome tug-of-war ensues. To this cautionary tale of a god brought low by a woman (as Samson is by Delilah), the spurned lover's ultimate response is to dynamite part of a mountain down upon an unintended target—his goat-girl mistress who gave generously of herself and loved him without reservations. The book is spotted,

like its high mountain trees, with set "sublimities" during which
the identity of the hero and his natural surroundings is alleged. We
enjoy bliss as well as suffer its attendant tears. Ferguson, whose
viewpoint I have been taught to value, greatly admires this novel, as
do many others. "This is a book," he says, "that reaches effortlessly
and deeply into the soul. . . ." But I am more inclined to share the
opinion of a contemporary reviewer: "The new book is characterized
by the same cheap phoneyness which has marred so much of what
Hamsun has written." To the main body of this novel is attached a
wholly misguided epilogue which I would advise the reader to skip.
It kills off the protagonist of the previous text in a place, at a time,
and in a manner that run from most unlikely to ludicrous. Critics
have extended themselves to justify the existence of this appendage,
but it is, like the blindfolded man's stab at the donkey, pinned far
from its intended place. In this instance, the defense maintains, the
author has created a purely fictional persona to narrate the work,
rather than a man (as in *Hunger*) who must undergo its victimiza-
tions. But the distance between the tale and its teller, in Hamsun,
is that of the thinnest thread. We can learn from his biographers
that this book is a dramatization of one of his courtships, and the
incidental characters (as in *Hunger*) are all clippings from his life.

Hamsun employs symbols too—shoes, slipper, shot-off toe, dogs
by the half dozen, bird feathers—that he stirs around through his
tale like ice cubes in the punch their appearance is expected to land.

Hamsun also lived according to the clichés which cling to the art
of writing: that it is a solitary occupation requiring hours of absorbing
and profound meditation; that it asks for patience during dispiriting
periods of sterility, requires continuous vigilance against the vanities of the self, as well as a ruthless indifference to the matters of
ordinary life when they chance to interfere; it tells him to trust in his
genius, yet retain an almost naive acceptance of inspiration when it
arrives. As a specifically Norwegian writer, he would be expected to
challenge received opinion and the aesthetic efforts of his predeces-
sors; he would defy tradition, whereupon tradition would award him

for it. Ibsen's outrages were expected of him; writers were supposed to send their works to scout out country customs and, by attacking them, to initiate change. Both writers and their readers lived as much upon scandal as the fishermen on their fiords, and adored the exposure of shocking thoughts and feelings as much as the public nakedness they pretended to deplore.

Early in his career Hamsun made much of his attachment to purely aesthetic ends, and certainly his interest is not in the social realism of many of his contemporaries; but his intentions aren't artistically pure either, and conceal the behavioral excuses his writings create for him, the personal vendettas they provide, as well as the other rearrangements of reality that suit his purposes. "Language must possess all the scales of music. The writer must always, unfailingly, use a word that pulsates, that conveys a thing, that can wound the soul so it yelps." Hamsun also likes to boast about his scruples as an artist, but in the twenty-eight years between *Hunger* and *The Growth of the Soil,* he wrote twenty-six books. How many of these could have been *Madame Bovary*? Later on his publisher will remark, "During the course of the last seven years he [Hamsun] had written over 1,500 book pages." Translation, of course, is always an element that must be apologized for in the estimation of any literary work. Each language has its own musical scales and its own syntactical and rhetorical structures. As far as I can tell, Hamsun's principles are most steadily upheld by those ideological loyalties that express his embattled sense of himself. When you write in frenzied bursts, in such amounts, there can be little time for prolonged concern about art or even the graces of daily life. His private estimate accompanied the manuscript of *The Road Leads On* (about yet another vagabond lover), and was more accurate: "Some good stuff and some garbage, just as in every book."

Hamsun's dislike of democracy seemed, for much of his life, to be a cranky possession of his own; but the rise of Hitler to power in Germany changed that.

All over Europe little schools of disappointed people appeared, prepared to follow the führer's lead in malice, ruthlessness, and noise. Here was a leader who resembled Hamsun in his simple origins, his maniacal ambition, his artistic genius, and for the ordinary world his contemptuous disdain—a figure in whose shadow he might walk without seeming merely a second shade. The defeat of the Germans by the beastly English in World War I was as unhealed a wound for Hamsun as it was for most German citizens.

In a Festschrift to celebrate Hamsun's seventieth birthday (1929), German praise was overwhelmingly present: Gerhart Hauptmann, Heinrich and Thomas Mann, Jacob Wassermann, and Stefan Zweig were among the many who complimented him then and regretted it later. In honor of the day, Max Reinhardt staged one of Hamsun's plays and it enjoyed an impressive run. Half a million copies of *Hunger* were in print. Germany loved him close up as well as from a distance. When Hamsun visited in 1931, his hotel room was filled with flowers, letters, and gifts. Irritating journalists pursued his touring party, but by their persistence made it clear that Hamsun was still news. While his entourage traveled through southern Germany, Hamsun hummed and smiled. However, the moment they arrived in Milan his mood changed, and during supper at the station he tried to straighten the prongs of the forks; noisily complained he couldn't decipher their maker's mark; and then attacked the spoons.

The smell of power is more seductive than musk and more damaging than first- or secondhand smoke. Initially Hamsun's life story had been merely disgusting; it now grew grimly dismal as he falls in with the quislings, jockeys for political position, and supports the German occupation of his country even when it begins its reign of terror there, arresting gentiles as well as Jews. His public utterances weren't nutty the way Ezra Pound's were, and had a weight in his country whose heft the American poet could only imagine. Hamsun takes his prestige and his fame to see the führer; then in that presence pleads the cause of his countrymen—commendable if his concerns weren't so callously selective. But the leader wants to talk literature, not politics, and is quickly made to regret his agreement to meet with the argumentative novelist. Hamsun has no influence after all: after all those words, that accumulated pile of work, those impressive sales and badges of honor. Nor did Hamsun's diatribes against the English defeat the hated islanders. Nor did the realization that he could not rescue a single citizen from the Nazi camps and their deadly chambers alter his attitudes. After the war, when legalized revenges were being undertaken, Hamsun's wife, Marie, who surpassed his Nazi sympathies in fervor (her children's books were also a success in Germany), though hating her husband only as thoroughly as he her, was convicted of treason and sentenced to two years in prison; but Hamsun, in an exercise of national hypocrisy, was hustled away into a psychiatric hospital and the company of doctors who were expected to find a kink in his crock and an excuse to save the state from an embarrassing trial. At the end of their investigations, however, the patient had to be pronounced healthy for his age, sound of mind, and competent in his dealings with the world.

The trial would be Hamsun's finest moment. Every step in the proceedings justified, once again, and before the public, the worth of his dearest beliefs. He stood alone, as his memorial statue in winter will, its shoulders only colder because of the opposing gale.

Retired to his farm, Hamsun was neither a country mouse nor a rodent exiled by his city. Some years before, he had settled on being the squire who owns the barn, though presently down on his luck, what with all those penalties demanded by the state. And it was the barn's cats that killed the rats. As for the afterlife's awards: "I have never been attracted to the honour that might come with big bronze statues of me in Norway's towns. Quite the opposite: each time I have thought of these posthumous statues, I have wished I could benefit from their value now—bring on the cash!"

KINDS OF KILLING

In order to prepare private citizens for the military, a humiliating and painful bullying is generally prescribed. Its aim is to inculcate obedience and create callousness. Leaders must be resolute and heartless, prepared to send any enemy "to their deaths, pitilessly and remorselessly," as the führer demanded. Next a campaign of denigration of the chosen opponent is undertaken. This is designed to reduce the humanity of the enemy, and to prepare a social web of support for behavior that is basically cruel, immoral, and normally disapproved. It strengthens every aspect of one's plans if the society that you represent brings to the project a tradition of paternal domination and abuse, reaching from the family (in Germany's case) to the kaiser and its final station, God. Deep feelings of injury, inferiority, and large reserves of resentment—the fresher the better—are nearly essential. Any widespread unhappiness within your country can then be directed at the scapegoat selected, by every available instrument of indoctrination and propaganda. If the enemy can be enticed to return fire, that will help solidify the nation's resolve. Since a saw's cut is painful either way it moves, the soldier knows that it is safer to risk death at the front rather than execution in the rear. A general sense of uneasiness helps, as if you knew someone were watching where you walked, reading your mail, and overhearing your talk. This atmosphere of anxiety can be sustained when the agents of power are pitiless. The master craftsmen of the Third Reich, whose state-of-war posture is so painstakingly studied in this superb but disheartening history of bad behavior, had set their sights upon Poland at the time the third and final volume of Richard Evans's masterwork begins (*The Third Reich at War*, 2009, source of the following quotations), and had made all the necessary preparations I have just enumerated.

Although preserving the purity of the bloodline is a commandment of tribal behavior, the Germans had expanded its meaning to include concerns about inner strength as well as physical health and racial genetics. Now the blood *in* the bloodline, not just its course, could be studied, and this gave to the most primitive of superstitions a scientific appearance. Dressed in laboratory coats, euthanasia could also be embraced. The Poles, like the mad, the ill, the old, and others at the edge of death, were incapable of a full-fledged human life. They carried disease, lived in filth, were born almost too stupid to breathe; their incompetence was as catching as the lice they bore; they should be confined to the muddles they made and their ignorance encouraged. Germany's earnest efforts to rub out any influence Polish intellectuals might have on their society, by removing them from their own lives, seem odd when dealing with such a presumably dumb bunch.

The novelty of the war that was beginning with the German attack in September 1939—aside from the journalistically popular concept of blitzkrieg—was its unusual aim: not the defeat of another army but the destruction of a population. From Germans already living in Poland the SS formed militias of men whose grievances with the indigenous population reached murderous levels with astonishing ease, and bands of "red legs" of this sort, obeying only the orders of their hearts, began organized shooting parties. The size of the payback for alleged Polish atrocities was 4,247 on October 7; by November, in Klammer, two thousand had been added; near Mniszek ten thousand more Poles and Jews of every age and sex were shot at the edges of the gravel pits that were to serve for their graves; in a wood near Karlshof, eight thousand more were massacred. The cleansing continued, picking up speed as efficiencies improved. Finding so many murderers among ordinary people had not proved difficult. Moreover these unconscionable activities were not the result of a long harsh military campaign and disappointing losses, but were available for use the moment the war began, with its immediate, immoderate, and overwhelming victories.

The German army, when it began to do its part, specialized in burning any village in which the least resistance was encountered. The SS, as well as regular police, were initially disposed to carry out the murder of specific persons instead of the anonymous many, and to be singled out might be a victim's only victory. This slaughter was ameliorated (the comforting phrase cannot be read without a grimace) when the authorities recognized that Germany had a serious need for workers, with so many men gone from their jobs and away for the war. Every available body was then rounded up and sent off as a labor replacement wherever those were needed in the Fatherland. The "recruitment" of foreign labor was a considerable preoccupation of German bureaucracy during the entire war, and eventually included putting to work prisoners of war from both fronts. Many a Polish house was emptied or a village stripped of its population, so that looting and pillaging became a military habit, and the rape of women almost an invitation. The greed of many in the high command was as huge, and as frankly bragged of, as Falstaff's pride in his belly. Hitler wanted to establish a museum of stolen property in his hometown of Lenz. Göring desired to display his art as he did his hunting trophies, above the many sofas furnishing his numerous *schlosses.*

This great war was not one war but many, fought in different places, under different circumstances, and at different times; but the German troops remembered to bring with them to new encounters the bad habits formed when they invaded Poland. Their behavior was still able to produce surprise. "Where is the traditional German sense of honour," wrote one inhabitant of occupied Athens. "They empty houses of whatever meets their eye. In Pistolakis' house they took the pillow-slips and grabbed the Cretan heirlooms from the valuable collections they have. From the poor houses in the area they seized sheets and blankets. From other neighborhoods they grab oil paintings and even the metal knobs from the doors." Of course, the pillowcases became bags for bearing off heirlooms, while the knobs, if metal, were needed back home. Looting was rarely random among the officer class.

Like a monstrous babe born from the brow of Rabelais, this war was only a few months old and already it had become a major crime against humanity. The German government, noticing that too much booty was escaping the clutches of the state, simply announced in October of 1939 that it had acquired for its own use the contents of the entire store. Acquisitions then began in earnest. The army took over farms and anything else that might supply food; universities lost their scientific instruments; every iron object, length of copper or zinc downspout, steel girder, tin saucepan, and—yes—doorknob was scooped up, melted down, and sent to work in the mills of the Reich. "Even the Warsaw Zoo's collection of stuffed animals was taken away." There appeared to be a bounty on Polish priests, who were deported, incarcerated, shot. Schools were closed and their equipment destroyed. Businesses were commandeered and landed estates requisitioned. As the winter grew harsh, the German police borrowed the Poles' sheepskin coats if they saw a serviceable one pass in the street. In town after town, the names of the avenues and alleyways were replaced. In sum, everything Polish was banned, burned, stolen, eaten, removed, imprisoned, or deported, and sooner or later entire populations were slaughtered far more carelessly than cattle.

Some senior German officers, who still believed in the traditional rules of engagement and the gallantries of military etiquette, and who were therefore increasingly disturbed by the rapacious behavior of the militias, began to protest and to make arrests, but Hitler immediately issued an amnesty for acts motivated by "bitterness against the atrocities committed by the Poles." Colonel-General Johannes Blaskowitz, who was at that time Commander in Chief East, complained in a memo to the führer of the horrible atrocities that now shadowed the conscience of the country, and of crimes the state would see reason to regret later; but many officers were only too happy to hand whatever brutality they saw or guilt they bore over to the SS, and soon Blaskowitz had another, much less important post. Demotions were lessons to others.

The grander aim behind these persecutions was the emptying of Poland of its Jewish/Polish inhabitants in order to fill it with repatriated Germans. After all, if you are going to acquire a bigger house, its previous owners should not be still flushing the toilets. Expulsions could be rather prompt—twenty minutes in some cases—and the journey cold. One trainload delivered the bodies of forty frozen children, dead on arrival but at their proper station. Eighty-eight thousand Poles and Jews of Posen were whisked away in this fashion during early December of 1939, to be sorted out. Relocation took more time, and a lot more money, since the genuine Germanness of people who had often lived for years away from the Fatherland had to be verified, fakers detected, Jews and weaklings weeded out, and some recompense made to the winners for their losses.

Page after page rolls by the reader's eye bearing these, even now, astonishing statistics—shocking, revolting, numbing, relentless—that sum up how many broken families, beaten bodies, and murdered men and women, how much loot and illicit booty, how many cruelties had, during this month or that, in simple village or chaotic battlefield, been undertaken and accomplished. The record is rich with irony. For every sincere member of the master race there were those who took bribes from the Jews as often as they took their lives. While the big—the organized—war went on, small wars everywhere flared and flowered. When food became scarce, the black markets had specials. The vast government organization had more cracks than any comedian, and up and down them thousands of busy creatures scurried, carrying baskets of fruit, tins of fish, bundles of carrots, barrels of oil, bolts of silk, as well as the traditional cigs, booze, chocolates, and lingerie. I wonder what one day's collection of screams might fetch.

With acres of their fields burned, crops requisitioned, and farmers enslaved, the population began to starve. Rations, if you were a Pole, came to no more than 669 calories a day. Jews received 184. An officer's spit might contain that much. Robbers roamed the roads and forests. Diseases spread as the body's resistance also failed. In France, when Germany overran it, refuges fled one city only to fill another. Friends turned upon friends. Denunciation replaced *"bonjour."* So the campaign of extermination was going nicely. Thin women were the only ones around but nonetheless inviting, exchanging syphilis for a few hundred calories of love.

On the eastern edges of Poland, where the Russians were employing very similar methods of murder and deportation, conditions, though sometimes different, were no better, and the killing contest, at an admittedly rough count, continued to turn out a draw. Jews scarcely knew which way to run; nor dared they stay in place, since anti-Semitism was, in Poland (as it was in Hungary, Romania, the Ukraine) a flourishing native plant. Evans is succinct: "The deliberate reduction of Poland to a state of nature, the boundless exploitation of its resources, the radical degradation of everyday life, the arbitrary exercise of unfettered power, the violent expulsion of Poles from their homes—all of this opened the way to the application of unbridled terror against Poland's Jews."

Is this particular mistreatment of the Jews entirely the result of years of Nazi propaganda or even of ancient misgivings? Is something more going on? Because even if I think no better of my neighbor than I do my dog, I treat my dog rather well, and can find the time to feed her, pet her, train her, walk her around. Even if I think of my neighbor as a leper, I might be expected to wish no more for him than removal to a colony; moreover I might be assumed to think of my leper's daughter as disgusting and far from desirable, when in fact I cannot wait to take her in my arms as roughly as necessary, her skin as intimate to me as mine, and then to enter her every aperture. Do I not care where I send my sperm?

The previous volumes of this history will help the reader confront such questions, because they chronicle the historic events that led to National Socialism's seizure of power in Germany (*The Coming of the Third Reich,* 2003), and then to its solidification (*The Third Reich in Power,* 2005). This particular period in history has given rise to a myriad of questions, some perhaps odd, others almost mysterious. For instance, only one conglomeration of events can be called "the Holocaust." To write of "a" holocaust suggests there might have been others, and damages this one's almost sacred status. Is, then, its singularity enough to deprive it of any place in a customary causal path so that history cannot account for it? Or is the Holocaust just the largest of a class of catastrophes, like eruptions, hurricanes, and landslides are? How many must die to achieve the number necessary to count as a holocaust? Fifty thousand? Four hundred thousand? Three million? Is it like deciding that among winds one is the windiest?

Perhaps it is how well organized and sponsored these massacres were that makes them so special. They were a real corporate enterprise, involving the apparatus of a nation-state. On the other hand, Croats, Hungarians, Romanians, including the Poles who were picked on, even the French and the Dutch Nazis, eagerly helped out. Many other issues are theological, such as wondering what God's purpose was in levying such punishment upon the Jews. Questions of this kind do not trouble historians much. On the other hand, the failure of nearly every element of humanistic interest and accomplishment in Germany to dissuade, slow down, or oppose the actions of the state, borders on total, and this sad futility is discouraging to those who thought that "higher culture" included a more refined morality. Is the fact that older generations of Germans were more likely to disapprove of mass murder due to the younger ones enduring an earlier and longer period of brainwashing, or just to their higher level of testosterone?

There are several strategies one might employ for lessening the guilt of the Germans without denying the occurrence of their crimes. A number are currently operating in the guise of (fraudulent) memoirs or romanticizing movies. A few such are cited by Jacob Heilbrunn in an article for *The New York Times*. Heilbrunn remarks that "the further the Holocaust recedes into the past, the more it's being exploited to create a narrative of redemption." Recently, stories of German opposition to Nazi actions have become particularly popular. There is, however, little that is exotic or particularly daring about the occasional leaflet campaigns that the Social Democrats managed to set going as late as the summer of 1934. Evans, in his second volume, points out that "[b]y this time, almost all the other leading Social Democrats who had remained in Germany were in prison, in a concentration camp, silenced or dead." Even those who would endeavor to kill Hitler were mostly motivated by their conviction that Germany was finally losing the war, rather than by any deep-seated objections to his policies. At least, that was the opinion the *London Times* found in its reviews of *Germans Against Hitler* by Hans Mommsen (translated into English in 2008) and *Luck of the Devil* (2009) by Ian Kershaw. Although one dead fly may ruin an entire porridge, an innocent olive will not render benevolent a poisoned glass.

Richard Evans is a veteran of these revisionist wars, having earned a few medals for his testimony at the trial of one of honesty's enemies, David Irving, who had the chutzpah to sue Deborah Lipstadt (a professor at Emory University) for libeling him in her book *Denying the Holocaust: The Growing Assault on Truth and Memory* (1993)—a careful exposure of this movement's bowel-like (regular, hidden, contemptible) strategies. Evans's evidence has been presented in his own *Lying about Hitler: History, Holocaust, and the David Irving Trial* (2001). Irving lost his case, but these apologists are not easy to discourage. They lurk about the edges of conflicts like this, especially now that the Internet lends its facilities to any voice that cares to attach a pseudonymous name or academic title to a site from which they can fire off innuendos, profit from ignorance, and cast suspicion. Another excellent exposure of revisionist methods can be

Kinds of Killing

found in Pierre Vidal-Naquet's *Assassins of Memory: Essays on the Denial of the Holocaust* (1987.) If there are any purely "intellectual crimes," denying the reality of the Holocaust is surely one of them.

Still, one excuse that I rather like is the presumption that any group of people, finding themselves in the same sort of situation, their histories stocked with similar resentments, would act in a comparably vengeful fashion. Suppose that I have been a pitiful powerless person my whole life, and the child of similarly helpless victims of war, humiliation, and economic collapse. Now, suddenly, finally, I carry your life in my holster, I can act with impunity and at whim, but I must remind the world of my elevation by repeated demonstrations, the more vulgar, petty, and disgusting the better. So after I have raped this Polish-Tunisian-Greek-Gypsy girl, who certainly deserved it, I shall invent little sadistic extras to demand of her: that she cleans the public latrines with her blouse. Jewish bystanders shall be required to doff their silly hats. Polish scum shall be made to lie flat in the mud and kiss dirt. While they are thus prone I shall try not to wobble when I walk upon one of them, but they are incorrigibly lumpy.

But it was the Romanian members of the Iron Guard who did the human race proud when they forced two hundred Jewish men into a slaughterhouse, flayed them from their clothes, and made them walk the line to their stockyard executions, after which their corpses were hung up on meat hooks that had been run through their throats. Those German "doctors," who looked upon the Jewish children in their hands very much as we do laboratory mice, yet wishing to erase any evidence of their experiments upon them, considerately shot the kids full of morphine and had them hung on hooks for SS men to yank as one has to tug when extricating clothes from a crowded closet.

"Croatian Ustashe units," perhaps out of friendly rivalry and to demonstrate that you didn't have to be a Jew, "gouged out the eyes of Serbian men and cut off the women's breasts with penknives." They also carried out clever sting operations by promising amnesty to any villager who converted to Catholicism and then beating to death with spiked clubs the three hundred who showed up at a Glina church for the conversion ceremony. Sometimes they just used ordinary hammers.

And to those making inquiries later, I shall say I did so because someone wearing the appropriate suit of authority or religious habit said it was okay. I shall say I did so because I've had a rather hard life myself. I shall say I did so because I am really scared of these flat-black-hatted machinates whose evil ways I've heard about on the radio. They are moneylenders, evil connivers, members of the Red Menace. Just look at them: dirty and diseased, bearing beards just begging to be tugged, eating grass like meadow cows. Down what dark twisted avenue of delight does this delight await me? And if I were a member of the Iron Guard that day, would I now—would anyone?—excuse myself by saying those Jews deserved the punishment of the slaughterhouse?

Well, we were preoccupied with our lives at the time, and didn't notice.

Is it somehow more or less awful if one man kills another hand to hand, or by bomb from a plane, or with a signature at the end of a page? What legitimizes murder: being a soldier in a nice tidy correctly declared war? Or a marine who is taking part in an unprovoked and preemptive attack? Perhaps we are considering a civilian who does in one of the enemy with a hay fork, or a member of the militia who acts in obedience to an order and delivers a merciful shot to the head of a prisoner kneeling before a pit previously prepared for his folded form. What is the degree of difference?

Contrary to common belief, monoxide fumes can be ghastly; reports about how it feels to be buried alive are slight; hanging is far too slow a method; poison is also unpromising. Is it okay to kick in a kidney because its owner is dirty, wearing the wrong clothes, clerks in a hardware store, is a disloyal Red, a moron, merely blind, walks with a limp, or should these people be sent to hospitals, psycho wards, and other capitals of euthanasia?

How should I know? I was preoccupied with my life at the time, and paid no mind.

Do we really have to fuss a lot over who deserves to die? Chance or whim does in the unlucky. Other times it is death by doctor, lawyer, Indian chief. Preemptive strikes against progeny, including mass sterilizations, were studied. "Senior SS officers fantasized about such methods being applied to 10 million racially inferior people, or to Jewish men needed only for labor. . . ." These were happy times for serial killers, and for those who needed to let off steam in order to seek anger relief. I wonder if the statisticians who are so devoted to numbers have calculated how many commonplace outrages were committed under cover of the general criminality. Well, you must know that the Russians are massacring millions too. And after the way I—we—they've been treated, what did you expect? The Jews took it lying down. Starvation, disease did it, whatever it was, not I. The Americans dropped that bomb, didn't they? Listen, I let the Warsaw Jews have their own mayor. Because it was winter, a load of young children froze while enjoying their train ride. Some things can't be helped. A few hearts failed from fear of being gassed, or waiting in line and being last. But, gee, there are more Jews now than ever. More Poles too. And that proves that there were never as many killed as has been maintained. Look at what the Allies did to Dresden. What gas chambers? I don't see any gas chambers.

When are we to know we have the final solution to the Jewish question? When we shall not have to live in the world of their awareness.

Richard Evans's three volumes of disagreeable details, masterfully ordered and presented with ruthless clarity, are not centrally concerned with actual fighting, although a good account can be found there. His indictment is principally based upon the political and cultural climate that created a monster out of an apparently civilized nation-state. And it does not fail to quote from countless witnesses whose eyes had to shed—like tears—their disbelief of a barbarism for which only the human species could find the evil energies.

Whether one must wear a yellow star . . . excuses are inadequate; whether one is banished from the queue for daily rations . . . excuses are inadequate; whether one is murdered in an unimaginably mean way . . . excuses are inadequate; whether that wretch whom I shot from a passing window turns out to be twenty or two thousand destined to crumple into open graves . . . excuses are inadequate; and if we feel rage . . . well . . . welcome to our ambiguous skin: victor hates victim for making him victorious.

Murder machines, such as those gas-driven engines of death that the Germans designed to facilitate their task, are the sort of thing that catches the popular imagination, but the quiet, at no point wholly observable method of starvation is the ultimate choice: profitable while being cheap, and requiring no implements, no death chambers, no immediate executioners either. Disposing of the bodies when you have shot five hundred in the woods, or at the end of a week of inhalations when you have more corpses than you know how to discreetly burn, becomes an increasingly sensitive and annoying problem; so it is comforting to contemplate how economical starvation is, beginning with the victims feeding on themselves, thus reducing smoky fats, with a good chance they will finally fall upon those of their own who have fallen, and endeavor to devour them. For sport, in some camps for captured Soviet soldiers, guards would bet on which dogs might leave upon their prisoners the most damaging tooth marks, but this was purely for entertainment and not very efficient for murder on a mass scale.

If you kill all the Jews, who will remain to accuse you? Scarcely anyone else will care and many will be quietly grateful.

The war against the Soviet Union began as felicitously as the invasion of Poland: many quick and easy victories, rapid advances, inconveniently large numbers of captive soldiers, much pillaging, including the seasonal collection of winter coats, frequent rapes, pointless vandalism, random killings, and the gradual re-realization that prisoners might be better used as workers than starvelings. Nevertheless, of the approximately 5.7 million Soviet prisoners,

"3,300,000 had perished by the time the war was over." As if anticipating the counterclaim (which is supposed to alter one's appalled reaction), Evans immediately continues: "By comparison 356,687 out of about 2 million German prisoners taken by the Red Army, mostly in the later stages of the war, did not survive." Moreover, many died in Soviet camps from the same straitened circumstances the general population suffered. They starved; we starved; he, she, or it starved with happy uniformity. Even curtains at windows grew thin.

As if to demonstrate who among the barbarous was hun in chief, the Nazis frequently attacked fine homes and furnishings as if the mirrors were shooting back. Soldiers burned Tolstoy manuscripts when they arrived in Yasnaya Polyana, and in Klin drove motorcycles back and forth over sheets of Tchaikovsky's musical scores. Mostly, though, soldiers complained of the miserable conditions of life that Russian villages offered them. "Partisan resistance prompted further reprisals, leading more to join the partisans, and so the escalating cycle of violence continued." This inevitability, ironically, seems to have escaped the notice of present-day nations. Still, what is the use of an upper hand if you can't spank someone with it?

Success has its penalties. The advance was so rapid that many Soviet troops were passed like hitchhikers on the road, and these unattached men joined the local partisans, made a nuisance of themselves behind the lines, and earned for others as well as themselves reprisals, which often meant that hostages would be executed, many by hanging from suitable trees, which often spoiled the view higher officers had from their very temporary accommodations.

Snow and cold began to kill people without regard to race or place of origin. Once more the Jews were going to lose their coats. The eyes of the troops wept in the face of the wind and it spoiled their aim. Their swollen feet had to be cut from their shoes. And Polish lice were now a third force. Like the lice, the Russians were too numerous. Killing them all was impossible, though corpses fell like falling snow into growing heaps. It did begin to look as if the enemy had better shovels.

One of the many shocks this book delivers is the reader's realization that—after following a trail of murder and usurpation through two and one-half volumes, during which death is more frequent than the words, cruelty and conflict more common than punctuation, murder spread equally over all its pages—the killing is now going to begin in earnest. "There is also some evidence that Ukrainian nationalists in Lemberg nailed bodies to the prison wall, crucified them or amputated breasts and genitals to give the impression that the Soviet atrocities were even worse than they actually were." I'm glad they had a good reason. Despite the fact that some Ukrainians were mighty busy beating Jews with the poor man's arsenal—clubs studded with nails—the Nazis complained that their attempts "to incite pogroms against Jews have not met with the success we hoped for."

Entire cavalry brigades were now assigned the task of destroying Jews. One such group especially distinguished itself by shooting "more than 25,000 Jews in under a month." At first, the executioners were not to waste bullets on women but simply to drive them into the Pripet Marshes, the greatest area of swampy woodland in Europe, where they might drown; however the marshes were deep enough only for wading, so the women, like the men, had to be shot. The Germans were not to be slowed by these defeats. They found ravines, and in the one called Babi Yar, after undressing and lying down in neat rows—victim placed upon the just victimized as blanket upon sheet—the Jews were bulleted behind the neck to a total of 33,771.

Men cannot imagine such numbers. They can only perform them.

Any reluctance felt by members of the military was overcome by an anti-Semitism almost as old as their age, by fears of reprisal for themselves, because of the shame they felt at being taken for sissies, and on account of the payments in plunder that fed their greed. "The great majority of officers and men took part willingly . . . and raised no objections." In some cases, Serbian prisoners would be used to collect from a fresh kill of Jews the contents of their pockets, and the soldiers would risk giving these people penknives to cut off ring fingers. A handy chart, of which there are many, shows by means of variously striped shades the numbers killed in the area stretching from Leningrad in the north to Vilna (248,468), from Minsk to Kursk (91,012), Kiev to Stalino (105,988), and Taganrog to Simferopol (91,678) during the years 1941–43. Only once more shall I give in to outrage and cite another particularly instructive moment among thousands that might be chosen, in order to draw your attention to Hans Krüger, head of the local security police in Stanislawów, Galicia, who threw a picnic for the shooters to enjoy between shootings, and oversaw the massacre "with a bottle of vodka in one hand and a hot-dog in the other. . . ." You may think this picture is simply grotesque. There is another in which we see an officer so horrified by the sordid conditions in which some Jewish children were being held that he approved of their immediate execution in order to spare them further pain. This exhibits a concern that might be expected for chickens.

By now (July and August of 1941), few soldiers were squeamish; their Austrian officers were still eager; shooting Jews was a sport as habitual as bowling on weekends; and anyone handy might be murdered just to meet the monthly quotas. The instruction that came down from Hitler was to kill "anyone who even looks askance." Evans is quite clear about the evidence that "many people in the senior ranks of the Party and state administration were fully informed of the massacres being carried out by the SS Task Forces in the east."

By the time the United States entered the war, the expansion of Germany's murderous ambitions had grown from one of forcible Polish relocation to pogroms that involved the whole eastern front, subsequently to the entire continent of Europe, and bore unmistakable signs, finally, of global aspirations. This would mean that the assimilated Jews of Germany, who had lost their homes and many possessions but otherwise were "merely" harassed by a lengthening list of petty bans on buying flowers or being forbidden to sit in deck chairs, to rules denying them cats, would now be removed to camps in the east. The boxcars began their tryouts for grainy documentary movies. Between November of 1941 and February of 1942, fifty-eight trainloads of those "useless eaters" who were declared unfit for forced labor carried fifty-three thousand Jews to camps in the east.

Who could have imagined there were so many Jews; that just removing them to overnight ghettos in Poland or the Ukraine would put such a strain upon every mile of track and every engine's boilers; that so many departments of government would be required, soldiers to shoot them, munitions to facilitate this, guards to control them, shovels to dig and to cover their graves? Better methods had to be found for both death and disposal. Perhaps those employed with such success in the programs of euthanasia might be brought into play—sealed chambers and car exhaust—and camps built solely for death's purpose. So thirty gas vans were built in Berlin. They could kill sixty at a time, an improvement of ten over previous model years. Occasionally a child survived whose mother had so severely swaddled it the fumes could not penetrate the cloth. It was a doubtful stroke of luck, since the guards would smash such babies' heads against convenient trees.

Timing became important. Himmler had to bawl out one over-zealous police chief in Riga who had a trainload of Berlin deportees killed too promptly, thus possibly alarming those Jews still in Berlin and causing them to be more difficult to handle. The range of extermination now clearly included the whole of occupied Europe. Yet it was the twentieth of January, 1942, before the infamous Wannsee meeting on the final solution to the Jewish question took place. No final solution seems to have been reached, but a semifinal one was. Elderly Jews would be sent to old-folks camps. Since the holding stations were about to take on the balance of German Jews, the Eastern Jews who presently filled them would have to be eliminated to make room. Gassing vans were amply available. Jews able to work would build roads and die on waysides. "Extermination through labor" was not a new idea, but it was an economical and effective one. There was no need to coddle these creatures, for when one perished another was available.

The propaganda machine was making its own carbon monoxide. Everything the Germans were doing to the Jews, the Jews had done to Germans, or would do if they could. They had started the war; they were eating away at the Reich's magnificent culture; they wanted to destroy Germany as it presently stood. Goebbels instructed the media to be unrelenting. "The Jews must now be used in the German press as a political target: the Jews are to blame; the Jews wanted the war; the Jews are making the war worse; and, again and again, the Jews are to blame." I do think Goebbels had begun to believe his own lies, but could an entire nation be deceived by nonsense so palpable it . . . But I forget. Nazism was a secular religion. Its sacred book was *Mein Kampf*. The Red Menace embodied another form of worship that held *Das Kapital* to its heart. Their godfathers just weren't in heaven, and could use the phone. Whether Jew or Christian, Nazi or Commie: they all had plenty of practice living in illusion and hating one another.

During the years 1941–43, Berlin Jews, who were not supposed to have their composure ruffled by hearing the worst of bad news, heard the bad news nevertheless and escaped by suicide. It was a wonder there were any trains left able to carry munitions. The idea that many people still didn't know what was going on represents another wild lie. If the Jews, who weren't supposed to know, knew, everybody did. Like the disciplined lines of white crosses at Arlington, numbers representing the sizes of the shipments march across Evans's text. Perhaps these pages more accurately resemble a schedule of departures than a cemetery, but their meanings are the same.

Jews were not the only victims of the Nazis' murderous frenzy; nor, on the eastern front, was the Soviet army Germany's sole enemy; because the moment the Czechs began to act up they were sorted out for deportation, sterilization, and execution, just as the Poles had been, and—as always—the Gypsies too, who were consistently preyed upon, as well as other racial odds and ends. When Czech partisans managed to assassinate their region's SS protector, Reinhold Heydrich, they hoped to provoke from the Nazis their customary kinds of retaliation, in order to reawaken a resistance movement that Heydrich's policies had managed to frighten or lull into passivity. In so doing they demonstrated how easily the same gloves of callousness that the Germans wore could be put on, and how well the fit was. Lidice was only the notorious part of the cost.

Until November of 1941, the extermination camps had not yet been built. A score of SS officers would run them; Ukrainians, taken from their own camps and given special training, would provide the raw manpower; and a few specialists recruited from the victims themselves (tailors, carpenters, cobblers, *und so weiter*) could supply the standard operative skills. All that otherwise might be needed, aside from the airtight gas chambers, were some houses for the SS, and barracks for the auxiliary servants of the industry. These camps were extraordinarily efficient, except that sometimes the wooden killing boxes began to leak and had to be replaced by concrete ones. At Belzec, the first of these specialized death camps, seventy-five thousand Jews were gassed and their bodies burned in its initial thirty days of operation. Eventually, the number would approach six hundred thousand.

Jews still in Poland were at full alarm, and many had to be killed in their houses and on the streets before their trains departed, they had become so obstreperous. Lest we focus our dismay too narrowly: Poles stood by and laughed at the sight—laughed then looted.

The second camp was modeled after the first, except it was housed in a brick building. However, hot weather caused the corpses in the burial pits to swell and rise from the ground in small hills. This putrefaction began to contaminate the local water. A horrible smell was pervasive and seemed to beckon rats and other scavengers, so the SS filled a pit with wood and set it on fire, but bodies that were already all bones burned badly, even when placed on grills and turned now and then, as you might on a company cookout. Cremations continued to make problems, and scientific studies were undertaken to discover the most efficient methods of getting air to and around mounds of corpses so the fire could breathe. As the Jews, naked, their possessions confiscated for auction in Berlin, were driven to the gas chambers by biting dogs and men with whips and iron bars, their wails of despair and screams from pain were alarming others, so the SS recruited a small orchestra to drown the hubbub by playing local hit tunes.

When, in April of 1943, Himmler ordered the camps closed and their presence erased, the job was almost done, although the task had become more difficult, and on several occasions a few prisoners of war and a passel of Jews had broken out, killing several guards and embarrassing officials. The Germans covered some sites with shrubbery, trees, and flowers, but this concealment remained rudimentary, although even the most inadequate erasures would give comfort later to those who denied the existence and/or operation of the gas chambers. By the summer of 1944 grave robbers had arrived, looking for the gold that might have been missed, only to turn up bones and rotting clothes.

Evans supplies very instructive details of the camps' procedures so that we may measure just how flourishing evil can become when provided with healthy circumstances. The novelty of Auschwitz was the use of a chemical pesticide called Zyklon B, whose most active ingredient was sulfuric acid, and whose lethal fumes were discovered by an accident that asphyxiated a cat. It was used in obedience to the following directions: "The men were herded into the room, the doors were sealed, then powdered Zyklon-B was shaken down through holes in the roof. The warmth generated by the bodies packed into the chamber below quickly turned it into a deadly gas." Those chosen for work detail had a serial number tattooed on their left arm that is now notorious and essential to the cinema.

Some camps were for show, like the back lots of movie studios, and were unable to make direct contributions to the killings, only mislead chosen visitors about them. In a few ghettos (Warsaw is the best-known) there were uprisings as well as scattered signs of individual resistance by the Polish underground; but what slowed the German war on humanity (besides the Soviet army) was simply the size and consequent inefficiency of it. Evans ascribes the principal cause of the monstrous behavior required of its organizers to their "visceral hatred of Jews," but the word *visceral* tends to beg the question. How was anti-Semitism, so patently false in all its ages of activity, able to lodge itself in so many minds and thereafter weaken—no, remove—their moral character? How, in general, do people become slaves of foolish ideologies, support them with treasure, allegiance, and time, and act, at their behest, so vilely, so contrary to their own interest? History is full of absurdities masquerading as absolutes. Like whooping cough, beliefs get to children early, make their symptoms chronic, hold out useless hopes, and offer vain excuses. It is reason's business to disbelieve, but the voices of reason have as much effect here as frogs in a swamp.

This book has many themes which a reader might follow instead of the bloody course I've chosen, such as the struggles for power among the many Nazi administrators when any one of them is trying to obtain status, protect his perks, or strengthen his grip, during both sweet times and sour. Women as a rule did not have such problems. They simply served. Generals, however, were a dime a dozen. Hitler repeatedly replaced one medal bearer with another and blamed them for trying to save their troops when the order was to die. Meantime, in the midst of a war that was not going well, there were other wars that developed a personality of their own the way Verdun did during World War I: such as the siege of Leningrad (". . . the city's inhabitants were starving, eating cats, dogs, rats, and even each other"); the struggle for Stalingrad ("even those who were not hospitalized were sick, starving, frostbitten, and exhausted"); or the Battle of Kursk ("the greatest land battle in history").

Setting cities on fire seemed the favored method of bringing death from the air. Evans's description of the raids and incendiary bombings of Hamburg is especially graphic. Although troops did get dug in, as they had in World War I, panzers brought fluidity to the front line that matched the maneuvers of armadas of planes.

As all the wars that made up the Great War began to go badly, so did the temperament of the German people, and their enthusiasm for it. It could be observed that party members no longer wore their party badges. After the bombing of Hamburg, angry citizens who observed that symbol in the street might tear the insignia from the wearer's coat. A contemporary parallel would be the way the American flag once flew in front of American homes and rode around on American cars until Iraq turned drearily boring, embarrassing, and deadly, whereupon the flag no longer waved o'er the homes of the brave. The Germans could become audibly grouchy if the government cut their ration of bread, but not so much when it killed Jews. By this time in the concluding history of the Third Reich the numbers in the text no longer refer to those of murdered undesirables or captured soldiers but to bushels of imported wheat, the total of factory workers building airplanes, or the limit of calories allowed each citizen; and the narrative, always heavy with statistics, is likely to sink out of the view of the eye.

In the aftermaths of heavy and repeated bombing, dazed German citizens were forced to find places among the ruins of their cities to bury bodies wrapped in paper like parcels, since the cemeteries were full and incineration was not feasible. What could burn, had. The dead were hidden in mass graves amid household furnishings—beds, jars, pots, clothing, carpets, cabinets—strewn about in a tumble of plaster, bricks, and stones. The picture Evans paints contradicts the view, frequently held, that the bombings did not have any noticeable effect on the German people's will to fight. That will was weakening rapidly, as were those of the armed forces, increasingly beset on multiple fronts, misled by Hitler's intransigence, and compelled by the Soviets' superior numbers to retreat. Such cohesiveness as remained depended upon a continuing hatred of Jewry and Soviet Communism, loyalty to their comrades in arms, and a realistic awareness of the consequences of defeat, as well as a fear of their own officers, frantic to maintain discipline, who were fond of courts-martial and the firing squads that shot thirty thousand men as a result of the incredible three million trials ordered for numerous offenses. The Reich also began to lose allies—Bulgaria first, then all of Italy, whose failures Germany was required to punish by corralling 650,000 soldiers for chain gang–style labor (50,000 eventually died in harness), and executing 6,000 others who resisted.

As the German armies fell back they enjoyed the classic revenge of burning any handy hospital, town, field, or manor they encountered, as well as employing some of the lesser forms of vandalism: feasting in occupied homes; stealing bedding, toys, clothes, shoes; and relaxing after their larger exertions by trying on the owners' hats, smashing what would readily smash, and leaving toilets aswim with their stools. Jews were required to ransom themselves with gold. This could occasionally work. Members of the partisan resistance were sometimes shot in conveniently located catacombs, an admirable economy of means. The German troops did not fail to use geography as a weapon, flooding the Pontine Marshes back to pre-Mussolini levels and reintroducing malarial mosquitoes, which produced ninety-eight thousand cases for them in two years, not all deadly, although the Germans took the local quinine with them when they fled. Straight-out germ warfare was unusual for the Nazis, who preferred more indirect methods—to overwork and starve their victims until they fell ill of disease.

Death is the repeated motif of this essay, and necessarily of Evans's masterful book, because death and the threat of death were the principal tools of Nazi rule—the noose, the gas, the gun. For citizens, a list of actions punishable by death might begin with the use of a weapon while committing a crime, hoarding food supplies, damaging military equipment, or making faulty munitions, and end with anything that hindered the war effort, including an injurious comment. Criminals serving a term greater than eight years were too costly to the state to keep swaddled in prison's comforts, and were likely to be packed off "for extermination by labor." Many, due for release before eight years had passed, were retained until they qualified for this extinction. "So many executions were taking place in Germany's state prisons by this time that the Ministry of Justice allowed them at any time of the day instead of, as previously, only at dawn." And the prisons filled and emptied like bowls of peanuts on a bar.

So hospitals, prisons, courts, police, ordinary murderers, labor gangs, suicides, soldiers, Gestapo, the SS, partisans, local militias, enemy fire were all active agents of death, death from all sides the way a billiard caroms: death that fell from the air, death borne by swampy water, death that opened from the earth as if every furrow were a mouth, death by whispered denunciation, death by every means imaginable including highway accidents, common fevers, cancers, strokes, and old age. Yet only one Nazi unit was called the Death's Head, indicating considerable restraint. Of course, there was little need for public boasting about the regime's death-dealing skills. The two Christian institutions (the Lutheran and the Catholic churches) were quite aware of the killing sprees in their countries of residence, but remained mum out of fear of reprisals, either from the regime if the Nazis won or from the Jews if Germany lost. This also may have been the most common attitude among the general population. "From 1943 onwards, they were mentally preparing themselves to deflect this retribution as far as they were able, by denying all knowledge of the genocide once the war was lost."

That the war was lost only increased the feverish pace of the killings, which were now defended as a moral necessity, a task to be completed despite temptations to tenderness, and because the cleansing was almost complete. Himmler's message was: The world may condemn us for carrying out such an unpleasant assignment, but somebody's got to do it. The Jews who remained to be gassed lived mostly in Hungary, whose Admiral Horthy had refused so far Hitler's requests to hand them over. The German army moved in and immediately began carrying out their obligations by transporting 438,000 Jews to Auschwitz before Horthy was able to put a stop to their shipments.

Once a repressive regime begins to stumble, there will be many ready to help with a push, but in Germany every sort of opposition had been so effectively frightened into silence or rubbed out during the time National Socialism reached or solidified its power that even Hitler's most ardent enemies remained compromised, divided, and weak. The Prussian conservatives were often guilty themselves of ordering Jews into camps, or willing, as a postwar gesture, to repeal the legal rules against Jews only because "the very small number of Jewish survivors would no longer constitute a 'danger for the German race.'" For some, discrimination was legit if murder wasn't.

The plots to assassinate Hitler were often ham-handed and always unlucky, but they led to lots of death anyway, as the conspirators were executed or killed themselves—to the sum of five thousand. For those arrested, the firing squad was preferred, and for the suicides the revolver or poison capsule were both more popular than the grenade. For the cinema fans, films were made during which numerous traitors were hanged by a thin rope to slow the strangle, and their pants pulled down for the purpose of postmortem humiliation. Hitler particularly liked these showings. Under the policy of "leave no possible enemy behind," wives, children, cousins, aunts, and uncles of the plotters were sent to Ravensbrück.

V1 and V2 rockets bore the same old bombs, only the method of delivery was new; however, nuclear weapons were unique to life and death equally. The scale of their killing could not yet be clearly imagined, but it was believed to be considerable. It would be the ultimate triumph for a death-mad world and would, again, put the German nation at the wheel. Had Hitler wished to hurry the appropriate research, there still would not have been time or materials enough to complete the project. Hitler did not have any enthusiasm for nuclear physics anyway, because it was an area of study he felt belonged too intimately to the Jews. There was at least one very promising nerve gas, but it was difficult to manufacture without killing many of its makers, and continued to have the same flaws poison gas has always had: it blows where the wind goes. As Albert Speer admitted, they also had drones on the drawing table, jet planes, and heat-seeking missiles, but these advancements would have to wait for the Americans, who would have German expertise to aid them.

Kinds of Killing

In the last days, Germans began killing one another: to settle old scores while pretending the enemy was within. It was nearly as if anyone who looked gloomy should be shot. But they were still killing with dedication if not cleverness and invention. Five hundred and sixty-five inmates of a woman's prison were, in the middle of an icy winter, walked to another jail thirty-six kilometers away. They kept falling over one another until only forty remained. From households there was little to loot, but women were still available for rape. Former dignitaries, foreign and domestic, who hadn't been murdered yet but held hostage instead, were executed forthwith. Those in prison for whatever reason were killed simply because they were handy, just in case, and because the Jews were already dead and someone should be dying. "Sick inmates were shot in their beds. . . ." Advancing armies made the murder industry in the concentration camps a matter of some urgency. Yet evidence of gas chambers, shooting locales, and burial parks had to be removed too, and it was difficult to clean up and kill at the same time. Russian prisoners of war, retreating along with German troops, died of weather, deep snows, and neglect. Killing was now casual wherever you were in the combat zone. Death marches so disorganized they "meandered across the country, even doubling back on themselves" at least emptied a camp by scattering bodies over treks of sometimes 250 miles. Nothing but surrender or the arrival of Allied armies slowed and finally ended this last deadly tantrum.

The Germans had failed to drown women in the Pripet Marshes and had neglected that form of murder almost altogether, but now, as if wishing to fulfill every possibility, regional leader for Hamburg Karl Kaufmann loaded ten thousand leftovers onto three ships tied up in Lübeck. These vessels were by happenstance bombed by British planes, and most of the prisoners, crowded into holds like slaves, drowned when the ships exploded, rolled over, and sank.

When the Red Army reached Auschwitz it found many corpses, but the SS had left seven thousand prisoners in some stage of life, and they had not destroyed every evidence of the camp's activity.

"Russian soldiers painstakingly catalogued 837,000 women's coats and dresses, 44,000 pairs of shoes and 7.7 tons of human hair." Finally, the Germans had acquired enough coats.

The Nazis were down for the count, but the count was only at nine when Allied warplanes kicked dozens of towns nearly out of existence (Dresden, most infamously), and the Red Army arrived to repopulate the ruins by raping the women who remained. They brought with them destruction, pillage, theft, rape, murder, and savage revenge. Death, it seems, was also an Allied deity.

Evans, after his usual sober and responsible account of how the end came for Hitler and Goebbels, writes: "The deaths in the bunker and the burned-out streets were only the crest of a vast wave of suicides without precedent in modern history." This penultimate killing was sometimes done out of an ancestral sense of honor, or from the shame and indignity of a trial that would brand them as criminals, or to avoid the mistreatment of their displayed corpse, or out of despair for Germany and the failure of their enterprises; but not often because they were wrong, not because they were guilty, not because they were moral monsters and could no longer bear the creatures of evil they had become.

Afterward, death would add still more to its roster with trials and hangings. Not just the guilty paid its price. In what was perhaps the final irony, many survivors of the camps would kill themselves because they were alive.

The Biggs Lectures in the Classics

FORM: *EIDOS*

I want to begin by imagining what may be an imaginary world already: the animistic environment of the early Greeks, a world given to us by Henri Frankfort, F. M. Cornford, Bruno Snell, and E. R. Dodds, among others, and one which Gaston Bachelard cited as the first stage in his theory of Western scientific and philosophical development. How many have made the early Greeks say what they wished them to, because what they have said to us is mainly in bits and pieces, in a language we don't know how to pronounce, and in words that refer to a world we have lost, if we ever possessed it, a world we have filled with our own feelings, like those of a childhood we want to think was happy and promising beyond all expectation. Our own awe built those temples and we were the ones who worshiped there. Even when, almost with relief, we decide that the glorious Greeks were really just as mean and murderous as we are; sometimes as stupid as their sheep; still worse, that they watered their wine; our revisions are but patina on the columns of the temples where the great statues stood, where Socrates discovered the immateriality of the soul, and, in the plays, Agamemnon died.

If we think of it now as primitive, and a phase of human growth that's been happily left behind—the childhood of our civilization—it nevertheless served as a bed of extraordinary seeds, for it was in fact a fruitful way of feeling if not thinking about life, one that's been admired and sought and celebrated by poets of every type, tongue, and time. Bachelard himself, at first interested only in the tendency of the scientific spirit to shed previous theories like snakes their out-of-season skins, and to move on to ever more abstract and arcane conceptions ("Nature must be made to go as far as the mind goes," was his famous phrase), later in life saw the importance for the arts in following a contrary path back to instinctive or elementary ways of perceiving, basic forms of feeling, immediate modes of thought, and the methods used by those who have nothing but their thumbs to solve their problems.

Bachelard treated concepts, and the words that represented them, like patients in analysis; that is, they were made of dynamic, interwoven, often antagonistic layers. As an idea struggled through history it bore some of its past along with it, just as enduring institutions do, so that the new was like paint applied over old coats. Moreover, past meanings were constantly reinforcing, interfering, rendering vague or ambiguous, theories that contemporary thinkers sometimes employed in ignorance of their historic complexity. An idea may have grown up to be stoic, studious, and severe, but it has preserved some inward space where the child it once was can still wail, an imp misbehave, and a lazybones lie in a hammock to have a snooze. A concept like *cleave* could even find itself in contradiction to its own beginnings, and etymological paths were often as tangled as twigs.

In that same wonderful work on the nature of science that Bachelard called *The Philosophy of No* (1968), he suggests that for each key scientific term, like *mass*, for instance, an epistemological profile be drawn up which would indicate how much of its current use was really as advanced as the science of its time, and how much of it was still made up of the meanings it had acquired during earlier stages. The first of these periods, the subject of the present inquiry, was that of animism, the richest, most poetic era of all, which Bachelard, in his scientific hurry, passes over as swiftly as a shadow. When I try to clear a tree from the land I am attempting to farm, it will resist me, exert its will, order its roots to grip the earth more firmly, stiffen its bark against my saw, fall, if it must, upon my ox and plow. Here energy and mass are sibling rivals—my energy, its mass; my insistence, its resistance. In phase two—one of realism, though of a naive sort—I shall judge anything to be heavy that makes me work to move it or simply looks big. Mass will be a permanent property of things, while energy will express itself through my sweat, grunts, and curses. In animism, to be brief, things are as heavy as they want to be; in realism, they are as heavy as their color and size suggest (the darker the denser, the bigger the beefier), or as heavy as they are difficult to lift. No one will be surprised if the same stone has more than one weight. If we ask why things have any weight at all, the answer will be the same as Aristotle's concerning gravity: because it's their nature.

In an animistic world there are no integrated selves—the individual has yet to be imagined—and anyone's response to some event will involve a mix of desire, emotion, and thought in a stew that confounds distinctions, because whatever confronts the hunter is an equally unstructured aggregate of powers and properties. Nietzsche called life at this level Dionysian. Like an animal in a herd, one is immersed in an ocean of incident. The herd flees as leaves are blown, in the breath of one alarm. Of course, we do not *know* this; we infer it from what is absent from their recorded vocabulary. Conjecture is the uneven ground we tread.

The third stage, which Bachelard calls positivism, introduces quantitative measures in every case it can. Instruments objectify and standardize what were formerly relative and subjective qualities. It is no longer as cold as the frozen pond, as cold as the woolly caterpillars predicted, or as cold as it feels to the cheek; but it is as cold as the mercury registers. What was heavy to me and light to you, because you were muscled and I was not, is now a phenomenon reduced to units, numbers, and their measurement while they sit on the sensitive tray of the scale. When a well-known philosopher with whom I went to graduate school was asked how his new baby was faring, he replied, holding his hands wide in the way we do for fish, "It is seventeen and one-half inches long." His answer was one of pure positivism, the tongue of quantitative measure, including especially the *it*.

The transition from realism to positivism can be observed in the earliest methods of measurement, when uniformities in the movement of the heavenly bodies were used to understand phases of more disorderly change. One traveled "many moons," or at least movie Indians did. Often, however, more modest regularities were employed. An eighteenth-century missionary reports that in the tribe whose souls he was saving, "They would indicate the size of a herd of horses by stating how much space the horses occupied when standing next to one another." A farmer saw the size of his land in terms of the time needed to plow it; a day's work was his oxen's "yoke"; another unit was made of as much wood as a man could chop before dark. The human body was a veritable bureau of standards: feet divided the stride, horses stood hands high, arms held out wide created a fathom, and when those closed in a hug, what one could hold of cut wheat was a sheaf. The farmer even put his carts, baskets, staffs, and buckets to work within this method of metaphorical measuring. A barrel was called a tun when full of grain, and a tun of land was as much as could be planted with the seed from such a container. Spelled with an o instead of a u "it became a measure of salt, coal, and the cargo capacity of a vessel," all this according to Henri Frankfort in his book *Before Philosophy: The Intellectual Adventure of Ancient Man*.

There were no meter bars in Paris or little weights to place upon the grocer's scale, so a kernel of corn might be chosen to make the comparison (hence *carat*) or the pit of a date. Time was similarly divvied up. Forenoon, in Sanskrit, was *samgava*, "the time when the cows are driven together." In the evening, quitting time for the Greeks was the moment when one unharnessed the oxen. The Russian peasant, always hungry, saw the day as made of stretches of work "between meals," and the Anglo-Saxon *undorn* carries a similar significance. "Let's try to get this done before happy hour," we still say, and "let's have lunch" still designates a time free of work's routines.

The positivist period, sometimes characterized as one of pure empiricism, is paradoxically a time of wariness concerning the senses. By this time philosophers and scientists have become so skeptical about human testimony and the reliability of experience that they begin to replace our fragile faculties with machines, devices that will not be swayed by urges or conniptions, except when the scales are made to lie by cheating merchandisers. Man is no longer the measure when man is measured.

In Bachelard's scheme, when positivism has lost its scientific popularity and become passé, it is supplanted by rationalism, a phase dominated by the figures of Newton and Kant and abetted by the calculus; but the mind is a restless and fickle lover, so this simple rationalism is subsequently replaced by its complex or complete version as shaped by Einstein, only to unseat itself (as these overthrows go) to become discursive rationalism, a development that is dominated by quantum mechanics and all its statistical companions. String theory inhabits the most recent realm, sometimes called surrationalism by people who like puns.

The old ways are never entirely abandoned. We still find measurement and standardization essential to our lives: how can we confidently buy bolts, do our nails, run tabs, gamble, broker, bank? And we are often more emotionally comfortable with a world that's alive even when it happens to be kicking. Animal magnetism is a date drug, good looks are everything, and diamonds are forever. But we need calendars and clocks so all of us will get to work on time and keep the company of men a company. There is around us, as there once were gods, legions of invisibles with rules and regulations that it isn't wise to flout. Seas rise and suns explode; viruses lurk and whales talk. A billion messages trouble the atmosphere and no one reads the urgent ones. Once we were a will within a world of wills; now we are a weed in a wall of indifference.

Rationalism is as suspicious of reason as empiricism is of perception. The empiricist, in front of any evidence, will say, "Let's see that again," and insist on the purity, as well as the repeatability, of laboratory circumstances; while rationalists set limits to reason and establish physical principles, like Galileo's laws of motion, that could never exist in the real world, only in perfect vacuums and unrealizable circumstances that are nevertheless ideal for perpetual-motion machines or squared circles. Instead of letting us puzzle our inadequate heads, the rationalist devises a calculator, and dreams, as Leibniz did, of a perfectly logical language whose grammar would forbid error. Despite their vigilance, rationalists allowed a lot of animism and other such stuff to slip forward unobserved. Ontogeny does recapitulate phylogeny, as Ernst Haeckel famously said. The idea of inertia, for instance, scarcely inert itself, would pop up again in Spinoza and Hobbes as the law of self-preservation (all things act to preserve the state in which they find themselves, Spinoza said), and even reappear in Freud, who insisted that the human body always acted to reduce its stimulation to a minimum, either by fleeing it or feeding it, whatever worked. What it really wanted was to remain inert. Romanticists called this "the return to the womb," or "the death wish," and shivered. At that time it was believed that the womb put a perfect pocket of silence about its infant. No one realized then that Mozart's music had been issued a pass. Nor did it forbid the cultural calamities of boxed wine or secondhand smoke.

Laws and principles are sometimes developed simply to save hypotheses from further embarrassment, and these are usually furnished with mysterious ideas like ether, wavicles, or phlogiston; others simply do not advance at the same rate as their fellow notions and become, in Bachelard's terms, "obstacle concepts." Not all ideas are meant to help the mind; some are there to hinder it. Nor are all ancient beliefs false. That man is a part of nature appears to be more valid a vagueness today than the view that human beings are special and apart, a belief that functions only as a dismal and desperate blockage of our mental arteries.

Although science may use *cause*, philosophy *substance*, or theology *soul* in a distinctive way, individuals living and thinking and coping on a day-to-day basis may actually have a profile that reflects their own particular personality and intellectual character. Some of us will feel persecuted by a lengthy red light; others will clock it and prepare to mail a complaint; a few of us may even admire the wisdom of such a simple system of permission and restraint. In any case, there will be concepts (or more vaguely, words) which will have special significance for each of us, terms that will usually provoke an obstinate opposition, a boil of ire, or a benevolent feeling of approval whenever they appear—totemic words, talismanic or irritating. In my case, this is certainly true. I have taken the opportunity these lectures perhaps did not intend, to investigate the backgrounds of three of my "hot Homeric buttons," proceeding as if they had been appointed to the cabinet or nominated for the court: a favorite, *form*—an enemy, *mimesis* or *imitation*—and an old drinking buddy, *metaphor.*

Suppose Homer's shepherd has nodded off while tending his flock, and the arm on which he has cradled his head has also fallen asleep. He wakes to find it unaccountably numb and unresponsive. It prickles as it rouses itself. Or he missteps while climbing about on the rocks, and puts his foot where he did not wish it to go, or he sneezes repeatedly, perhaps hiccups, suffers cramps and spasms, grows weary without reason, and, most particularly, dreams. These are just a few occasions in which his body may not seem to be his, but apparently has ideas of its own—is, in fact, its own boss. When Rainer Maria Rilke saw a man afflicted with Saint Vitus' Dance jerking spasmodically on a Paris street, he wrote of it as if it were a case of limbs in revolt, a loss of the body's essential commonwealth. The independence of the penis is notorious.

Homer's shepherd would have less sense of revolt than this, since he would have no central self, no conception of a unified body, because it was "comprehended, not as a unit but as an aggregate," as Bruno Snell suggests in *The Discovery of the Mind* (1984). His limbs would be his as his goats were his, often off on their own; it would be his own legs that walked like Rodin's *Walking Man,* all stride; and it would be two accommodating cheeks that blew into his pennywhistle air from lungs that wanted music. In this world, you know who you are because of the way you are greeted; it is the eyes of others, as they see you, that you see. Again, as Snell argues: "there was no one verb to refer to the function of sight as such, but . . . there were several verbs each designating a specific type of vision." And these were defined in terms of facial attitudes—staring, gaping, peering, gawking, squinting—each representing how one looked when one looked.

Although whatever elements of nature the shepherd encountered would be aggregations much as himself, he was not personifying his world or peopling it with creatures—filling an otherwise empty cupboard—because, as Henri Frankfort insists in *Before Philosophy* (1949), "primitive man simply does not know an inanimate world . . ." His world is given to him already "redundant with life, and life has individuality, in man and beast and plant, and in every phenomenon which confronts man—the thunderclap, the sudden shadow, the eerie and unknown clearing in the wood, the stone which suddenly hurts him when he stumbles while on a hunting trip."

Language was relatively holophrastic, and with different words for different unanalyzed activities, it offered no clue to the parts or interrelations of what was named, as if *gallop, canter,* or *trot* bore no more resemblance to one another than knitting, swimming, or a headache. Some aspects of reality were more torpid than others, but even a rock could be roused, and would resist when struck or moved. In Greece, particularly, dry riverbeds might leap to torrential life overnight, springs gush forth from stone, trees speak, animals plan, the heavenly bodies coast across the sky like ships bearing gods. Actually, they *were* ships bearing gods.

We are still inclined to kick the coffee table that has barked our shin, or think ourselves persecuted by a run of bad cards, or blame black cats for Halloween's rain. We may observe that "spring is late this year," or believe that good weather is paid for by bad. We tactfully don't blame God for sending a great wind to destroy our trailer; instead we thank Him for letting us escape with our lives, even though we are likely to feel "under a cloud," cursed, and pursued by the Furies. Families, like the Kennedys, have fates—and to have a fate is never a good thing. Causes that I am used to will feel natural, and the appearance of their effects will be expected, as Hume has explained, purely out of habit—birds flock at evening because they always do—it is when they act otherwise that I take particular notice and perceive their behavior as an omen, because it is the untoward that signals the presence of the gods.

With only sun, moon, and stars to measure with, my sense of space and time is likely to be elastic, determined by expectation and awareness. The distance to Grandmother's house, as we sleigh ride over the river and through the trees toward it, is so much longer than the route and runners we slide home on; the time it takes for this lecture to pass may seem painfully extended, but once it is over, and its audience is asking itself with puzzlement what was said, there will be so little to remember, it shall seem to have lasted no moments at all. The paradoxes of subjective time have been often remarked. Space has the same elasticity. Around us there is always an area that remains ours and must not be invaded. We shrink it for travel on the subway train, and expand it sometimes on an empty avenue so that someone's stare, though it comes from across the street, feels intrusive. Whatever feels secure, welcoming, familiar, is home. So our one home may have many realizations. That Goldilocks has been there in our absence, though nothing is damaged or missing, is still felt as a violation. While there is but one origin of life, one paradise, one Armageddon, Day of Doom and Judgment, there are many couplings, gardens, battlefields, or pits of hell that fit the bill. In short, the same place can be in many places at once like a Holiday Inn, and occur in more than one time too, as New Year's Eve does, if the ritual is right, the occasion propitious, and the time zone different.

Skills, traits, habits are properties that belong to people like hats, so that a man can misplace his courage ("lose heart," as we still say), or find that, during the night, his eloquence has been stolen from him as Ulysses' was, or that he can't hit the curveball anymore. What to us might be as purely phenomenal as shade or a river's reflection, or utterly relational, such as the placement of a knife by a plate or a cup in its saucer, or as abstract as the Pythagorean theorem to the pre-Classical Greek, is as much a material thing as a shield or a bowl of soup. It is extremely difficult for us to envision it now, but the problem that presents itself to Socrates in the *Phaedo,* as he begins to examine those comforting arguments for the survival of the soul, is made more difficult by being the reasoning of a realist that has been contaminated by animistic dispositions, and still further confused by rationalist assumptions that are as daring as they are mistaken. A brief look at the passage might pay dividends, provided the market stays bullish.

We might be able to maintain that life continues even when death threatens it, if we can insist that living and dying are activities that form a single continuum—the living of one thing is the dying of another. This strategy is one of the first Socrates suggests as a remedy in the face of his own demise. The rationalist that is stirring within him recognizes that terms which act as significant contraries, such as *short/tall* and *hot/cold* or *living/dying*—their meanings being mutually dependent on each other—must be defined together. Now we call them co-relative terms. In addition, he assumes—what rationalists suppose with characterizing regularity—that linguistic connections mirror natural, non-linguistic ones, so that not just the knowledge of *good* and *evil* (to cite a notorious instance) are necessary to each other, but that good and evil themselves are Siamese twins. As an animist, Socrates proposes that these correlatives are causes of one another: only the living may die and those who die do so while alive, and do so only having brought about more life— "opposites come to be only from their opposites" is the preferred phrase. Being dead, in short, is a steady and active business. Similarly, the small comes from the large, the cold from the hot, and vice versa, because without *up* where would *down* be? (An aside: for such things the positivist needs only his scales. It is either ten or twenty centigrade, and there is no value in using vague words like *hot* or *cold* when the precise and objective are at hand; so if the baby is eight and a half pounds, well within healthy limits, terms like *large* and *small* lose employment. Meanwhile, the rationalist replaces both felt warmth and measured temperature with the improved or impeded movement of molecules.)

Not only does Plato confuse things of no degree—like life and death—with things that have more degrees than a commencement—such as hot and cold, better and worse, living and dying—but he cannot, in the moment he has Socrates making the argument, understand how, by adding a small amount to another, you can make it larger, for the small should make something smaller as a bit of salt makes it saltier; nor does he grasp how a number like four can be larger than three yet smaller than five at the same time. If I put one bagel in my sack alongside another bagel, I have not made two bagels, for two cannot be made; these bagels were two all along, as if they were brother and sister, one formerly in Paris, the other in Peoria, now united in Toledo. This confusion will not last. Plato will get it right eventually, but his difficulties indicate how novel the notion of relation was, how tenuous the hold even the master's mind had on abstract ideas.

The outstanding example of the materiality of thought among early Greeks is their treatment of numbers. They often counted by using pebbles (since bottle caps weren't available) and formed them into geometrical patterns by placing them at the intersections of imaginary lines the way they are still displayed on the face of dice or on dominos. (Braille, I believe, is also animistic in just this way.) In such a scheme, two becomes an oblong, three a triangular number, four a square, five pyramidal (the first three-dimensional number), eight the cube, and ten (the sum of one, two, three, and four, and stacked in rows in just that way) turns out to be the sacred Pythagorean equilateral triangle, called the Tetractys of the Decad, by which the cult swore its most binding oath: "By him that gave to our generation the tetractys, which contains the fount and root of eternal nature," as G. S. Kirk and J. E. Raven report in their book, *The Presocratic Philosophers*. These pebble patterns were not mere representations. They were the numbers themselves, and numbers were physical properties of things like roundness might be of pie. Aristotle observed that "the Pythagoreans, because they saw many attributes of numbers belonging to sensible bodies, supposed real things to be numbers—not separable numbers, however, but numbers of which real things consist." They could be cut apart or divided, added to or subtracted, and so on. Temple columns stood in pebbled rows and spoke their patterns to the sky. Because they were things, numbers could be squared or cubed, and their roots similarly found at the feet of their forms. Other maneuvers time has forgotten. If you squared two by adding two pebbles, you could triangle two by adding one, or hang another in the space above four to make the pyramid called five. The triangle of three was six, and that of four the holy number ten. At parties you can astonish your guests by pyramiding the champagne flutes or doing triangular roots.

Numbers were also something new because, as Euclid wrote, "a number is an aggregate composed of units." Each one of these units was named *one*. These ones were not aggregates, but indivisible as the soul is alleged to be in the *Phaedo* or atoms are for Democritus. The Greeks hated fractions with the passion of a schoolboy: one-sixteenth, for instance, would be understood as one among sixteen, like candies on a plate, and not, as a shaving from a stick or a chip from a block, a piece of a larger unit. To be one of sixteen instead of one-sixteenth is a redescription that would make any modern spin doctor proud.

Calculations were not initially inhibited by the materiality of this mathematics. Rather, proofs were concretely visible—demonstrable in a literal way. To square a number you pebbled it as a square—sixteen made a splendid formation—and you could see at a glance that four was its root or base. You could cube a number in the same way. You just needed a lot more stones and some sticks to support them in an extra dimension. If you created a right triangle that had a horizontal base of three and a vertical of four, you might then form squares against each side—sixteen high and nine at bottom. The square that you would have to erect on the hypotenuse would always be the sum of the squares of the other two sides. See it. Believe it. Counting of this kind could conclude any argument.

Moreover, discoveries about numbers came easily and in droves. Since, as Kirk and Raven remark, "Greek thinkers were very slow to apprehend that anything could exist without spatial extension," most of their advances had a strong geometrical component. Triangular numbers, it would turn out, were the sum of successive numbers, while square numbers were the sum of successive odds, and oblong numbers the sum of successive evens. Six was discovered to be the first "perfect"—that is, a number whose factors added up to its own height (1 + 2 + 3). Distant observers such as ourselves are able to see the intrusion of animistic impulses at every level of these mathematical investigations. The word *perfect* is already a clue. Numbers whose factors added up to the same number (such as two, three, and five, whose factor was one) were called *amicable,* while those whose factors amounted to more than themselves (twelve, for instance, 1 + 2 + 3 + 4 + 6) were *excessive,* and those that fell short (like nine, that possessed only one and three) were deemed *deficient.* Numerology was getting a foothold. Justice would be described as square and therefore equal to four.

Aristotle, whose remarks on the Pythagoreans are the basis of most of what we know about them, was aware that the number three had a beginning, a middle, and an end. But it can be seen so only if its triangularity is admitted. Three is the model for the first great aesthetic form as well: home, departure, return, or that of the sonata, or the rhyme scheme a-b-a, and that dialectic in which the fixing of an identity—hi!—is followed by the finding of difference— uh-oh!—before the discovery of similarity or resemblance—aha!—is reassuringly made. Of resemblance, more ahas later.

Gradually, the idea that everything was alive became modified, and life withdrawn from some things like savings from a bank; but as the withdrawal occurred, the questions of just what the elixir was, and where the difference between the living and the lifeless lay, went unanswered. When the élan vital was universal it scarcely needed to be explained—everything lived, and lived in its own way—but the bodies that littered the battlefield, unlike the same ones that had, shouting, swung a vigorous sword before, had ceased breathing (was that it?), were motionless and soon stiff, became pale and cold (did life dwell in the heart like a hearth with its heat?); and blood in drying puddles could be regularly found near the wounds the fallen warriors had sustained (surely that was it); because life was clearly something that came and went, danced away, maybe, like motes in the air do (so some maintained); it was as physical as a muscle and might live in one place rather than another, or perhaps had parts, for flowers were alive as well as bees, as well as the women who valued both blooms and honey (perhaps reason resided in the head, the passionate part had a room in the heart, while desire—all our vegetable loves—had to make do with the gut); yet was it not soon a rule that whatever died did so because it came apart? So if the soul (as life stuff got called) were to be indestructible it would have to be indivisible; however, blood (a likely candidate for what it was) infused each so called part with its warmth, and went out of lifeless limbs like a light.

Within this swirl of issues, and the first movement toward some system of classification, the notion of form began to acquire meaning. Its development depended upon other ideas, of course, which were equally inchoate. How was one to understand where a living thing's living began, and where its edges ended? Two kinds of definition emerged. One was dynamic and understood form to refer to territorial rights, like those demanded by birds or hunting animals (it has been said that wolves marked these limits by peeing on rocks and trees), or by tribes that posted warning signs, including the skulls of enemies, on the borders of their lands. The form of a thing was that area whose touch or intrusion drew a response. The other definition was static and seemed to have been based on the silhouette; hence the importance of the shadow something cast, and the visual outline of an entity—in short, its shape, for the origin of *eidos* (that which is seen) lies in *idein* (to see). The early draftsmen's renderings of men and animals were probably outlines of life, while, for the dynamic definition of the term, the drawings they did were like maps. The suggestion of the dynamic was that the life force moved around and the pattern of its movements—its responses and its sallies—were its form. The experiences men had of instantaneous travel while drunk, in dreams or hallucinations, when mad or merely vividly imagining, were convincing. Meanwhile, the static sense of form said, in effect, that what had been an aggregate of elements—arms, elbows, eyelids, hair, and ears—*soma*—was now understood to belong to a single purposive whole.

Change, then—these inexplicable alterations of habit and routine—could be understood in terms of a change of form or shape or even residence: a *meta morphosis.*

When the Greeks began to study change (which was almost right away), their model was metamorphosis, or change of form, but what was form or shape? Something so rigid it didn't change, or something so malleable it was a part of the problem? Some of the pre-Socratic philosophers had differed over which of the famous four elements was the one real substance of which all things were made—fire, water, or air (slighting earth somewhat, although, especially for them, *matter* was the right choice); but it was Parmenides who provided the first rationalist argument, since Thales had offered only the realist's commonsense observation that water frozen became a solid, and when heated turned to air.

The argument is classic. One has to admire it. When anything changes, there has to be some part of the changing thing that does not change; otherwise we would not recognize it as having altered, but, at best, as having been replaced. In sentences like, "Wow, Achilles, how you've grown, once so small and now so tall," the subject remains as steady as nouns in that position always do, only the predicate *small* has shifted its spelling slightly so that Achilles can don the toga of a stripling. Even when the gas station on the corner is demolished and its buried tanks dug up, the lot stays put. Otherwise we should not know that anything had happened to it. We do not say, "Why, Fred, you're Ned now, what a change!" unless Fred has married his boyfriend and taken his name. Not only is there something unchanging in change *it*self, *it* underlies *it,* and even makes *it* possible, whatever *it* is. These days (from Aristotle on) we might say that form was the unchanging substance—the skeleton, the DNA, the fingerprint, the eyeshade; and indeed one's identity— for others—may rest just there; however, for Parmenides the visible provided only adjectives and adverbs, borne to their nouns by verbs like Trojans proffering their dubious gifts. As Frankfort puts it concerning Egypt, "only the changeless is truly significant." For Parmenides multiplicity was equally suspect. And his attitude prepared Plato also to deny ultimate reality to it. Many sheep are grazing on the hillside. But each is a sheep, and the class of sheep is one class, though its members may be a multitude. The class, moreover, is without flesh, bone, or blood, and therefore cannot decay, did not come to be, and cannot pass away. Sheep and goats belong to two different groups, but both are included in *animal,* which is one and pure and perfect. *Und so weiter.* Till we reach the form of the good, or Hegel's absolute—whichever comes first.

Why is the class so separate from its members? Because the members vary indefinitely and inexplicably (there are black sheep and skinny sheep, dumb sheep and dumber sheep), while the definition that determines which ones shall be called *sheep* defines only the nature of the class. As far as their species is concerned all members are identical. Sheep are sheep the way business is business. And if all the sheep in the world were eaten, the class would still be as real and thinkable as ever because an idea has a quite different ontology. To reach such refinements of objectivity and abstraction—to see the Form Forest rather than a forest, the Form Tree not a tree—

Parmenides, Plato, and Aristotle had to take steps no other culture to that time had taken. And if Socrates and Plato did not discover the human mind, as Bruno Snell maintains, they invented it. The psyche, as they conceived it, may have never existed—certainly the soul was given little chance of being a reasonable conjecture after it left Aristotle's hands for those of the Romans and the Christians—but it was the first abstract idea, which is like the invention for the mind of the wheel.

If it was Socrates who first began to sense that the soul was everywhere structurally the same and strangely immaterial, it was Plato who transformed our understanding of language and meaning, because he began to see words as altogether abstract, and as designating universals. A possible exception to this might be proper nouns like *Achilles* or *Socrates, Fido* or *Bill's book,* each of which refers to a specific empirical thing. Slowly, one of philosophy's most distinguished arguments fell into place: the argument for the Forms, an argument I should like to perform for you now, not as it was born, through piecemeal appearances in the *Dialogues,* but as it can be recovered, like a pot, from its shards. Aristotle refers to five arguments for the existence of the Forms, but his references to them are so brief and almost by-the-way that many commentators are inclined to think the Forms had to be entities with which his audience could be assumed to be familiar. Plato does not develop a technical philosophical terminology like Aristotle. He had to cope with the wayward language of daily life, and in that sphere *eidos* most usually meant the outline of something "sensible" or "visible," so by students of Pythagoras it could confidently designate the shape of numbers. The shapes of the numbers were geometrical figures. At that moment the move toward abstraction was on its way. And the building of the proof began.

STAGE ONE

One: the premise.

We do have knowledge of some things, most reliably of geometrical figures, expressed as definitions of circles, squares, triangles, and the like.

Plato assumes that knowledge is a matter of definition—What is X? What is Y?—and maintains that we know everything in the same way—knowing Greek and knowing Homer, knowing what and knowing why—and that there is one and only one definition that legitimately belongs to each term. This is a common rationalist desire, but no language will satisfy it, because words have always been as slippery as the convictions of a politician, and their ambiguities convenient for human exchange.

Moreover, to anticipate a principal objection to the proof, an animistic thinglike character is still a part of Plato's conception of the Forms, as is a standard of "perfection" which tends to conflate immateriality with superiority.

Two: the choice of example.

The definition of *triangle* (to pick a handy figure) includes the fact that it must have three enclosing sides which are straight lines meeting at three points, with the sum of the interior angles equal to 180 degrees.

In the *Phaedo,* Plato uses the example of two sticks and wonders whether they are of equal length. The issue is not the sticks, of course, but the idea of equality and its representation.

Three: the first fallout.

The argument asks us to draw a triangle (on a blackboard if in a modern classroom; on a piece of paper, since you may try this at home; or in your mind's eye). The argument then asks whether you really believe that you can make a triangle that truly fits the definition, because no triangle you might try to construct will have perfectly straight lines, actually meet at points, or have angles equaling 180 degrees. Even with the best instruments you would fail, if only by a molecule.

The second fallout.

Nor could we find a triangle in nature anywhere, because nothing we should find could possibly conform to the definition. And if there were one that we'd found or somehow made, we wouldn't recognize it, because our instruments could not measure the properties it would be required to have.

Our problem is that we started out designating points with pebbles. Greeks assumed that points had dimensions and that a straight line took the shortest route between two of them. This materialism seemed far more sensible than supposing points had no dimensions and that a straight line (one dimension) went from nowhere A to nowhere B without the wherewithal to do it. Or was a compacted row of no-dimensional spots. Or was the path of a point like the trail of a plane. Without dimensions you simply cannot be: you cannot be located; you cannot line up for inspection; you cannot travel from Nowhere to Noplace.

Zeno's paradoxes make a fundamental contribution to the argument. Zeno points out that between any two points A and B, a line can be imagined that is capable of being divided in half (at C), and that segment (AC) further divided in half (at D), while that part (AD) also can be cut in two (at E). This can go on longer than anyone has the energy for it. Yet if points have dimensions, and any line is divisible into countless numbers of them, every line is—we hate to say the word—infinitely long. Moving from A to B would be equivalent to picking up an infinite number of points and putting them, like pebbles, into a sack—namely as impossible as undesirable. If, however, points are without dimensions (heretofore unimaginable), picking them up will be only a figurative exercise that will get you nowhere. To pass through an infinite number of points in a finite time is as impossible as doing so in an infinite time, for one amount cannot be picked and the other cannot be passed.

One of the outcomes of this famous, and justly admired, argument is that geometrical figures cannot be figures found in our space, a consequence of which Zeno does not appear to have been aware. But Plato is. Space with its extentions—those fundamental properties of early Greek materialism, and every materialism since—is not geometry's subject. A mathematical defense of this would have to wait for Descartes, who was able to transform geometry into algebra.

The third fallout.

Our knowledge of *triangle* (which we admitted we had at the opening of this proof) did not emerge from an observation of triangles, either found or formed. The definition is neither empirically derived nor empirically verified; nor does it have as its subject anything empirical.

Corollary to the third fallout.

The things we call triangles, since they are not triangles, but nevertheless are recognized as "triangles" in contrast, say, to "circles," must be copies of triangles, or imitations of triangles, or representations of triangles, rather than mere words for triangles, inasmuch as words do not mimic, in any sense, their referents.

Indeed, the same may be said of Galileo's renowned principles of motion. None of these laws are empirical either, and the Leaning Tower of Pisa trick was just that—to fool the eye into believing something only the mind knew was true; for, of course, in nature bodies always fall at different rates, and nothing in motion will ever move at a uniform speed for very long. Galileo, as Galileo avers, was an ardent Platonist.

Form: Eidos

Meeting the first objections.

Maybe we could derive our idea of *triangle* from observations of them by simply choosing one, either found or constructed, to serve as the standard (as some imagine the meter bar in Paris does). When we do that we always cheat, because we begin with our knowledge of *triangle* intact; we are only pretending to be ignorant. Suppose we tried to define *hiccobite*. We probably would have no idea how to collect our candidates, though the shrewder among us might begin by canvassing bars. Moreover, in order that any one thing serve as a standard, either the whole of that thing serves (down to the zerkin they commonly wore) or, if a zerkin is chosen to provide the norm, the same thing can be said of it, as was said of the hiccobites—who, for all we know, although members of a joyous monastic order, are almost perfectly peevish when questioned.

All right, then say hello to the possibility that we could induce the idea of a perfect triangle from our perceptions of innumerable imperfect copies. Alas, that is exactly what has happened, leading us to believe these material things are triangles in the first place. The recognition that X is an imperfect triangle requires prior knowledge of perfect ones, including all their perfect parts (straight lines, intersections at those mythological points, exacting angles), just as the judgment that the two sticks are unequal requires a previous grasp of the idea of equal length itself.

Plato will give the previous objection this much: if our minds have the knowledge of *triangle* in them before our eyes have ever encountered any imitations, seeing these copies may lead us to recall their more perfect counterpoints. This is the first appearance of the Doctrine of Recollection, which will undergo its own metamorphosis, emerging as a belief in innate ideas. Its most recent manifestation can be found in the work of Noam Chomsky. Since, in order to recollect our knowledge of oblongs, squares, and triangles, we have to have first forgotten them (else we could do Euclid in our cradle), the doctrine requires the initial appearance of the concept of repression, too, later put to profitable use by Freud and on many a patients' bill.

We have now completed stage one.

STAGE TWO

This knowledge of *triangle* which I have is not something personal and subjective because, first, the same definition is arrived at separately by different persons at different times; and secondly I don't think we would want to admit that if I stopped thinking of *triangle,* or if I myself ceased to exist, that the idea of *triangle* would disappear or die with me. And if we all went the way of the hula hoop, the ideal circumference of its vanished hip swaying would still be πr^2.

So this knowledge is entirely independent of all men's minds, as all truths are. That is: there is the Idea or the Form Triangle; there is also the general conception that geometers have of *triangle* at any particular time, which may be equivalent to the Form Triangle, depending upon the state of their knowledge; and there is my notion of what a triangle is (my understanding of it), and finally there is the idea which I am presently examining in my consciousness, and this may include only part of what I know. In short: $E = MC^2$ was true before men existed at all; nor did it come to be the moment Einstein thought it or wrote his paper; nor did it wait to exist until its truth was admitted and its proposal gained currency.

This plane triangle, then, of which I have a degree of knowledge, is an objective, independent, nonmental, and universal Form. We may discover it, explore it, and understand it, just the way we discovered, explored, and now understand Iceland.

STAGE THREE

The generalization principle.

We can take any noun, so long as it is not a proper name, and sing the same song about it. No man, however many weights he lifts, can exemplify manhood completely. No woman, even as armless as the

Form: Eidos

Venus de Milo or, like Helen, worth a war, can embody beauty utterly, and if we think of Form in the radical new Platonic way, and not as the sculptor, in terms of visual shape, the distance between what we would now call the connotation of a noun (its definition and accumulated meanings) and its denotation (things like ties, socks, soap, and even courage, justice, and love) grows wider than oceans, rather as wide as are different modes of Being.

These Forms are still too much like things, despite Plato's realization (after some hesitations and confusion) that the Form for disreputable stuff and surly deeds (feces, for instance, or wickedness) does not have the property that it denotes, because the knowledge of evil is a good thing; knowledge of anything, the nature of mud, the kinds of cloud, types of thieves, is good. The Idea Long does not have to be long, or that of Triangle triangular. But the Idea of the Good is good nevertheless, Beauty beautiful, and the Goluptious, I suppose, goluptious.

We have seen the idea of Form travel from its territorial sense—a tribal boundary—to the narrower notion of a physical edge; it then became further reduced to an outline, like a silhouette or sketch. Plato transforms it by giving the concept a new ontology, removing most of its material characteristics, and treating it the way we tend to treat a universal. As rationalists, we shall henceforth understand that we have true knowledge to the degree we can express it mathematically, and see the world through the grammar or the structure of its modes of representation. Rational discourse will be more in touch with reality than the world is, for the world of Becoming, as Plato puts it so memorably in the *Timeaus,* is the qualitative expression of quantitative law. Through all these alterations, the idea of form remains central to the determination of the identity of things, whether it is the tribe, the kind, or the slowly evolving sense of self. With Aristotle, as we shall see, form is returned to objects first as structure, then as function; the world is not merely an imitation, but is a thing made real by its own essential nature. For both philosophers, it is a work of art.

MIMESIS

If Greek theater had deep religious implications, as some think, and often functioned as a ritual would, then the actor on the stage, his features obscured by a mask and robe, might be thought to be a mouthpiece for the gods. If the play were significant enough, the words powerful and rich and wise, a moment could occur in his impersonation during which the divine spirit entered him; the soul of the actor who, a moment before, had been reciting the playwright's words might, so to speak, stand aside, and his speech take on an imprimatur its actual author could not lay claim to—their metamorphosis would be obvious to every ear—for (in a switch no different from Zeus's frequent changes of form to further an amorous prank or political ploy) these words would be severed from their source of utterance in the actor and from the hand of their author as well; they would participate in the divine; while the audience heard the speech of nature as they had in former times, when leaves whispered and torrents roared and the world, more than words, was alive.

Nothing has changed. When the text sings, the reader listens, and soon her soul sings too; she reenacts thought and passion's passage, adopts Chaucer's, Shakespeare's, Milton's tone; her head echoes with sounds no longer made by Henry James, who is but a portly poor old bachelor, after all, and she is not the she of household worry either, or lawyer at her legal tomes, but these words are the words of Sophocles, then, of Oedipus just now blind, and the world is the world it once was when the world was alive.

Like most words, *mimesis* is a nest of meanings. Shadings fly from it like fledgling birds: imitation, representation, replication, impersonation, or portrayal do for Plato; nowadays we could add copy, counterfeit, dupe. Grammatically different forms of what is called "the mimesis group" designate the action of mimicry—or the actor, mime, or mockingbird that performs the tune—while others aim at either the subject of imitation or its result, or sometimes indicate the arena of representation itself: the agora, law courts, or the stage. Mimesis calls the theater home, some say; it is derived from the dance; it belongs to mockery and mime, not always silent, and is often concerned with events and situations in daily life; no, it is the creation of effigies—statues, scarecrows, voodoo dolls—it is the means by which we call upon the gods. But did these meanings of mimesis really compete, or is the competition to be found in the disputatious pages of contemporary scholars, who prefer one meaning (theirs) over others, much as if, in a mulligan stew, one conferred honor and dominance to six pearl onions?

For Plato and Aristotle, I think, the word is still a wardrobe, but it is stashed backstage, where the masks are kept and the chorus instructed. The actor becomes his role, we sometimes say; but what does the role become? I remember that Shakespeare says very little about Hamlet's weight, nor does he give Iago thin lips and an evil nose, as Dickens would be sure to. How can I impersonate a creature whose visible form is unknown? Merely claim to be he or she? Zeus dons and doffs bodies the way we do clothes. Clouds are camels one minute, streaming hair the next. Some things, like Proteus, have no fixed form, so I could claim I was, while in my workaday togs, one of the sea's moods. In many paintings Jesus is as blond and blue eyed as a Nazi.

If Socrates has a snub nose and thyroid eyes, his portrait should have the same painted nose put in the same painted place, and the same swollen eyes painted as protruding—paint for point and point for paint over the whole head. But what good is a likeness *when it is the reality of the thing that should be captured*—should be, yet can't be—not in another medium. Once, when the world was young and still alive as liquor, the soul itself might slide from fern or face into the leaves that covered Eve and Adam, or love pass from the lover's adoration into the heart of the adored. But now, when the gods are called upon to come from their own play into ours, how could the transfer be effected?

A god enters, but speaks Sophocles anyway, having, as some say, no mind of his own. In the theater it is only the words that can achieve the change. The music, the moving limbs, the spectacle, from painted drop to gaudy robe and dancing lads, add their emphasis, their rhythm, their emotion to the speech, but what, when Apollo approaches . . . what will . . . what will the god say? And the gods will have the character the poets give them; the gods will wear whatever raiment can be sewn; the gods will do as they are told. . . . But a person whom the audience knows well, such as Socrates in Aristophanes' satires, will have to have at least the demeanor Athenians are used to. Certainly this is true of Plato's own challenge to the dramatists. *The Dialogues* are nothing less than the theater of reason where Plato's Socrates plays the role of the real one. There is an irony in this that has not gone unnoticed . . . by Gunter Gebauer and Christoph Wulf, for instance, who write: "There is an element of contradiction in the fact that Plato criticizes art as mimesis in principle but at the same time works mimetically in producing dialogues in which artistic elements are present."

In the early dialogues, Plato may be considered to be presenting Socrates to us in his full historical reality, in which case the philosopher's mimetic skills are governed by historical concerns; whereas, in dialogues of the so-called middle period, Plato's interests are more and more "artistic" and "fictional." But I suspect that Socrates' great speech that concludes the *Apology* is about as faithfully mimetic as Pericles' Funeral Oration in the imaginative reenactment of Thucydides. Nevertheless, Pericles must sound Periclean, and speak as the occasion demanded, just as Socrates must press his case for suicide in the *Crito* because so many are alive who know he did so.

But if the features of the person to be represented have to be created, the chances are they will replicate the characteristics chosen by the first imitator who undertook the task and did Buddha fat and Hamlet thin, Desdemona blond because Othello's black, Jesus fair with a light beard and wavy hair, handsome as heaven—as if he'd been there; because the audience has attended these plays too, and knows what Apollo came arrayed in apart from light, and what suited the Furies and Clytemnestra's moods. Although each author interprets the myths in his own way, what Electra says has to be in harmony with what Electra was in her last show, her previously recounted story, her rap sheet. Otherwise she'll not be she, and fool nobody. The operatic custom that permits a fat Carmen to shake the flats when she dances her fandango will not travel any better than the local wine. The success you might have in making yourself similar to somebody else will depend upon the ignorance of the audience you intend to fool, and the success, in creating a tradition, of any previous proponents of your scam. Plato knows there are no gods, that the gods are merely Hesiod's manner of speaking. How much of Homer did he honor as the truth, or were the poets liars in every rhyme and line?

I bring this unpleasantness up because it may help us to understand the relation appearance has to reality. If reality remains unknown, then Punch is Punch and Judy, Judy, both as real as the husbands and wives in Devon or Westphalia they might have been used to represent, or as present in the world as the warring forces of good and evil. Furthermore, bowing before a curtain of ignorance, any appearance may choose its cause and claim it. I can be said to resemble my uncle Fred only by those who know both of us. If no one knows, no one can gainsay it. If no one knows, no one will care.

Plato became convinced that Parmenides was too quick to dismiss this world of incessant change, too eager to move on (itself an act of deception) from its illusions to the eternal unshakable plenum that Being really was. These fleeting appearances had to be saved, yet they could be accounted for only if they were explained; and they could be explained perfectly provided this world were indeed a play, much as Shakespeare and others would describe it. It could be saved if the mime it made were as successful as the speeches of Aeschylus and Sophocles, and the world were understood to participate in the Forms through its acts of so eloquently copying them, reality descending to touch our lives like the gods once inhabited the speech of Prometheus, perhaps, or Athena as she made her vows.

And doesn't Plato say in the *Laws,* when the playwrights clamor to be allowed to ply their trade in his second-best state, that

> we also [Plato's imperial *I*] according to our ability are tragic poets, and our tragedy is the best and noblest; for our whole state is an imitation of the best and noblest life, which we affirm to be indeed the very truth of tragedy. You are poets and we are poets, both makers of the same strains, rivals and antagonists in the noblest of dramas, which true law can alone perfect, as our hope is. Do not then suppose that we shall all in a moment allow you to erect your stage in the agora, or introduce the fair voices of your actors, speaking above our own, and permit you to harangue our women and children, and the common people, about our institutions, in language other than our own, and very often the opposite of our own. For a state would be mad which gave you this license, until the magistrates had determined whether your poetry might be recited, and was fit for publication or not.

Appearances are to be saved by being explained, not improved. It is important to the psyche that this world not be understood to be a deliberate lie, rather just a necessary one. Poets, it is true, do not make things up out of whole cloth. There *was* a Troy. It *was* destroyed. But they are song-stitchers of low employ. They make quilts out of scraps and tatters, castoffs, rags, and misfitting sweaters, which warm as well as the purest wool—a good that frugality might celebrate—if warming were the reason for the sheep.

Plato was, of course, aware, as many now who peruse these texts or attend these tragedies are not, that committees chose the plays that would compete; that money had to be raised for their performance, much as we squeeze uniforms from our local merchants to doll up our children's soccer teams; that politics was always an issue; that religious implications were rife; and that the aim of the citizens who performed these tasks was principally the reaffirmation of common ideals, and the strengthening of community spirit and purpose. It was important then that the dramas appeal to the public, cause the right sort of stir, and be accounted successes.

In the Athens of this time there was another contest: that between the poets, priests, philosophers, and politicians, for the power that the approval—the applause of the people—might give them. So that they might lead, they claimed to bear the solemn burden of the truth, a burden that many liars are eager to say they carry like an Olympic torch to light the public way. Plato's complaints about the poets, in this context where the truth of things is at stake, are, I think, entirely appropriate and right, because the truth, in the politician's oratory, arrives arrayed in rhetoric fit to the public's fears and wants, while in a poet's mouth, such truth becomes the sweet taste of the line, not the hard design of science or the rigor of philosophical argument. Rhyme, of the sort I have just employed, might be sugar to the ear and thus agreeable to the mind. Although sophists like Gorgias might make a public show of their rhetorical gifts, it was the mimesis of the drama that most frequently encouraged passion and desire to rule the soul. In the arena of the theater, people sometimes charged the stage, shouted angrily, and even fainted. None of this was known to be a reaction to the premises of an argument.

Plato is critical of the mimesis of the poets and the painters because he has made Truth and Beauty predicates of the Good, as every puritan has since. But he has plenty of positive use for mimesis in his own great contribution to aesthetics (in addition to the *Sym-*

posium, of course), namely the cosmological dialogue the *Timaeus.* This dialogue, cast in meaningful mythological terms, is a description of the making (the poesis) of the sensible universe. The Demiurge of the dialogue is a creator par excellence—the best, in fact, that could be imagined—and he will be responsible for the existence of appearance as well as its relation to reality.

From the Beginning there existed Being, Non-Being, and the great Receptacle, Space. Being is understood as the realm of Forms, and these are formulas, as I prefer to see them, expressible in mathematical terms. The epistemological essence of Platonism (I shall foolhardily say) is that we shall recognize that we have knowledge in any sphere to the degree we can express it mathematically. In any case, these Forms are arranged in a hierarchy topped by the Good that contains them all. It does not, however, contain them the way Aristotle's idea of Being contains all that really is, for Aristotle's formulation is always in terms of genus and species expressed in extensional language—as spaces, or classes, or sets. For Aristotle the widest, the most embracing class is the least informative one, and to say of anything that it has Being is to say the least possible about it; whereas, for Plato, the Good is an integration of other Forms the way flavors blend or colors mix, and we can find in this intentional interpretation remnants of animistic and naively realistic thinking, because Plato's daring formulae are like recipes interested in the qualitative flavor of ideas rather than classes that can enter a large sphere as dogs might join cats in the realm of pets without altering either their own nature or the habits of cats, or even the defining properties of the class of pets in general. You can't mix paint with that expectation. The figures in a formula do not alter just because they have been put near one another, nor do the words of common speech become other than they are; but the words in a poem and the colors in a painting are as responsive as flesh is to an amorous touch.

The realm of Forms has Being but it is not alive. Only the soul is alive. It is the moving principle, an intermediary between Being and the created world that it will animate. The Forms are the Demiurge's model. His palette is the chaos of sensible qualities Plato calls Non-Being, though it is scarcely nothing. It is called Non-Being because it is a mess, because without order there can be no Being. And what are these qualities? Colors, noises, feelings, I suspect; flavors, pains, probably? Aches wandering around without knees or any other place to inflict; smells that have never known noses, sours apart from their whiskeys, and every adjective as it would be if bereft of its noun—unattached, meaningless, waiting to modify. They are adrift like sea wrack in the Great Receptacle, as Plato calls it. In the womb of things to be. Time will be created as the moving image of eternity, but emptiness has always been, and here it serves as the canvas for the artist, the place the pigments will finally find their regal robes and handsome face.

With every element prepared, the Demiurge makes the Pythagoreans look smart by fashioning the frame of the universe from such simplicities as their treasured right triangle, whose figured image, when flipped so that one shape lies provocatively upon another, causes a rectangle to appear, and when spun creates a cone, and by various whirls around its hypotenuse produces whatever geometry requires, since spheres are cones rolled the right way.

Three important factors in creativity are singled out, and these three remain as resolutely present now as they were then. The Demiurge must suffer some things to come about through sheer Necessity: space is what it is, the qualities are what they are, the mural's wall is but ten feet high, and there is an oval window in it; the words of any language, its grammar, its historical contexts, are as given as a flaw in the sculptor's marble, or as the nubble of the canvas that requires it to be sized, or the fact that the blonde the studio has cast in the lead has a lisp more prominent than her notorious chest. On the other hand, many things come about through reason alone, when the Demiurge's intentions are nowhere impeded. Finally, for most effects, the Demiurge must "persuade necessity," as Plato puts it. Here the artist's skill is at its utmost: that flaw in the marble becomes the center of the composition; necessity is not merely the mother but it is the entire household of invention; and what could not be helped is made a help, or as the formula would later be: for the artist, the arbitrary is a gift to form.

Reality is not alive. It is the Pythagorean world of numbers and as still as the plenum of Parmenides. But think of the plight of the Forms. Put yourself in their place. You are a law of motion yet you do not move, nothing moves, there is no performance. You are the way things would change if anything did but it does not—a falling body would go splat if there were bodies and if they fell, but they do not; or you are the definition of a species extinct before knowing life and have only imaginary members; and though you are an object of knowledge, you will never know what knowing is or, like a castled virgin—flaxen-haired beauty herself—what it is like to be seen, longed for, touched, loved.

Plato never tells us why the Demiurge felt that need . . . to create an inferior realm, a necessarily imperfect copy of the Forms, a realm of Becoming . . . but I think I have suggested a reason. The Forms have what Aristotle would later call "second grade actuality"—the kind that things made for a function possess while waiting for that function to be realized: the tool in the box, the book on the shelf, the manuscript at the bottom of a drawer, a talent not yet discovered, young men at puberty before being killed in a war. The realm of Forms will not be perfect if it remains as pure as Plato at first imagines it to be. So its image is required. The Forms have implicit denotations. What does it mean to say that there are theories, laws, explanations, definitions without the heat, movement, makeup, character, or morals they delimit, regulate, and rule? Reality needs appearance to complete it.

The world needs souls if the world would be moved, and souls need poets to move them. Pythagorean formulae that resemble those for the harmonic mean are mixed like ingredients for a Christmas loaf by the Demiurge, and out of these numerals soul stuff is rolled into orbits and raised into spheres: the passage of the planets and the ceiling of the sky with all its stars becomes the soul of the world, now understood, in purely animistic terms, to be a living breathing animal, within one of whose countless furrows we live like mites, mostly ignored. Such an amazing dream.

The movement of the planets is rational; therefore it is circular, another bit of animistic logic which prefers cycles: the daily sun, those of human generations, the phases of the moon, the periodicity of women, the revivals of the seasons, and the return of past times like comets from a long journey. And while such perfection the circle has suits the planets, who resemble real gods—un-Olympian, unanthropomorphic, undeterrable—it will not do for man or any other living things whose perfection falls far short of even the twirling of a top. Now comes a moment in Plato's account that is straight out of the atelier. The demiurge may not make man more rational than he is, yet his touch will do just that, so, having created reason, fashioning the lower parts of the soul is left to the planetary gods, subordinate workmen, and from them our vegetable lives and our animal instincts are made, as if the background of a mural were left to the master's best pupils to practice on. Frank Gehry cannot be expected to have designed everything he signs his name to.

These identical three-part souls are sown throughout the universe and bring to life the bodies they enter, with the curious consequence that a carrot will possess as full a soul as the rabbit who fancies it or the hunter who snares, and it will be the inadequacies of their respective bodies that will determine individuality. Souls have no more individuality than a plastic drinking cup. So if you are smarter than I am, it is because your body (hence the lower orders of the soul) has less influence on your thoughts and actions than mine has.

That is to say: you are better ruled. This is another mimetic element in the Platonic system, and develops from a proportional metaphor: the soul resides in the person as the person resides in the state. The soul, it seems, is a little kingdom that may be run well or badly, depending on whether it is governed by reason or by passions and desires. The political entity that Plato calls the Republic has a soul as well. It is composed of the three classes of citizens in the state:

guardians, functionaries, and workers. Of the cardinal virtues, three are particularly appropriate to the structure of the soul and the ruling organization of the commonwealth: temperance suits the workers, who are mastered by their appetites, as fruits and vegetables are—breeding and feeding; next, two kinds of courage, of body and spirit, are appropriate to the soldiers and administrators; while wisdom, of course, is special to the guardians. Justice, the final virtue of the four, is the harmony in each soul that is reflected in an analogous harmony in the state, each element performing its proper task.

Using this scheme it is possible to describe governments in terms of the balance of the classes in them, and whether the citizens have been properly sorted out. Tyrants, who were as plentiful then as they apparently always are, furnished examples of city-states ruled by the worst rather than the best, and democracies (by which Plato understood a government largely run by tribes or demes, with officials chosen from them somewhat at random) little better run than if they were not run at all.

We have not yet passed through the entire mimetic chain. If the Forms are definitions—definitions of functions—they are also instructions, and the world of appearance participates in the forms (one meaning of *mimesis*) by carrying out these instructions, though how specifically Plato never makes clear. Any bed, for instance, will exhibit the physical laws that make its structure suitable for sleep, a need that human beings have, according to a form's program for us. But we do not dwell in this world the way trees or stones or beds do, unconscious of their surroundings. Is what we see when we see, and feel when we touch, a copy too?

It would be too much to expect a culture that has just discovered the self, just made the distinction between appearance and reality, located abstract ideas as if they were stars from another hemisphere, and begun the foundations of logic as well as the entire remaining table of contents for philosophy, to have driven its epistemology so quickly into subjectivity as later the Enlightenment would; but in the *Theaetetus*, Plato has put his pedal to the metal. He fashions for us another amazing sexual metaphor. Such images appear to be his specialty.

He conjectures that when we see, rays emanating from the eyes encounter, as a searchlight might, other rays reflected by or sent forth from objects. These rays intermingle like passionate limbs and from their intercourse are born twins (which, as we know, are a sign their mother has suffered trespass as well as the owner's tread over his rightful property). Then the eye *sees*. That is one child. And the object *becomes* white. That is the other. After all, what has Plato's favorite word for our world been but that of Becoming. Perhaps Plato has imagined one too many rays, though today we wallow in frequencies. Still, if I blow the dog's whistle, his ears hear, and the whistle grows loud. We would probably say: for him; but the Greeks don't doubt the public nature of appearances. The world is as external, as objective, as the façade of the palace at Thebes. And Oedipus enters for all to see.

In Plato's day, art was becoming more mimetic by the minute. And that meant: more faithful to appearances. Figures were now individualized, not so hieratic, symbolic, and formal; casts were being taken from the bodies of athletes to the scandal of the connoisseurs; decoration was looser and less geometrical; paintings which deceived the eye were marveled at (Plato was not pleased that painters were proud when birds pecked at their painted grapes); drama was undergoing the same slow transformation: had not Agathon—the writer whose victory in the theatrical competitions the *Symposium* celebrates— had he not introduced, for the first time, nonmythological elements? And what was one to say about Euripides' sensationalism, and his vulgar pandering to the passions of the populace? Aristophanes had made fun of the saintly Socrates before the Athenians murdered him. Artists were in cahoots with the priests who looked after the numerous sanctuaries that had sprung up as if piles of rock had been watered into bloom, and votive objects and other offerings to the gods had collected in the precincts of the shrines like leaves in a windless corner. The politicians, moreover, had led the people into an ill favored, unfortunate, and lengthy war. Plato's attitude would become a familiar one. Mass culture has been eating away at high culture's cookie for as long as baking has been a business. Sculptors were manufacturing huge heavily bedizened statues for the public to marvel at, and countless pretty boys in marble toes or ladies dressed in plump breasts and long thighs that Roman pillagers would later resell to the Latin bourgeois, received the ardent admiration of the masses—not just then, but, in the guise of Roman copies, since.

What a pleasure it was to produce reasons that copying was so detrimental to the rational spirit, and put painters in their place, because the people and scenes they painted were already artifacts, already appearances, already removed from reality by at least one degree. Falsehoods follow falsehoods like pilgrims to their shrine. The world loves the flattery that all likeness intends.

However, that very character of mimesis is essential to the educational process, much of which must take place before the age of reason, and therefore very often by means of imitation. The youth must be provided with proper role models—to employ one of our popular euphemisms. Plato has still another use for his proportional metaphor of the divisions of the soul and state, because when we are infants, we are also as vegetables; we eat and excrete, cry and kick, and our parents are expected to supply the moderation that would otherwise be lacking. As youths we are controlled by our passions, and we must be taught to bleed for peace instead of drill for oil, to direct our feelings to their appropriate objects, to love the good and hate the ill informed. When adults, we rule ourselves. This is an ideal, of course, because when the state is badly managed, its citizens remain children; they fire their guns into the sky; they die for the wrong causes; they allow their passions to be stirred by raucous music; they read only one book.

Alas, for consistency, if we tell only nice things about Zeus and his fellow loungers on Mount Olympus, so that the youth will have something to be devout about, we shall have to tell lies, for the gods are as wicked as you and I, and don't rule the way guardians are supposed to. Lying is not a seemly exercise; nevertheless Plato recommends a shield of lies to protect the innocence of the people and enable them to be more easily managed.

Yet one more proportion can be lined up alongside Plato's controlling metaphor, namely parallel levels of knowledge. When the appetitive portion dominates, the soul lives in a state of ignorance, is psychologically a child, and should be allowed only a workman's productive role in the ideal republic. He or she depends upon successful *praxis* to make do, and learns a trade by imitating those who already have it. Skills, like casting bronze, are passed down from master to his sons like recipes for stews, and may include good, bad, or irrelevant advice, often a surprising mingling of superstition and good sense. Administrators are allowed *doxa*—opinions—beliefs that, whether right or wrong, are not supported by satisfactory reasons. Only guardians possess the *Logos,* theoretical knowledge, the justification that makes some opinions sound.

These three levels of "knowledge and education"—*praxis, doxa, Logos*—match up with the parts of the soul, and those with the stages of human growth and psychological types, and those with the classification of citizens along with their appropriate virtues, to form the soul of the state; and in every case the connection is established through mimesis—mimesis as either impersonation, participation, or copy—and one in which Form is made manifest through the order it lends to illusion.

If Plato is prepared to put every meaning of mimesis to use, and make it a modest philosophical jack-of-all-trades, Aristotle appears inclined to confine it to more purely aesthetic contexts. Either because of the fragmentary character of the *Poetics,* its sketchy lecture-note quality, or its immense concision, there seem to be more flagrant misrepresentations of its contents than most early tracts have had to suffer. As Stephen Halliwell points out, "the philosopher's concept of mimesis has played a vital role in the long story of Western attitudes to artistic representation, [but] that role has often been mediated through the reworking and misinterpretation

of his ideas, especially those found in the *Poetics*." I would suggest
that the philosopher's concept has not played a vital role, after all,
but only misconstruals of it have, much in the same way that the
Bible has suffered from its readers, so that what it has been taken to
mean, not what it means, matters. Falsehood and error have played
a far larger role in history than truth and correctness, for falsehoods
always find a way to be convenient and of use.

Even if Aristotle had said, "Art is an imitation of nature," the words
he would have used—*techné, mimesis physis*—would have given the
game away; for each of these terms has considerable philosophical significance in Aristotle's work and, understood in that context,
make the formula one I, at least, might love, instead of this infamous
sentence's historic meanings, all of which are vulgar and abhorrent.
Aristotle says he is going to investigate one of the productive arts—
the craft of making poems—and that investigation will involve dis-
tinguishing poetry's genres and their particular effects, defining the
elements that comprise the craft, especially how to turn traditional
plots into decent drama, as well as whatever else proves to be perti-
nent during the course of his study. And he will begin, as he customarily does, with first principles.

He could have said he was going to study the skill of a pilot of
ships, whose aim is a safe arrival in harbor, or that of a physician,
whose purpose is healing; but neither is a part of poiesis—the productive arts. He could have made his subject the sandal maker's art:
what kinds of sandals there were; what end each was designed to
serve, and how you went about making them: the tools you would
need, the materials you might choose, and so forth. But, you might
say, in that case where does mimesis come in? Some animals have
padded paws; some have hooves; some skins are as leathery as
gloves. But we have no such protection from the sharp stones of the
road, so the cobbler remedies that lack, not by imitating hooves but
by following the hints thrown out by nature, and bringing shoes into
being mechanically without any thought of resemblance, only one of
function. The principle of change lies in the cobbler, and is clearly

external to its object, unlike the fabled acorn that follows genetic instructions. When the artisan goes to work, he makes things by *following the pattern of nature* (that is the right rendering of *mimesis* here): *it* makes lava, *he* manufactures plastics; *it* grows talons, *he* invents corkscrews; *it* encourages eagles, *he* runs after rats with baited traps.

There are some things in nature that need to be fixed, and there are others that aren't there at all, but ought to be. The physician mends; the cobbler adds. Potions that physicians might need, our chemists sometimes supply. It will be like that with the craft of poetry. Tragedy, it will turn out, is a purgative, and good for the body politic—an analogy that has its origins in Plato, but one that Aristotle is happy to continue. He was the son of a physician, after all.

There is another consequence of Aristotle's treatment of poetry as a craft. As Gerald Else remarks, "There is not a word anywhere in the *Poetics* about the persons Homer and Sophocles. The artist does not produce *qua* man, person, individual, but *qua* artist; or as Aristotle says, with his special brand of vividness, 'it is accidental to the sculptor that he is Polyclitus.'" Another example, updated from Plato: the art of medicine is a body of knowledge which the physician internalizes. Then when Dr. Weisenheimer cures my gout, it is the art of medicine that does it. When he botches the job, he does so as old Joe Weisenheimer of Louisa Alcott Lane. When the Romantic poets fly their kites, it is the wind that keeps them airborne. They just think it is their own hot air.

So poetry is placed among the productive arts. In the most businesslike fashion possible. I don't think one can stress this placement too strongly. As Gerald Else concludes, "His treatise is not a discussion of 'poetry' in either, or any, sense of the English term; it is, in all sadness and sobriety, an analysis of the nature and functioning of the *art* of poetry and of its species." It is not *about* Sophocles' *Oedipus Rex*. And those species: what are they? They are the epic (which is recited), tragedy and comedy (which are performed), and dithyrambic poetry (which is sung by a chorus). Flute and lyre music are also deemed imitations. Aristotle goes on to say that some arts use color and shape, but all the others employ the voice, or are at least audible.

Aristotle resides in an oral culture still. Moreover, he knows that the written word can resemble only other written words. "The cat sat on the mat" in no way imitates its situation. When Creon enters in a snit, however, his words enable the actor to impersonate his character, mimic his tone of voice, and say what he might say under the circumstances. We also know that he won't talk American, though he does in this translation.

> Citizens, I have come because I heard deadly words spread about me, that the king accuses me. I cannot take that from him.
> [*Oedipus the King*, 512–514. David Grene translation.]

The stage directions, "Creon enters," do not imitate an action; they order it. The words Creon speaks do not imitate his state of mind; they express it. However, Creon's speaking them—his tone of voice, his choice of the Americanism "cannot take that from him"—do help the actor impersonate Creon's character and consequently could be said to be an imitation.

In the case of music, both Plato and Aristotle seem to find it especially infectious—that martial music makes one martial, that lullabies lull, and so on—that is, they encourage participation, but it is the dynamics of music, more than anything else, that is transferable, and it is music, too, that achieves its harmony through the formal relations of its sounds and the manner of their production, since the Pythagoreans had presumably discovered a connection between tones and the length of a lyre string. Its harmonies and disharmonies affect the morally important emotions; indeed, as Stephen Halliwell puts it, they are "*enacted* by the qualities of the artwork. That these qualities are 'in' the (musically organized) sounds themselves is inferred from music's capacity to convey emotional-cum-ethical feelings to the audience."

Mimesis

In a previous lecture I observed how Plato had argued for a division between the realm of Being and the world of Becoming that could be crossed only on a bridge of mimesis. The Demiurge uses sensory qualities to imitate the Forms: the things of this world impersonate their real counterparts, and gain their secondary and only reality by participating in them. Aristotle, with so much common sense it seems daring, does not have a gulf he must cross, because his forms exist in every instance of their kinds. They are sunk in their particulars like posts. If all the members of a species are there, in that species, because they have "the same form," then might it not be possible to imagine a situation in which a form customarily found in one place was found in another as well? A musical score possesses a note structure that the performer follows and reproduces in the piece he plays; moreover, the auditory waves that microphones capture and transfer to digital tapes can boast that structure too, as a disc's grooves do. It might be only a metaphor, but music's moods and the emotional coloration of our consciousness could share similar dynamic relationships without in the least having the same content.

Ultimately, Aristotle interprets the form/content connection first as a structure/function relation, and finally as one of potency and act. To understand this we have to remind ourselves of Aristotle's classification of causes into four kinds, because they apply to the sources of action in a tragedy, and to the course of mimesis there, as surely as they do to nature and life generally. Every event has a material cause. It is made of something, sometimes several different kinds of thing, and this matter must be considered, when confined to artistry, as canvas and pigment, words in a language, sounds from a flute, stone from a quarry. Every material will have its own actuality (the idea of something that is pure potentiality—prime matter—is entirely conceptual); that is, marble will have that stone's qualities and forms. These, however, will be the basis for the many things it might do or become. The efficient cause is simply the work done in order to realize those potentialities; it is energy enabled by tools and directed by skills, in the sculptor's case, so that out of the marble a marble fawn emerges.

The formal cause is what will be later called the object's essence, and like the material cause is a combination of what the thing actually is and what it can become because of what it actually is; however, the formal cause is its definition, and determines what a thing is destined to become or do if allowed to express its nature. In the case of a work of art, the formal cause, as I've said, lies outside the thing itself and resides in the artist. Nothing grows into a marble fawn on its own, though flesh and blood fawns do. Those principles of change that reside within an object or event are said to be its entelechy—its direction of self-realization. The final cause is, of course, the end at which a course of action aims, the fully realized deer, or statue, or polished skill.

All this is elementary Aristotle. What scholars seem less inclined to do is to apply Aristotle's physics and metaphysics (even his ethics and his logic) to the principles of the *Poetics*. If we do that, many obscurities become immediately clear and the concision of the text understandable. For instance, a tragedy, Aristotle says, is the imitation of a morally serious action—clearly one that has taken place, or might take place, in the ordinary life of extraordinary people—in such a way as to show how its consequences follow inevitably from its nature. These consequences invariably involve the loss of eudaemonia, well-being, or self-fulfillment, not merely for the individual but for the society. So often catastrophe is the result of excess: of success, as if a vine choked the tree it twined upon; or certainty, as if you bet your life on your ability to guess right; or duty, pursuing what you think proper against every advice; or of innocence, or loyalty, or honesty itself, so often not the best policy because virtue is the way to ruin.

Aristotle advises the plot maker to concentrate upon a single unified action, and therefore one that is definable and has a beginning, a middle, and an end. His advice is not as simpleminded as it sounds. It has to do, as he says later, with raveling and unraveling, tying the knot, and untying it.

The beginning of a play is complete when the dramatist has established a situation that implicitly contains the conclusion. It is the planted seed. Henry James used to feel that his beginnings always needed more material put in them to support the story, consequently that they grew too large, so he studied various methods of foreshortening. For Aristotle the play's course—the object of its mimesis—must resemble an entelechy. The play's middle occurs at that point in the arc of an arrow's flight when its rise weakens and the course of its return becomes inevitable. This is often seen as a reversal of fortune, since the action was initially regarded as a good and wise one, and prospers in that guise, before showing its true self, and reversing its direction. The conclusion is the completed actualization of what was there to be realized from the beginning. When there are many subordinate plotlines the trick is to find one fulfillment that will satisfy them all.

The infamous unities of one place/one day are suggested only because such a confinement makes far easier the disclosure of consequences. A tragedy should move like a syllogism from premises to conclusion. The fewer premises the better. The ordinary world rarely offers us such a sight, because there are too many competing courses of action. The seed of a tree must not only cope with the earth it finds itself in and employ the moisture and nutrients that are there, but it must compete with other plants for its light and food, avoid being munched into oblivion by a deer, stand up eventually against the elements, and dodge disease, the sawmill, and the forest's fires. History is an account of accidents, collisions of causes, and its results are always maimed. Thousands are throwing their basketballs at the same basket. History hears only the din of disappointed ends. There is no song that isn't interrupted almost the moment it's begun. History is wreckage. Whereas the tragic action grows like a plant in a nursery or a bacterium in a laboratory. No one is permitted to knock it from its stand; no diseases darken its leaves; no worms chew its blooms. We can therefore see what it will be; what it is in its inner self—a complete action as rounded as a racecourse. Who better than Kant to warn us against actions with unintended consequences, advice that, given early, nevertheless comes to our politicians too late? Tragedy drops one small smooth pebble into a calm pure pond and then measures, whereas history tosses a handful of gravel into a raging sea on a foggy day. That is why poetry is more philosophical than history. History's universals are all dead or dismembered.

Oedipus sees his own tragedy unfold and is the best spectator for his own blinding. He learns that what he never intended to happen, fate has seen to. The play that so fascinated the Philosopher does not imitate our world. Nor do Galileo's mechanics. When has a kid slid down a slide the way a kid would if the kid were an imaginary kid computing the rate of his passage along geometry's inclined plane? Utopias, like Plato's *Republic,* attempt to control causes and consequences, generally with ludicrous results. Better a plausible impossibility, Aristotle remarks, to the consternation of countless commentators, than an implausible possibility; because history is nothing but the implausible, the unpredictable, the incredible concatenation. A good play's movement is inexorable. It is, in that sense, the equal of any argument. In real life, people recover from incurable cancers—occasionally. And nearly always in bad movies. We complain of such conclusions. We blame them on Hollywood.

Aristotle wants his action to be performed by a powerful person so that the consequences will escape their agent and implicate the state. All of Thebes is suffering, the chorus is quick to tell us. Tragedy is a massive loss of opportunity. Right or wrong, Aristotle always makes sense.

The artist brings things into being the way nature brings things into being. Art adds realities to the world that were missing from it, and that well might belong here. That is Aristotle's sense of mimesis: it does not make copies of things. It does not end with a likeness. It is, instead, an investigation, an argument, a realization.

METAPHOR

Meta- means "between," *meta-* means "with," or *meta-* means "after."
Metempsychosis means "to travel to another life." *Metamorphosis*
means "to alter shape or form such as the transformation of cartilage
into bone, worm into butterfly." *Metaphysics* means "to go beyond
material things the way the book that comes after the *Physics* in the
collected works of Aristotle treats of first principles." *Metalanguage*
means "to look down on the language of Use from the language of
Mention." It is the tongue for speaking of tongues. *Metanoia* means
"to repent, to change one's mind." *Metalepsis* means "the exchange
of one figure of speech for another." *Metaphor* means "to move to
a strange place, to be a word that wakes up in an unfamiliar bed, a
substitute for an injured player, another eye in another sky." *Phrein,*
the back half of metaphor, means "to bear on one's body as the scars
or wounds of argument and war are borne." It means "a likeness, a
trace, a spore." It means, in general, "to carry, wear with honor, or
hold dear as one cherishes a grudge." So *metaphor* means "to carry
between, to bear with, or to look after." What it does not mean is a
simpleminded transfer of a word from one place to another like a
rider who changes buses; it does not mean a word out of order; it
does not mean a word with an unfamiliar function.

The section of the *Poetics* in which some of Aristotle's observations about metaphor are contained is often treated by even the most dedicated commentators as an abberation. Gerald Else, who lavishes 670 pages of exegesis on this little book, is blunt enough: "The three and one-half chapters [which deal with grammar and metaphor] are omitted from this study for three reasons: (1) they are technical to a very high degree . . . and bristle with special problems . . . ; (2) to a degree unequaled by any other part of the work they have to be treated in a special context, that of the development of 'grammatical' study in Greece; and (3) they have very little—astonishingly little—connection with any other part of Aristotle's theory of poetry." Else goes on to wonder whether these paragraphs are even genuine. A few more pages are devoted to metaphor in the *Rhetoric,* where, we are told, Aristotle provides over twenty examples; however, some of them are so obscure, because they are cited out of context, as to defy analysis, and G. M. A. Grube advises the casual reader to skip to the next chapter.

It does not help that Aristotle uses *metaphor,* as Plato does *mimesis,* in the widest possible sense, taking on its meanings as one embattled takes on all comers, or that he appears to reduce the figure to a word, a noun. He classifies nouns with his customary relentless analytical intelligence into "current, strange, metaphorical, ornamental, newly coined, lengthened, abbreviated, or otherwise altered," a strangely disorderly list. Then he says: "A metaphor is a word with some other meaning which is transferred from genus to species, or from species to genus, or from one species to another, or used by analogy." This is called by contemporary commentators the substitution theory. They do not like it, and no wonder.

It is important to remember what Aristotle says metaphors are not: they are not strange, that is, foreign, unless we were to say, regarding the president's stated reasons for invading Iraq, "his soufflé fell"; and they are not ornamental; that is, they are more than merely decorative, for instance, if "the employee's flattery left lipstick on both of his bosses' cheeks," then whether the image were merely decorative might depend on where the cheeks were.

Aristotle's own examples are problematic. He says that the expression, "There stands my ship," shifts from an implicit genus, which he claims is that of lying at anchor, to one of its species or kinds, namely "to stand." However (in English, at any rate), one's posture while lying at anchor would be quite different from that assumed when standing. Both are species of being moored, but to stand at anchor means to be at the ready, to show mostly your masts, whereas if you lie at anchor you are hull down, and most of the crew will be ashore. The proper genus for lying and standing should be simply at anchor. We can leave G. M. A. Grube's version for S. H. Butcher's translation, but it is not only awkward and tautological but laughable as well: "'There lies my ship,' for lying at anchor is a species of lying." Philip Wheelwright, to take our chances there, gives us, "'Here stays my ship'; for being at anchor is a species of staying." However, it isn't clear whether *being at anchor* isn't the genus and *staying* the species.

Aristotle's instance of species to species is "with the bronze drawing out his life," or "cutting with the stubborn bronze." To refer to a sword by the matter of its blade is already a doubled case of part to whole—*bronze* for *blade* and *blade* for *sword*. *To draw out* in English means to entice an exit or disclosure, as a character in Henry James might "draw out" one friend to speak about another, or a lady's wink in the hall draw Cedric from the dining room, or, more strongly, the phrase may mean to siphon or extract. "Cutting with the stubborn bronze" sounds like the same synecdoche—*bronze* for *blade*—with animation added like oil for an engine, but in this instance Aristotle is referring to a bronze bowl and the ritual of sacrifice. The English word *stubborn* will possibly take us still farther afield.

Only by leaving the language in the Greek can we be sure we have the right image. When the word that makes the metaphor moves into place it brings a fresh context of meanings the way a new owner fills an old house with his furniture. The former occupants, and all their stuff, fade into the background and lurk there like ghosts. The literal never likes to lose its place. Telemachus complains that Penelope won't bring to an end the constant solicitation of her hand, while the suitors "continue to bleed my household white." The metaphor is built of a triple ratio: blood stands to body as money stands to household; bleeding is to body as expenditure is to wealth; and white is a sign of sickness or weakness the way one's bank balance, by adding an ı, becomes blank. Moreover, as Homer later informs us, this expenditure of wealth is partly the result of the thirsty princes "draining the broached vats dry of vintage wine."

Although the simplest imagery is not simple, we use it easily and all the time. Actually, "all the time" is a hyperbole like Aristotle's example of a transfer from species to genus: "Odysseus did a thousand noble deeds." The genus that *thousand* stands under here is the idea of *many*, Aristotle claims. We are certainly familiar with this sort of exaggeration. "I have a million things to do this morning." "I innocently asked her to dinner, but she ate enough for forty men." The crucial thing about any hyperbole is: How far do we blow up the balloon? When do we think we have exceeded every norm sufficiently? One only has to sense the different effect the image has as you go from what may be only a likely enlargement to one surpassing the imagination. "I have sixteen things to do this morning." "You don't say! Well, I have thirty things to do this morning." "Yeah? but I have a million things to do this morning." Set that acceleration against: "I have thirty-eight things to do this morning" "Tough luck, kiddo. I only have the square root of forty-nine things to do this morning," or, "I have a god-awful lot of things to get half-done by noonish."

The literal version of this bit of unhappiness would be, "I have impossibly many things to do this morning." The impossible is philosophically suspect. Is it possible to have degrees of impossibility or is it like being dead—never a matter of more or less? Telemachus is probably exaggerating, too, when he insists that the bleeding of his household has reached the paleness of white, but we would have to have some knowledge of his finances to be sure. If the Ulysses Trading Company's stock went up, he might be in the black again. This complex metaphor (complex because it is made of many interlocking images: his household has a human body; the suitors are wounding it; the wound is financial; the wound is deadly) demonstrates that hyperbole can lose or gain such a status, depending upon external circumstances. Robert Fagles's modern translation suggests that the suitors are leeches, and the word *bleeding* tempts us to consider the leeches' use as a medical procedure, an encouragement that is probably inappropriate.

Let us look at that move of species to genus again. This occurs when a species is made to do the work of (or stand for) its genus. "Odysseus did many noble deeds." "Oh? how many?" "A lot— thousands." Why wouldn't you just stay with "Odysseus did many"? I am forced into the hyperbole because I am afraid that my hearer may think, "Ah, sixteen," when I want him to understand that it was really quite a few. However silently said or quietly read, hyperbole is a shout. So precision is inappropriate. The shouter has no time to count: "Odysseus did sixty-six noble deeds." Moreover, the speaker has feelings about this information, as one who shouts usually does. "Charlie must have eaten a hundred of those peach pies!" Only the context will tell us whether the speaker approves of this voraciousness (the word *noble* supplies the judgment in Odysseus's case) or is revolted or simply amazed.

Species do not simply float around inside their genus like mist in a cloud. There are hierarchies, especially among the holier-than-thou: God the Father, the Holy Ghost, Archangels, angels, saints, and so on; there are onions: sweet spring yellow, white and hot, garlics, scallions, shallots, leeks, and bulb, Bermudas, Walla Walla, Maui, Spanish, and Vidalia. The country of classification is complex and not always harmonious, so the choice of what species shall be asked to stand in for the genus is crucial. The genus *Many* has as many classes as a university. If we want to say that the truth is an onion, have we a preference for the scallion, the Vidalia, or the leek? Is the truth long, thin, pale, green for much of its length, or round as the world? Perhaps it is merely irritating to the eye. The greatly inflated list is another kind of hyperbole, a consequence of structure rather than single word choice. Not only were there too many onions in the onion sentence, they were there higgledy-piggledy because different kinds of classifications were resorted to, not just different onions.

The relation of species to genus is nothing like that of part to whole. Your clothes are not a part of your luggage the way the bag's straps are, but they may be packed in your luggage to be pawed by customs or wrinkled by jouncing. Although a species of cat is "in" a genus, it cannot be chased by the pack called *dogs* up either an ideal or a real tree. Aristotle thinks of his analytical orders as we think of classes. These are conceptual spaces, usually represented as round, where other such circles are included and where, ultimately, individuals are put. Definitions determine the membership of a class the way golfers are admitted to the country club, so that when Homer says that the nurse "found Odysseus in the thick of slaughtered corpses, splattered with bloody filth like a lion that's devoured some ox of the field and lopes home, covered with blood, his chest streaked, both jaws glistening, dripping red—" he suddenly removes his hero from the human sphere where he was, and puts him in one made of wildlife. He does something else. He makes the slaughter more grievous but more tolerable, because Odysseus has become an animal, and one can expect no less than such relish and such ravening from a lion.

If our King Richard is a lion, he is as brave as the beast is considered to be by those who enjoy careless clichés, because the lion's fellow creatures know how lazy the snoozy fellow is, and how he prefers to prey upon the weak—ancient antelope and coltish zebras. If Richard is a lion, will he hunt like them? Will he have a pride? Will he wait until his wife has made the kill and then feast? Will its mane be Richard's beard, and will he run around on four feet? Metaphors have both depth and scope. They are as deep as their context allows us to take them. If the suitors are leeches, has the palace been built in a swamp where leeches lurk? The depth of a metaphor depends upon the number of other metaphors that are implicitly present. "Odysseus did a thousand noble deeds" doesn't have many offspring, although the sentence itself has two images—the hyperbolic number of deeds and, possibly, one other, regarding their "nobility." If Odysseus is not a noble himself, then his noble deeds are metaphorical (he did as nobles do, which might not be noble at all by our lights); but if he is one, then the phrase is somewhat redundant. When the writer extends his metaphor into a conceit (which is the name for such a device) he makes some of the implicit images manifest. For instance, if Telemachus were to complain that the suitors continue to bleed his household white while growing fat and black themselves, he would be developing and deepening his original image. He is saying: they are leeches. I really mean it. And there is a bit of hyperbole in that, because he can't really mean it.

For how long shall the suitors remain under the mantle of this metaphor? Till the next page? Next book? The remaining epic? Scientific laws have scopes; that is, they have an area of application: Boyle's law pertains to the behavior of gases; Darwin's theories have life only in the land of the living and not in the dirt and rock of that land; there is no Oedipus complex for chickens, though there may be one for the cock of the walk. King Richard may be a lion in the fray, but back home he is no fiercer than the baby Jesus. Shakespeare sometimes uses an image to help him organize an entire play. His metaphors are usually both deep and wide. *Finnegans Wake* is ruled by one trope.

So metaphors have depth (or offspring), scope (or extent of application), and a structure, something Aristotle is trying to unearth (if they are buried), disclose or reveal (if they are hidden), lay bare (if they are clothed), or reaffirm (if they have been challenged), stress (if they have been ignored), or reinforce (if they have been weakened). Enough of multiple choice; however, if a writer is to be read seriously she must choose her imagery wisely. Is the structure of a metaphor basically sentential: A is B? And how does it place itself among other meanings: Does it go there secretly? Dressed? Is it buried? Asserted? Proclaimed? Is it fixed like a post, a floorboard, or a roof?

When a part is asked to serve as a whole, or a whole is made to behave as a part, the justification for the move is often obvious, and indeed a literal statement can easily be mistaken for such a figure; for instance, "Achilles' blade killed many men." Since Achilles can wield his sword only by its handle, if he killed those men then his weapon was the instrument, but it is factually the case that only the blade bore the deadly edge, and it was that edge that did them in. Similarly, events that are causally linked to one another can be considered to form "wholes," and frequently one cause is chosen to bear entire responsibility. A bullet killed President Kennedy, a rifle shot him, and Oswald murdered him, so if I say that the bullet murdered Kennedy I am speaking metaphorically. Bullets don't lay plans. If I believe that Cubans plotted the Kennedy assassination, I may insist that the Bay of Pigs killed him. To these niceties one is tempted to say, So what? But whether the blade alone did it (having been given magical powers by one of the interfering gods) or Achilles did them in on his own makes a big difference. When the writing is good, to "So what?" there is always an answer.

Aristotle devotes more space to the proportional metaphor (which is a similitude expressed as a ratio) than he does to any other of metaphor's many kinds. Every one of these ratios will generate more metaphors, but they will generate them differently than Richard's lionheartedness or Odysseus's dripping jaws. Aristotle's first example is, once again, puzzling. "The cup is to Dionysus what the shield is to Ares; one may then speak of the cup as the shield of Dionysus, or of the shield as the cup of Ares." Is the ratio possible because the cup is what Dionysus, god of the grape, drinks from, and the shield is what Ares, the god of war, fights with; or is it because cup and grape are icons for these deities, and serve for them as heraldic signs; or is it that Dionysus defends himself from the world by getting drunk while Ares simply holds up his shield and cowers behind it? Similarly, we might say: "The elephant is the Republicans' donkey."

His second example is famous because it is famous. "Or again," Aristotle says, "old age is to life as evening is to the day; one may then speak of the evening as the day's old age, or of old age as the evening of life or the sunset of life." This is described as an analogy, but most analogies are literal. "The financial problems that the Smiths are having are analogous to [resemble, are of the same sort] as those the Browns are suffering." Aristotle's "old age is to life as evening is to day" is metaphorical because the comparison falls between two different but structurally similar temporal divisions. More such divisions can be readily provided. The proportion is a veritable machine of metaphor. I shall crank out a brief assortment.

1. Evening is the old age of day.
2. Old age is the evening of life.
3. In the evening of life one remembers the morning with a melancholy fondness.
4. These evening eyes no longer see so sharply.
5. The day is weary of its work and longs for sleep.
6. This symphony is the high noon of Beethoven's achievement.
7. We are in the teatime of this age, and familiar with its doddering.
8. Spring is the youth of the year and all its flowers are in school studying how to bloom.
9. For this regime it is almost midnight and the ravens sit silent in their trees.
10. Who shall care for me; my spring is past, my afternoons a memory, and even evening, to reach its night, must use a cane.

But we don't need my list when we have T. S. Eliot's famous example:

> Let us go then, you and I,
> When the evening is spread out against the sky
> Like a patient etherised upon a table.

Proportional thinking began with Plato's *Republic*. The tripartite division of the soul (the corresponding states of knowledge, opinion, and ignorance, of childhood, youth, and age, the three classes of citizens and their functions in the state, justice as the harmony of both soul and citizen) gives form to his utopia the way the similarly triune composition of the syllogism provides its dynamic, or, much later, supports the architecture of Kant's philosophy, and supplies the Hegelian dialectic with its force. We shouldn't forget, either, Plato's metaphysical trinity: Being, Non-Being, and Becoming, or his famous assertion that the Idea of the Good is the sun of the spiritual world, a proportion based on light as intelligibility. According to Plato's remarkable conjecture, our world is a work of art that embodies universal laws. Its qualitative expression imitates those laws, so those laws are, as they appear here, metaphorical.

Occasionally, Aristotle suggests, metaphors are required to provide new names where old ones are lacking. "At times," he says,

> there may be no name in use for some of the terms of the analogy, but we can use this kind of metaphor none the less. For example, to cast seed is to sow, but there is no special word for the casting of rays by the sun; yet this is to the sunlight as sowing is to seed, and therefore it has been said of the sun that it is "sowing its divine rays."

So when the problem set for the student is: if x is to sunlight as sowing is to seed, what must x be? then the proportional machine will promptly provide the answer: the sun's rays. It may be worth noting that the theory of light required will have to be corpuscular. But the proportion must be real. "Think of it this way," Aristotle suggests in the *Rhetoric*, "as a purple cloak is to youth, so to old age is—what? The same garment is obviously unsuitable." Perhaps we shouldn't speak of metaphors as being true or false, but some proportions are sound while others are obscure, forced, or skewed. We might rescue this one by associating colors with seasons (from green to gold or gray) and assign green to youth and gray to octogenarians.

A few paragraphs later, Aristotle upgrades metaphor from its place as a rhetorical and poetic trope to that of an important empirical talent. In the *Rhetoric* he describes metaphor, in addition, as "lucid, pleasing, and strange." This is well-trodden ground but it remains a minefield. The tradition has it that Aristotle said that the wise use of metaphor was a sign of genius; but it is probably safer to follow Grube's more restrained version: "The right use of metaphors is a sign of inborn talent and cannot be learned from anyone else; it comes from the ability to observe similarities in things." It was this ability that broke apart the referents of holophrastic language and is a characteristic of the analytic mind. In an animistic world a bard reciting a historic chronicle might be said to be *oldling,* while a boy saying his sums might be described as *digitmittering,* these words concealing from view any similarities between them—that of reciting from memory, for instance. When these wholes are seen as having parts that are different from one another—the agent, the action, the object of the action, or the qualities of each—then some of these elements can be collected and classified. The American butcher carves his chickens into pieces. He then places all the drumsticks in one cellopack and all the thighs and breasts in another. Plato has told us to carve reality at the joints, but the European butcher cuts his meat differently than we do, suggesting that he has his own principle of division. Nor does he understand why anyone would want to buy twelve chicken legs without thighs. Moreover, with the right sort of kitchen shears we can cut as we please. Nevertheless, to divide, sort, compare, recombine: these are the steps we must take to realize the Aristotelean universal. I shall try to show how metaphors perform them.

But we go forward in the face of Plato's opposition. He argues that without a prior principle of division no analysis can be made, and without a definition no similarities can be perceived.

Aristotle's preference for the proportional metaphor may actually hide what Aristotle valued in them. It was not, I would suggest, their meanings that entranced him, even when they were self-explanatory, such as "old age is like fine wine; its bottle may be dusty but its contents rich"; nor was it these metaphors' structural proportionality by itself, though that is what gives them their name, but the perception of parallel periods of natural change, sometimes three or four of these, often as many as seven stages (birth through death, dawn till darkest night, planting to harvest or to frost, the ebb and tug of the tide, the full and slivered moon, the needy, gleeful, then sorry phases of love). In the example calling upon the sun's rays, the structure is built of an action (casting, sowing) and the corpuscular makeup of the sun's rays. But these proportional metaphors actually are promoting a cyclical view of history, or, at least, a dialectical one, and therein lies their importance.

The syntax of the most modest metaphor (and what makes a metaphor modest, one might ask?) is [(subject) {copula} (predicate)]: Penelope's suitors are leeches. Determining what happens when a predicate modifies or attaches itself or couples with a subject is most difficult. Aristotle believed that (1) an identity is asserted (Sophocles is the author of *Antigone*), or (2) the class the subject belongs to is included in the class the predicate defines (tragedies are plays), or (3) the subject is said to be a member of the predicate's community (Sophocles is a playwright). In these cases, however, it is important to observe that, although the predicate is presumed to be *about* the subject (Sophocles is the author of *Antigone*), in two of them it is the subject that is the subordinate entity, either as a member of a class, or as a class included in a class. The subject syntactically finds its way to the predicate. Sophocles aspires, he knocks, he is admitted, but the class of playwrights remains indifferent. For Plato, on the other hand, a proposition asserts that the two forms that make up the subject and predicate meld or blend the way the ingredients of sauces or stews do, and the predicate becomes a property of its subject. Aristotle's interpretation is called extensional (because of its spatial treatment of classes and the verb *to be*), while Plato's is called intentional (for no reason I have ever understood). Another example: for Aristotle, when the schoolhouse is made red, the schoolhouse enters the class of red things, and predicates made of adjectives become nouns (red things); while for Plato the schoolhouse gets painted by that property so that a compound noun subject is formed, namely redschoolhouse, no doubt in honor of the German language that would arrive one day.

What about those suitors? They are making merry. They are bleeding the blood bank. So the leech becomes their predicate. But now it does not modify its subject in any ordinary way. Only in Kafka could they really become leeches. The literal account that lurks near Telemachus's figure of speech would say that Penelope's suitors are greedy guests; they are guys seeking to marry money; they are lotharios looking to get lucky with a lovely and languishing widow. Because Penelope's suitors are greedy guests, and greedy guests are costly to feed, Penelope's suitors are costly to feed. But notice something that Aristotle did not. He regarded universal affirmative propositions as having the form: all S is P, but we now know that these seemingly confident assertions are hypothetical and have a different structure: if x is a suitor, then x is a greedy guest. But only if.

The modification that a metaphor makes is far-reaching, reciprocal, and complex. The predicate of a metaphor may be interpreted as a lens through which the subject is observed. The predicate is a historically ragged system of meanings that are used to interpenetrate a similarly unkempt collection of concepts kept like house pets by the subject term. That is why many other metaphors are engendered by the parental one. When Odysseus eyes a little island near where the Cyclops lives that is uninhabited and ripe for development, he says, "No mean spot, it could bear you any crop you like in season. The water-meadows along the low foaming shore run soft and moist, and your vines would never flag." Homer does not say: these swamps are meadows, or even meadows of water, according to Robert Fagles, but water-meadows. What a lovely thought. I have seen such quiet stretches in a shallow lake where flocks of ducks light and delve over the terrain like grackles in a field of grain.

If we don't have a word for these soothing patches of resting water, perhaps a metaphor can supply them. This is certainly a function Aristotle finds appropriate. Such a metaphor divides one kind of water from another. It suddenly sees a certain stretch as pasture the way, in the mountains, tableland sometimes appears between peaks. But it does so violently, melting soil into moisture, reclaiming a length of lake for the land. Yet we can let this new name claim its referent by pointing to the way swamp grass grows up through the water until the surface disappears. Here hippos might wade or buffalo browse.

The legitimacy of the image is demonstrated by carrying it to lengths, but this exfoliation also "explains" it, leaves the image without a shred of mystery, unpacks its bag and tosses the contents on a bed, as I did by explaining that old age was like fine wine because its contents were rich. However, Homer's favorite images are often developed prior to their application. For instance, when the suitors are being slaughtered,

> Odysseus scanned his house to see if any man
> still skulked alive, still hoped to avoid black death.
> But he found them one and all in blood and dust . . .
> great hauls of them down and out like fish that fishermen
> drag from the churning gray surf in looped and coiling nets
> and fling ashore on a sweeping hook of beach—some noble catch
> heaped on the sand, twitching, lusting for fresh salt sea
> but the Sungod hammers down and burns their lives out . . .
> so the suitors lay in heaps, corpse covering corpse.

Metaphors announce themselves by being rowdy and by violating rules, either of syntax, as in E. E. Cummings's line "anyone lived in a pretty how town," or of semantics, by being manifestly false to fact, like, "I have a million dishes to do," or logically out of whack, such as Andrew Marvell's famous line, "annihilating all that's made / To a green thought in a green shade," or Homer's phrase, just mentioned, "lusting for fresh salt sea," if indeed it is Homer's and not the translator's; and, finally, pragmatically, by committing breaches of custom or decorum, for instance, the man who tips his tie instead of his hat in the presence of ladies, or the man who brushed his teeth with motor oil. Simply not done. Often it is only the context that lets us know why. "His teeth glistened so agreeably, he must have brushed his teeth with motor oil."

Sometimes, the vacation that metaphor takes from normality is set up by the poet himself, who reuses some earlier lines. Homer is fond of this trick. In the *Iliad* he tells us how a hurled spear, missing its mark, struck the ground: ". . . it was buried in the earth, and the butt of the weapon quivered; then mighty Ares took away its force." Our own eyes have no doubt verified this effect. But at another time the implement does not miss: "The spear was fixed in his heart, which in its palpitation made the butt of the weapon, also, quiver; then mighty Ares took away its force." G. S. Kirk, who cites this passage, does not approve, calling the image "artistically rather absurd," but we have read Kafka by now and may love the reversal of cause and effect. On another occasion, when so impaled by the pitiless bronze, the victim's eyes fall out. Stricken warriors regularly fall from the "well-wrought chariot" and their horses scatter. The death of combatants in movie Westerns is similarly standardized as they solemnly clutch their chests and slowly topple from stagecoach or rooftop to the mattress below. Then suddenly, Homer will have one of the slain fall headfirst into some soft sand so his legs and feet show and the horses trample over them. If this happened in the movies, it would be regarded as a form of slapstick, a visual joke, and very funny. Image B becomes a metaphor for image A.

Comparisons are commonly literal. "George is taller than Paul." "George is as easily riled as Steve." "Her hand was like ice"; that is: both were cold. But look what can happen when a bit of warmth is applied. "Her hand was like ice and melted in mine." Simile signals—words like *like* and *as* and *as if*—can themselves be used metaphorically. "His words were like cannon shots and scattered the populace." When Aristotle analyzes imagery he does so in the same way he translates Greek sentences for the syllogism. "Her hand was a member of the class of icy things." "Icy things are included in the class of things that melt." Therefore, "Her hand was a member of the class of things that melt." The predicate must always be the name of a class.

What a metaphor does, I think, is make a model; it makes a model the way the sciences often do; its construction resembles the pattern so ably outlined by Stephen Toulmin in his little book *The Philosophy of Science*. Let us begin with some examples from that arena.

Imagine a lone and leafy tree in the middle of a glade. The bright sun beats down upon it the way the Sungod hammered the netted fish. Beneath the tree, however, there is a cool pool of shade, the silhouette of the oak whose height seems so striking we grow curious about it. But unless a little bird tells us, we can only guess how tall it's grown. Can Odysseus, the wise and crafty one, help us out? Under his direction we gather a lot of empirical data, particularly the length of the silhouette. That shadow suggests to us that if we thought of the sun's rays as straight lines, as corpuscular beams, we might be able to understand our phenomenon in terms of Euclidean geometry, for we now have, to assist us, our disheveled empirical data on the one hand, and an abstract system of great power, coherence, and rationality on the other. The trick is to get the data into the demonstrator, which the principle of the rectilinear propagation of light will do for us. It was once taken to be a law, but it is now understood more commonly as a rule of representation.

If the ground contains the length of the tree's shadow, seen as a line, and the path of the light another, then a measure of the angle of its fall will allow us to construct a triangle whose perpendicular will be the height of the tree. What we must remember is that it was Euclid who gave us this knowledge, for we know quite a lot about right triangles, and so much less about the heights of trees. Our perceptions have been made to work within a system; they are now related to one another in a significant way; and the mind has made of the tree and its shadow in the glade an abstraction—a model—and if experience counts for anything, we know that models are always far prettier than the clothes they wear.

Let us move for a moment to another example. When Galileo presented the formula "distance equals velocity times the time," he performed a similar model-making action, for the law emerges from a diagram. On an x-axis, he marked out the velocity of his object on a unitary scale, and on a y-axis he did the same for time. These he saw as the sides of a rectangle whose area he could calculate very simply. Again, by representing data as lengths of a line, measured visual observations could be squeezed into Euclid. Let a point be an object, let the point's moving path be a line, its movement that line's length. Does the rectangle formed resemble its phenomena? Not in the least, apparently.

Suppose the world were a model. It would embody the Forms but would not resemble them. Its mimesis would be beyond copy in its subtlety. Its structure would be quantitatively graspable by the mind, its appearance appreciated mostly by the senses.

What happens when a model swallows another model? The same thing that occurs when one metaphor engulfs another. If Galileo made the practice and observations of kinetics into the science of mechanics, Descartes elevated everything by transforming geometry into algebra, and with that amazing move making calculus possible. Now, in what ways do metaphors manage similar operations?

One of the most mesmerizing though repellent images in the *Odyssey* occurs after Odysseus has slain the suitors like baby seals. The women who serviced Penelope's beaux, while they were waiting to find the favor of his wife are made to scrub the bloody gut-strewn halls and carry corpses out into the courtyard to prop them against the colonnade the way, in our West, bandits were propped on boards to have their lifeless faces photographed. The earthen floors were scraped clean with spades by the herdsman of Telemachus, and the dirt taken outside by the same condemned women, who were then herded into a cul-de-sac and hanged in a line—on a line—by this son and heir of our hero.

> . . . taking a cable used on a dark-prowed ship
> he coiled it over the roundhouse, lashed it fast to a tall column,
> hoisting it up so high no toes could touch the ground.
> Then, as doves or thrushes beating their spread wings

against some snare rigged up in thickets—flying in
for a cozy nest but a grisly bed receives them—
so the women's heads were trapped in a line,
nooses yanking their necks up, one by one
so all might die a pitiful, ghastly death . . .
they kicked up heels for a little—not for long.

That last pause before "not for long" has been much admired.

What is crucial to the success of this Homeric image is its implicit time line. Here is a case where the scope of a metaphor must extend to an elapsed text, not merely to the passages that shall come after. If we start the import of the conceit at the moment it appears in its verses, then it will not seem accurate or appropriate to the women's fate, because these are victims of Telemachus's rage and are dragged into the snare, driven there; they have not innocently fluttered into this hangman's hands. After they had scrubbed blood from furniture and walls, and carried corpses to a courtyard, they were not expecting the gift of a cozy thicket-protected nest. Nor, for that matter, were these nooses rigged in advance of their arrival. But long before, in the beginning of this adventure, they had flown into the arms of the suitors and enjoyed there much petting and great favor. And one can readily imagine how often Telemachus had pondered their punishment, possibly planning—among others—just this painful payback. In short, the scope of this metaphor extends for the length of the ladies' stay at the palace, and must do so or it will not work for a careful listener. To give it sense, we must carry the idea of innocence back to a time when there was some—when the arms of the suitors seemed safe.

However, we cannot place so much emphasis upon the duration of an image's operation as to ignore the impact of its initial appearance. The suitors were the first snare, the nooses the last. They were not lured there by Telemachus. Rather, like the hunter, he will enjoy the catch. As for an image's duration, this one has a distinguished history, for Sophocles will pick it up. In Amelie Rorty's version:

Metaphor

Wonders are many, and none is more wonderful than man . . .
In the meshes of his woven nets, cunning of mind, ingenious
   man . . .
He snares the lighthearted birds and the tribes of savage
   beasts . . .

These women were, first of all then, little birds. The image says that, like little birds, they sought safety. The thickets looked good to them precisely because they would not look good to others. In innocence they entered. Maids, servants, they were certainly without significant strength and sought protection. But were they innocent after all? Did not a dozen go "tramping to their shame, thumbing their noses at me, at the queen herself!" as the vengeful old nurse says, who tattles on them to Telemachus. Then they are strung up on a line like wash—but now I have carried this image cluster like a bunch of grapes, awaiting the critic's trampling, into another vintage, and its ending, another age.

Clearly our focus word is *bird* and its object the women. As the women undergo their metamorphosis, however, their nature will select from that collection of properties and behaviors that the birds possess only those which best suit their circumstances, for they are birds in the act of seeking such shelter as the shrub offers them, and that they do other things as well will be ruled out. In short, the metamorphosis will be partial. So we see them fluttering and twittering and hopping about until, suddenly, they are enmeshed, bound, their necks snapped, slain. The thicket is not a thicket either. It has become a net and nettled trap. Telemachus is now a hunter, his prey within a fowler's net, enacting a less arduous, more comfortable transformation. He has only to put on his predator's purpose.

These three operations—on doves, a thicket, the trapper—to women, ropes, and a bloodthirsty man—occur simultaneously in the reader, and without any recognizable work either, so that a system of similarities will have been picked out and many differences discarded in order to achieve a feeling, as well as an understanding and a rendering, of the scene. The factual content of this image is considerable, since Telemachus may well have hunted so himself. A modern sensibility may find the massacre pitiful (the text suggests it), and the famous pause—"they kicked up heels for a little—not for long"—cruel, but there is no pity in this passage, only triumph and the exultant glory of revenge. "How it would have thrilled your heart to see him," the old nurse says to Penelope when she's hastened to bear her the news of Odysseus's return and the slaughter of the suitors—"spattered with bloody filth, a lion with his kill!" Sentimentality is not seemly in a hero or a queen. After the carnage, when Odysseus purifies the palace, he does so to further rid himself of his enemies, and such stench or pollution as they might have left, not to cleanse himself of any guilt. Guilt has no harbor in a hero's heart.

I can only pause here a moment to note how images interconnect—one part of the text with another, one text with another—sometimes over great distances of time and subject matter. In our era, kicking up one's heels would suggest a return to the original frolic of the women. Another minor example would be the recurrent little twitch that takes place as life leaves its body, as though waving good-bye: the fish who flop about on the sand until sunburned, the spear that shivers in the earth and in the warrior's chest, the feet of the hanged women that bob about for a moment as leaves rattle in an errant breeze.

Images, like the sentences that contain them, possess—or should possess—a factual core in the form of a comparison: both women and doves are captured and killed; both leeches and suitors drain life-giving resources; both day and life have beginnings, middles, ends; and both the glowing brand in the following passage, and Odysseus in the protective bed of boughs and limbs he finds after his shipwreck, are conserving and saving their vital energies.

> As a man will bury his glowing brand in black ashes,
> off on a lonely farmstead, no neighbors near,
> to keep a spark alive—no need to kindle fire

from somewhere else—so great Odysseus buried
himself in leaves and Athena showered sleep
upon his eyes . . . sleep in a swift wave
delivering him from all his pains and labors,
blessed sleep that sealed his eyes at last.

Every metaphor, as I've said, will violate some fundamental canon of custom, some accepted fact of life or a rule of grammatical regulations that will signal to the reader its presence. Metaphors will create interactive models made of the intermingling of meanings during which the same term will alternately serve as object or as lens, as the field of disorganized data, and as the new ordering system. Odysseus's action (finding a sheltered place to rest after an arduous adventure) is to be interpreted in terms of an equally common practice (keeping a flame alive in the ashes of a hearth or cooking pit). Homer will carefully explain why one must do this: sometimes one is without a neighbor from whom a spark, like a quarter for the phone, may be borrowed.

As the glowing brand must be buried in nurturing ash, so must the weary body of Odysseus find rest and protection beneath the trees, their boughs and leaves. Another ratio. Another reason for Aristotle to approve of Homer. When Athena showered sleep upon our hero's eyes (according to Fagles), she would wash his weariness away, for showers have a pleasant reputation for cooling, restoring, reinvigorating. Sleep is to the tired body what showers are to the thirsty earth. More proportions. Another model. More approval. ". . . blessed sleep that sealed his eyes at last . . ." Fagles has it. "A slumber did my spirit seal . . ." Wordsworth put it. "Turn the key deftly in the oiled wards, / And seal the hushed Casket of my Soul . . ." Keats begs. When my eyes or my lips are sealed, it is so that no one else will know, through look or speech, the contents of my mind, but when sleep seals them, it is so that *I* shall not know, for a while, what *I* know.

Metaphors will possess scope and depth; they will be condensed or expansive; and they will exhibit those qualities of perception, emotion, thought, energy, and imagination that every conscious-ness enjoys when it is fully functioning. They will sense something; they will feel something; they will think something; they will want something; and they may imagine almost anything. They will see the snare that's been rigged in the thicket and that way see the women cornered, see them wave their futile arms and cry out; they will feel how deserving the women's fair necks are to have a noose around them, to have these bodies rise a bit past tiptoe because their previ-ous behavior has earned them their present deadly suspension; met-aphors will state the women's execution as plainly as a judgment, as matter-of-factly, as coolly as a morning dip; they will say so with a rhythm hard and measured as a march, full of drive and satisfaction; and they will unite these qualities to imagine how life, in a twitch, in a pause between words, departs the strangled birds . . . departs the shivering spear . . . departs the feet that once felt the reassuring earth . . . feet whose heels kick up as they may have also done when they were alive and lascivious in the arms of the enemy. All this can be found in that little pause, that moment of surprise that the end has come . . . just like the pause. . . . . that ends this series of talks.

Theoretics

LUST

My desires were never allowed to reach the lust level. That doesn't mean I don't know what lust is, for lust is an essential ingredient in life. Like most of the vices, lust is fundamental and necessary. Deep down it is a virtue, whereas the virtues themselves are surrounded by vices as boxers are by their sycophantic sponging entourages. This is why people with lots of "faults" are often loved, and why saints are despised while they live, frequently tortured to death, and admired only after they have expired.

Just as there are the greater and the lesser Antilles, so there are greater and lesser virtues. Neatness is one of the latter, and a handy example. The neat person believes that there is a place for every-thing and that everything should be in its place. The neat person is an enemy of history, erasing evidence of every party, pretending nothing happened—especially lust. Few things are sexier or more inviting than a rumpled bed. Neat people are fascists of the mop and bucket, the tight sheet, the silver chest. They never use the good dishes. They like the way it was yesterday. The order that neat people prefer is not creative; it is stifling. We need neat people, but only a few at a time. To pick up after picnickers in parks.

Yes, I'm afraid we need some neatness—to keep us from chaos. So long as neatness is not a cloak for custom. So long as neatness is not a nanny for the status quo. There is nothing neat about lust. Lust hates regulatory agencies. And when our children describe a situation as *neat*—a word they use, like *cool,* with infantile approval—they mean "easy," "that's a problem solved." Meanwhile, the disorder of their rooms keeps parents from discovering anything but confusion when they pry.

Truthful people are a big pain. That is their aim in life: to be a big pain. Because we naturally love lies. Lies are more fun, far pleasanter to hear, for the most part, and certainly more effective. In fact, they are called for. Parents pretend they want to know whether Gertie is screwing in the parlor and whether Peter is smoking pot in the barn. And if the kids tell the truth, as they are beseeched to do, they will be ragged and snagged and grounded unmercifully. So the kids learn. Lying promotes freedom. Lying guards privacy. Lying saves lives and wins elections. It describes things as they ought to be. Of course, we need to be truthful, but only on occasion.

Lying is a vice that succeeds, as so many other vices do, only in an environment of truthfulness. Remember the paradox: Cretans are liars, the Cretan swore. And retell to yourself the fable about the boy who cried, "Wolf . . . wolf . . ." one too many times. Vices need virtues and vice versa.

I am speaking, of course, about the little lies of daily life, not the big lies of priests and politicians, those who want to fix things and those who want things fixed. People who publically complain of sin so often privately enjoy it. Lutherans, for instance, don't like lust. Catholics and Calvinists are both against it. Mormons allow us several wives but it's not on account of lust. Baptists are not on lust's side. If you measure a man by the quality of his enemies, Casanova figures well.

The trouble with temperate people is that they are rarely temperate. All the temperance societies I know promote abstinence. "Nothing too much yet everything a little bit" is not their motto. No. *Nothing* is the operative word. "Masturbation in moderation" is not their motto. A truly temperate person doesn't play golf every day. A truly temperate person doesn't run more than a block a week. A temperate reader won't read all of Austen or a lot of Balzac. Temperate persons eat sensibly, which means they never diet. But those whose profession is temperance only rail against sex and alcohol, drugs and atheism. Professionally temperate people are cranks. Atheism they ought to like. Atheists admire the word *nothing*. But they probably don't admire lust much. Not a single favorable vote from the Methodists. Pietists—nix.

Piety is a nasty little virtue. Reverence for Pa the father, Ra the god, and hurrah the flag. Piety is respect for power and privilege, ancestors and the dead-and-gone deities. There is nothing in the world worth worship.

Adultery, on the other hand, cannot be too frequently practiced. If adultery were understood to be a virtue, and committed whenever opportunity offered, then we'd soon be unsure whose kid was whose, the hierarchical character of families would be disrupted, and the succession of paternal property would not succeed. Lust would be at last separated from the coarse and common activity of begetting. Going to bed with one person for the rest of your life? You've got to be kidding. Kidding . . . yes, kidding is the problem.

So what about lust? Let's compare it with gluttony. That will get us off to a good start. Satisfied lust isn't fattening. Satisfied lust may mean two people are happy. "It's the restiest thing thar are," Granddad used to say. It improves the skin, all that blood rising to the top like cream. It detenses the limbs so that all one's aches feel far away and in the past. Common courtship costs. You take one another to dinner, gluttonize, pay up, the heart burns. But lust is easily relieved without any outlay. You can easily eat too much, grow round as the earth, break wind, ache, but there is no penalty for coming twice. Sexual satisfaction raises self-esteem, produces a healthy languor, and leads to a happy life.

Sometimes sexual insecurity, rage, or various repressions masquerade as lust, but brutality and runaway promiscuity are not signs of an overpowering appetite, for appetites can be at least momentarily assuaged; rather such rampages are indications of sexual weakness, not strength. The glutton eats past satiation and should be carefully distinguished from the connoisseur, whose concern is in quality, not amount.

Traditionally, lust has had a touch of greed's indifference to its object, since it is, of course, the sexual impulse dialed up . . . and in its grip one is alert and on the prowl; one feels rapaciously alive, paying loving attention to one's friends and companions and anyone else who may relieve the itch. There are always those undiscovered chests, those untouched tummies, the straits of paradise.

Why would one want to put a stop to such a healthy high-powered connection to life?

There are practical reasons: babies, diseases, babies. But these problems can be readily solved. If we had the will for it. There are other things at stake: patrimony, power, possession, pride. Anyway, it isn't lust that is really being proscribed. The aim of lust's enemies is to deny lust its satisfactions in the hope that more governable behavior will replace it. Lust is thereby exacerbated, strengthened, multiplied.

Let's go back to the beginning.

God walks in the Garden to enjoy the cool of the evening. God makes clothes for Eve and Adam. God savors Noah's sacrifice. The smoke of a good goat. He has to descend from heaven to check out the Tower of Babel that is rising toward Him and would reach Him if He'd just wait. He is His own investigative team looking into the alleged criminality of the citizens of Sodom; however—hey, what's going on?—He has permitted the Snake to Inhabit Paradise. Moreover, He misrepresents the consequences to Adam and Eve of eating the fruit of the tree of knowledge. He must be fearful that Adam and Eve will become gods like Himself. I think He envies their nobility. After all, isn't He the Ancient of Days?

The sinful simply can't take this stuff seriously. Nor should they, for sin is virtue in the face of such pranks played against reason and nature's hungers. In the face of nonsense it is appropriate to giggle.

Decorum has its designs on everybody. It will chastise us, and charge us with flippancy. Perhaps we should take seriously ideas that have helped millions murder one another. Is it the numbers that should earn our respect?

God has one law, never mind how many the lawyers manage: obedience to the commands of God. That's why the laws must be accounted equal. For the same reason that Zeus cuts the ripe round people in half, according to Aristophanes in Plato's *Symposium*— though their roundness was perfection; and God scatters the language of Babylon hither and yon, destroying that unity along with its tower; God also punishes Adam and Eve for not doing what they were told. Hubris is at the root of it. Man may have been made in God's image, but he is only a faint and distorted reflection. He dare not presume to rival his Father and get to know what is going on.

What sort of knowledge of good, and what sort of knowledge of evil, results from eating the forbidden fruit? Is it knowledge by acquaintance, so that suddenly Adam and Eve lust after each other and go to it in the bushes? Is it knowledge by description— equivalent to reading a self-help book on how things are done? Is the knowledge basically, as some think, of practical matters: the way God's creation works, and how Adam and Eve can now command its laws; was it a skill acquired, like learning French, a gift for music and the lyre? Or is it more narrowly the inexperience of innocence destroyed by disobedience, and disobedience punished by shame, work, and death? The Garden was the good life. It sheltered the bliss of ignorance. Adam and Eve didn't know that either, although their subsequent exile—their sojourn in an evil world—is a condition whose character they now know well.

It was the juice. They bit into the fruit, and, as Rainer Maria Rilke wrote, "life and death entered their mouths." They tasted culmination. They ate pulp, the flesh that surrounds seeds. The fruit hid inside its succulent skin—an apple, a pear, or a peach. Or for the sake of resemblance, a fig. They awoke within these sensations. Lust sang inside them like a bird. And they saw they were naked.

The serpent, or jinn of the tree, never struck me as any more than an ordinary local imp. The devil dwells in this story's interpreters. Their motives, one and all, were malignant. It is the Saint Pauls of this world who give lust a bad name. Sexual feelings and their consequence recapitulate the fall and pass sin on, as miasmas were passed, as feuds were refueled, from generation to generation. The act of making more men and women makes the men and women genetically wicked. This doctrine creates a world of customers needing to be saved. Lust is thus the core feeling that inhabits all wrongdoing, because sex is its symbol.

Over time, people were encouraged to forget that disobedience was the original sin (Satan's *non serviam*) and to believe that sex was after all the evil agent. Adam and Eve were as little children romping around the plastic pool until some mom or pop began to make them put on bras and panties. And the apple got blamed for inviting its bite. Not the pear. Not the peach. Not the grape. Not the fig that furnished its leaf. But there were those—there always are—who argued that the tree was a vine, and that the serpent offered Adam a glass of wine.

Well, it was the juice.

There is no need to dignify this malicious little tale with any further interpretation. It simply became a useful moment for those seeking power to reinforce their views. Encased in a sacred text, guarded by a pampered priesthood, its allegorized message became central to Christendom's traducement of our sexual lives. Lust, which ought to be the feeling of life itself; erection and reception, which ought to be creative signs in whose physical exemplification pure delight is taken; the closeness passion insists on, whose loving intimacy of touch ought to yield the reassurance of one's acceptance; the ecstasy of release and its resulting relaxation, which should yield a sense of security and peace and serene renewal: all these gifts of nature to us were—not only by organized religions, but through cultural policies both social and political, and by the pandering of profiteers and traders—made to blush, to seem evil, low, and nasty, at worst like our fecal necessities—though obeyed, never displayed, praised, discussed.

"In their zeal," Rilke writes of believers in "The Young Workman's Letter,"

> they do not hesitate to make this life, which should be an object of desire and trust for us, bad and worthless—and so they hand over the earth more and more to those who are ready to gain at least temporary and quickly won profit from it, vain and suspect as it is, and no good for anything better.

Not only do these liars promise to rescue our souls from the ground where our bodies rot, they tell us our human nature and all the signs of life in our species have put us there, into the dirt we deserve. So if we give up life here, we may later have it given back to us up there. How stupid we must be to believe in that promise; to accept the honors afforded chastity, for instance, that prolonged and perverse denial of our present existence; to reject this world for a nonexistent other.

Of course, when lust must go about in black clothes and seek other outlets for its energies, in power and privilege mostly, or ally itself with pain and pursue its infliction, or substitute shopping or golf for its goals, growing moist only at the mention of money, getting hard at the prospect of rape or war, then lust will be said to be "Lust," one of the seven deadly sins, to be regarded with loathing and fear; then lust will be said to be selfish and interested in its own satisfactions; sexual organs will be places where favors are sold and money is made, not where joy is experienced; then lust will have to seek permission for its satisfaction by obtaining a license to drive from the state, permission from the Church to mate, and approval from family, friends, and credit card companies, but only to make babies and go into long-term debt.

Lust seeks another; lust is inherently social. Frustrated, arousals unanswered, the masturbator is sad and alone. Your own hand is not a fun date.

The lustful gaze—that great look that says, "I want it, it will please me, I shall please it in return, we shall merge more usefully than vehicles on the highway, we shall experience the interiors of one another, we shall burn like painless fires"—is thus not meant for men or women alone, and not perversely for vacuum cleaners or sheep, but for the sensuous appearance and shape of things, for the taste of fruit, the feel of silk and leather, for songs in another's throat, for a horse in stride, and strong rich lines of verse.

Lust is present in any desire that has a strong sensuous component, because lust is provoked by form and color, and moves closer for odors to get in on the action, and then for taste and touch to fulfill it, for it's not orgasm lust lusts for, but the juice of the orange squelching between the teeth, the touch of an inner thigh that transforms the palm, the smell of stew in a winter pot, snowflakes melting on glowing cheeks, wine rinsed meditatively in the mouth, the sound of "ah!" after a long indrawn breath.

To realize one is naked, rather than just one of the other girls and boys in the plastic pool, is what kind of knowledge? Is it knowledge of good and evil, or is it awareness of opinions fabricated by a society that has its reasons for lying and pretending and faking it? Adam and Eve saw they were naked; they saw they were naked because they saw, at the same time, that nakedness was wrong; they saw it was wrong because the tree of knowledge was planted and cultivated by a Santa Claus moonlighting for the Salvation Army.

Certain of our needs have a small range of satisfactory solutions: for thirst, water is the first and last solution; everything else we might drink—pop, juice, Scotch, soup—will be useful only because of the water it contains. For thirst, water is reality. No religion rules out water, only claims it for rituals. Hunger, on the other hand, can be satisfied in a thousand ways, so many of them can be safely forbidden.

Those who dominate the value choices in our societies, whether they represent business, military, state, or church, always try to regulate diet, clothing, off-duty activity, and sex. Eat veg; wear black;

pray while kneeling and making the right signs; take some days off; choose a chosen bride; don't dance; don't hum; don't fuck from behind; don't suck anything, handle yourself, or suck another self; don't enjoy; don't smear fluids; don't shout or move about a lot.

Hide her behind veils, voluminous folds, body paint, high walls, patriarchal laws; cut her clit, or her hair; slit her nose; trade for cows—these are sins—not a nipple reaching its full height in another mouth. Not baby time down south. Burn her alive along with the furniture. Bury her in your tomb, you stiff. Slice her heart out with a sliver of stone. Sliding out and in is just plain nice when it's done because it is just plain nice. Hey, at my wedding car, don't throw the rice.

> You think it horrible that lust and rage
> Should dance attendance upon my old age;
> They were not such a plague when I was young;
> What else have I to spur me into song?

Old man Yeats knew what was true. If you have no anger at this world, anger at its willful stupidities, its grim indifference, its real sins: its murdering hordes, its smug myths, exploitive habits, its catastrophic wastes, the smile on its hyena hungry face, its jackal tastes, then you belong to it, and are one of its apes—though animals should not be so disgraced as to be put in any simile with man.

Old age ought to know. Death will soon enough come to its rescue. Till the knowing ends, all that was wasted and wronged in youth—through ignorance, haste, competition, bad belief—all that was bored by middle age into one long snooze, has borne its juiceless fruit, and is now known for what it is: nothing has been righted here. Yet if desire can be kept from contamination, if it can be aimed, as one's fingertip, at the root's place, if it is not harnessed to the horses of dismal domination, but is allowed to be itself and realize life, then the flutter of an eyelash on a cheek will assume its proper importance; Wall Street may crash and the gods of money be smelted back into the sordid earths they came from; yet, unfazed, our heads will rest at least on one another, a fall sun will shine on the sheets, your nipple shall enter my ear like a bee seeking in a bloom a place to sleep; life shall run through us both renewed; we shall feel longing, lust for one another; we shall share rage for the world.

NARRATIVE SENTENCES

Let us begin with an example from Ford Madox Ford's *The Fifth Queen,* always a good source of sentences of every kind. Upon the opening of the novel we meet Magister Nicholas Udall, a teacher, who is hungry, cold, and drenched.

[1]
Ford Madox Ford. From *The Fifth Queen*
(Vanguard 1963 p.12 1908).

He stood in the mud: long, thin, brown in his doctor's gown of fur, with his black flapped cap that buttoned well under his chin and let out his brown, lean, shaven and humorous face like a woodpecker's peering out of a hole in a tree.

He stood   in the mud:
                                              long,
                        1   thin,
                                              brown
                                         in his doctor's gown   of fur,

with his black flapped cap that buttoned well under his chin
    and

let out	his brown,
	lean,
2	shaven
	and
	humorous face

like a woodpecker's peering
out of a hole   3   in a tree.

There are many things to observe about this early moment in the text. The lane in which Magister Udall is standing, wondering where to go to get dry, have a bite, and enjoy a wench, is suckafoot muddy. "He stood in the mud" puts him there quite firmly, but he is not unventuresome as a stick-in-the-mud would be. After the colon, there is what is commonly called a description—the man at this juncture—though not a complete or even extensive picture, for oncoming passages add that he has two books beneath his arms, and that they "poked out his gown on either side." Moreover ". . . the bitter cold pinched his finger ends as if they had been caught in a door." So there he is—with his learning and his loins—in a sack of wet fur.

The sentence is divided into two roughly equivalent parts (plus a metaphorical addendum), each announced by the verb phrases *he stood* and *let out*. Each contains a list of attributes that ends in a long mouth-shaping line. The most important word is possibly the preposition *in*. The context tells us that the magister is in doubt, and then that he is in the mud, in his doctor's gown, and in his black flapped cap. Not only is he inside, so are his books, warily peeking out. The repetitions of *out* only increase the importance of being "in"—inside, out of the elements, in an inn (if we may be permitted the pun), quaffing some mead, eyeing a maid. Once within he may look out at the weather as he now peeks out from his fur and his cap.

Clearly this sentence is part of a story and contributes to it, but what is the point of suggesting that it contains incipient narrative elements, especially when it possesses obviously contrary qualities? Narrative runs from its words, and it does so in two directions: first, it leaves the word for the actions and events the words, it believes, are there to designate; second, it looks forward to the words (and events) that are about to arrive. It does not like to dally over a meal; it bolts its food: salad only delays the steak that may itself be valued principally because its final swallow signals the onset of dessert. In music one would say narrative was "voice-led." Listen, however, to this masterful prose speak its piece: the magister stood in the mud, yes—"brown in his doctor's gown," "with his black flapped cap that," or should we revel in the movement of the vowels: 'on' 'in' 'ow' until the 'o's end in 'oc' and 'or' to be softly closed by 'ur.' "He stood in the mud: long, thin, brown, in his doctor's gown of fur." Hurrying on—is anything happening?—to the second *brown,* we read of "his brown, lean, shaven and humorous face," that has been "let out" like you let out your dog, or . . . And at this point we can stop to admire the woodpecker image at our place before the hole in the tree.

It is a sentence shaped and sounded, its words selected not merely to get the magister's boots muddy, or be obedient to syntax, but to have its own singular integrity, its own metaphored and modulated, its own rhyming, formally balanced, brown leather binding. Its plot is its own performance. Yet it is one of many like it in its paragraph, upon its page, well within its fiction. Just another little stroke of genius.

Prose cannot describe without beginning to narrate. Unlike events which succeed one another when we read (and only when we read, for the reader is the mover), features, properties, conditions stay awhile to be named one at a time as though the round faced and footed alarm clock were its ticks. We are aware that one tick does not cause another, that they are independently produced, but the word *tick* does cause the *tock* to appear, just as *brown* and *gown* become related, and, in balanced prose, one clause calls for its companion.

[2]

Sir Walter Scott. From *Waverly* (1814).

Waverly found Miss Bradwardine presiding over the teas and coffee, the table loaded with warm bread, both of flour, oatmeal, and barley-meal, in the shape of loaves, cakes, biscuits, and other varieties, together with eggs, reindeer ham, mutton and beef ditto, smoked salmon, marmalade, and all other delicacies which induced even Johnson himself to extol the luxury of a Scotch breakfast above that of all other countries.

the table loaded with warm bread,

                        both of flour,
                        oatmeal,
                        and barley-meal
1   in the shape of loaves,
                                                        cakes,
                                                        biscuits,
                                    and other   varieties

        together with eggs,
                    reindeer ham,
                    mutton
2   and   beef ditto,
                    smoked salmon,
                    marmalade,

                            and all other   delicacies

We cannot always find perfection, so we shouldn't linger over third-grade grammatical errors such as giving to *both* three choices (a vulgarity the dictionary reluctantly admits), or the awkward juxtaposition of *oatmeal* and *barley-meal*, or the foolish arrival of *marmalade* at the end of a list containing *beef, ham,* and *salmon.* We can be confident that our hostess, Miss Bradwardine, has not randomly belabored her table, but has placed the marmalade nearby the breads, where it belongs; nor has she placed crocks of flour there to identify ingredients, though poor Scott has—why not yeast and baking powder, or perhaps a rolling pin? I'm being a bit unfair to make a point: the contents of the table are spread out before Waverly, but for Scott the same situation requires a narration of nouns, ordered like events with a forcible forward thrust, and containing closure. Phrases like "and other varieties," and "all other delicacies . . ." trail off lamely, the last in an allusion to Dr. Johnson's well-known aversion to the Scots.

Rhythm is the principle propulsive agent, but sound patterns also serve to bind words together, to make us feel that *gown* is oddly the cause of *brown,* so that *brown* is no surprise. Just to prove I do not have it in for Sir Walter in particular, here is an example of what not to do from the aforequoted Ford:

[3]
Ford Madox Ford. From The Fifth Queen.

She wore a long dress of red velvet, worked around the breast-lines with little silver anchors and hearts, and her hood was of black lawn and fell near her hips behind.

Behind is a disaster, both in meaning, position, and reflexivity (if Scott can *both* it so may I), and grows worse as the years pass and usage puts even more behind in *behind.* At the end of a phrase, a clause, a sentence, a paragraph, a scene, a story, the reader needs to feel she has arrived, or at least that she is about to transfer immediately from train to bus or car. These ends, in short, may be modest and not sound the last trump, but an end is an end is an end. Notice that one more *end* than the three *ends* used already would be one *end* too many, a rule which also holds for the rose.

In a recent essay, I distinguished story and storytelling from fiction and its narration, an arbitrary and somewhat prejudical bit of name-calling, perhaps, although the distinction named is not. Stories exist outside any particular medium and can be filmed or played or told or inscribed. Moreover, there may be multiple versions, siblings, if you like. Copyright might get in the way; otherwise the story of Mrs. Wiggs and the Cabbage Patch could reappear as "Bela Lugosi and the Nightshade Bed." Or, in my version of Mrs. Wiggs's garden problem, I speak on behalf of the cabbages, and begin my recitation in the mournful middle of things, working forward and then back, back and then forward, leaf before leaf after leaf.

However, if I wish to change the three magic rings that motivate some fables into three gifted Frisbees, I shall have to retain the number three, and the Frisbees will have to perform quite analogous functions—do as the rings did—otherwise we won't be able to claim it as a version. I thought that at least six characteristics of the ur-tale would have to be retained if identity were to be claimed: (1) scale—the temporal size and sense of the events that make up the fresh version would have to harmonize with those of the original; (2) the causal or productive connections between those events would need to be parallel; (3) all patterns and repetitions, since they are so fundamental for form, must find the same place and role in both; (4) the aim or direction of the stories must mesh; (5) their principal meanings as well as the significance of those meanings would have to jibe; (6) and lastly, the justification for the existence of both tales as well as their telling need to coincide, or, in terms popular with earlier critics, the moral . . . the wisdom . . . the warning that attaches to each cannot diverge. Perhaps I should have added a shared rhythm to my list of essentials.

[1]

In long passages, even grotesqueries of scale can be disguised, but in a single sentence such ill-assorted company becomes glaringly evident.

Narrative Sentences

[4]

The dam broke, and on the very next day so did the elastic on my bat-a-ball paddle.

[2]

The causal or productive connections of the artful sentence should not be left to logical or grammatical form alone. As in the example just used, *and* is sometimes consequential. "The dam broke, and" is politely propellant.

[5a]

The dam broke, broke the bridge in half, halved the city hall on party lines, and lined all our roads with tarps on top of the drowned.

[3]

The patterns in a sentence like this seem a bit playful at first, so that, in addition to the expectations raised by "broke, broke" and "half, halved" a little lightness can be looked forward to, an assumption dashed by the rudeness of "tarps on top of the drowned." We can ease that somewhat.

[5b]

The dam broke, broke the bridge in half, halved the city hall along party lines, and lined all our roads with tarpaulins to cover the drowned.
Or "with tarpaulins of a size sufficient to conceal the drowned." We are aware that every word counts, but we rarely act as if that were so. Well, the shadow cast by the sentence knows.

[4]

The drowned are indeed the end of the sentence. Like water through the burst dam, it has been rushing in that direction.

But we can change the ending in a few words. ". . . with tarpaulins of a size sufficient to conceal the drowned from relatives now guiltily aware of what their vote against repairing the dam had cost." This is the story:

[5c]

When the vote was lost the damage was done, since the dam soon broke, broke the bridge in half, halved the city hall along party lines, and lined all our roads with tarpaulins of a size sufficient to conceal the drowned from relatives now guiltily aware of what their vote against repairing the dam had cost: wet basements, waterlogged cars, and missing dogs.

[5]

Quite similar things can be said about meaning as are said about story. I—not Ford—could have written: "Magister Udall's feet were planted in the mire; he was tall, not 'long,' skinny, not 'thin,' and generally furzy." To a story, and for most ordinary usage, these changes will not matter, because stories are as softly coarse as oatmeal, and in a story Magister Udall's stature can resemble any tall thin guy's; okay, he's thin, he's tall, he's fur coated; so what next? Get on with it. But to a fiction—an artful fiction—it should matter.

Here is a sentence, with its introduction, that can serve as an emblem for the art.

[6]

D. H. Lawrence. From *Sea and Sardinia* (1921).

"Our bus-mate came and told us we were to sit in the bus till the post-work was done, then we should be driven to the hotel where we could eat, and then he would accompany us on the town omnibus to the boat. We need not be on board till eight o'clock; and now it was something after five.

So we sat still while the bus rushed and the road curved and the view of the weird, land-locked harbour changed, though the bare masts of ships in a bunch still pricked the upper glow, and the steamer lay away out, as if wrecked on a sandbank, and dark, mysterious land with bunchy hills circled round, dark blue and wintry in a golden after-light, while the great, shallow-seeming bay of water shone like a mirror."

We, readers as viewers, sit in our seats. It is the bus that moves, and so, most immediately, does the view, but clauses arrive from places farther off: the bare masts of ships, the steamer that seems to have run aground, the circle of land that defines the bay; and they are as fixed in the scene as we are in our vehicle, while what we both frame acts as a mirror that holds its own motion motionless—the momentary pause of a twilight sky.

Kafka is plain as pie. His prose is as straightforward as a spear. It is the significance of the story, the meaning of the meaning, that both alludes and eludes us.

Difficult texts are rarely hard to read; they are hard to understand. This—may we call it a paragraph?—from Samuel Beckett's *Worstward Ho* can be hard to get a grip on:

[7]
Samuel Beckett. From *Worstward Ho,* (1983).

"Say a body. Where none. No mind. Where none. That at least. A place. Where none. For the body. To be in. Move in. Out of. Back into. No. No out. No back. Only in. Stay in. On in. Still."
But it is not because we don't know the words *say* or *place* or *move*. It's not a case of, "Strike the crossjack, we've struck a swarm of desperate Hesperioidea."

Similarly, the literal sense of a story—its "gist"—can be so evident its presence is never felt. Meanwhile, the significance hides. Parables are supposed to be plain to the ear and dark to every mind but an adept's. In Kafka's *Metamorphosis* there is a deadly tug-of-war between Gregor and his sister, Grete, for dominance, growth, and freedom. The passages that describe Grete feeding the family's resident bug with table scraps are easy enough to read; the meaning is clear, as is Gregor's gratitude; but the significance of this act, since it accepts, indeed insists on, Gregor's pitiful condition (unlike his parents, who are horrified), is far from a benevolent one, and, in the end, it is Grete who is described as spreading her wings like a butterfly. Be it noticed: another kind of insect.

The meaning of the Cinderella story is just what it says. The moral is that if you treat people badly you'll end up paying for it. The significance suggests another moral: we must look beyond the trappings of things to find values that are often hidden. But we should not forget that the wicked sisters were ugly and the ill-treated servant-sister was beautiful. Beauty will burst every stay it's confined by; the loser is never as handsome as the winner. If Miss Beauty falls in love with Mr. Beast despite his beastliness, is she rewarded for this mistake by his living a long hairball life? Not on yours! The Beast that Beauty loved is changed into a handsome prince whose hair is only where it should be. Is Miss Beauty so fond of the fur she fell for that she is dismayed by the change, wants her gorilla back, and falls out of love with the changeling as if she'd fallen out a window? Not a chance! She marries the fine fellow and gives him ten kids who resemble the head of their father artfully stamped on a gold coin.

Sentences are rarely so duplicitous. Their narrations are gestural. Sometimes one of them seems to be so wonderfully summary, nailed to the end of the story like a sign that serves as a cemetery marker. For closure, that is hard to beat. Moreover, the concluding moment must overcome its own awkward entrance. *Incalculably,* from a visual point of view, is perfect: *in calc ul a ble,* because the word breaks apart into channels that have no great significance by themselves; but from an audible angle, *incalculably* is unpronounceable.

Narrative Sentences

George Eliot. From the conclusion of *Middlemarch* (1872).

Her finely-touched spirit had still its fine issues, though they were not widely visible. Her full nature, like that river of which Cyrus broke the strength, spent itself in channels which had no great name on the earth.

But the effect of her being on those around her was incalculably diffusive: for the growing good of the world is partly dependent on unhistoric acts; and that things are not so ill with you or me as they might have been, is half owing to the number who lived faithfully a hidden life, and rest in unvisited tombs.

Stories love morals and here is a big one. Instead of writing "For the improvement of the world depends as much on unhistoric as on historic acts . . ." she says, rather awkwardly, "the growing good," and by doing so helps make memorable her conclusion. Having used *good* she must employ *ill* later on. From her particular heroine, Eliot rockets off to "the world"—not just the betterment of a few friends, a bit of England, or the nation as a whole, but that of China and Sioux Falls equally—only to return to "you and me." Oh, yes, she has as many hedges in her sentence as the fields do in her shire: "partly dependent," "half owing"; however, the last two clauses carry all before them, grant her heroine and her kind more than half the number "who lived faithfully a hidden life, and rest in unvisited tombs."

Lying inoffensively quiet yet forcefully present in the paragraph is the sexual story borne along by its imagery and defined by repetition and alliteration—*finely fine full*, for instance. Dorothea, finely touched, gave birth, not to a heroic king, but to many fine and modest offspring. This growing good, we must finally observe, is measured negatively—less ill. Nor will these fine folk be remembered for long. Their deaths shall be as unremarked as their lives.

With sentences set before us that are only partial instances of narrative qualities, let us turn to some more fully fledged, this next a sentence embedded in an article rather than a fiction.

[9]

Daniel Defoe. From "An Essay upon Projects" (1697).

There are, and that too many, fair pretences of fine discoveries, new inventions, engines, and I know not what, which being
advanced in notion, and talked up to great things to be performed
when such and such sums of money shall be advanced, and such
and such engines are made, have raised the fancies of credulous
people to such height, that merely on the shadow of expectation,
they have formed companies, chose committees, appointed officers, shares, and books, raised great stocks, and cried up an empty
notion to that degree, that people have been betrayed to part with
their money for shares in a new-nothing; and when the inventors
have carried on the jest till they have sold all their own interest,
they leave the cloud to vanish of itself, and the poor purchasers to
quarrel with one another, and go to law about settlements, transferrings, and some bone or other thrown among 'em by the subtlety
of the author, to lay the blame of the miscarriage upon themselves.

These days this paragraph would not be allowed to pass as a sentence. It would be cut by periods into digestible lengths like poultry,
for we have no fewer fools today than those who disgraced former
times.

In order to reach the "story" (i.e., gist) of this sentence we have to
dispense with the syntactical modifiers. "Pretenders to new inventions have led people to invest in and promote companies at such
supporters' expense only to vanish with the money before the scam
is discovered, leaving the investors to quarrel over what little is left."
Clearly, the "gist" could be expressed differently. It is beyond any
specific words the way a story is beyond words. Defoe chooses to tell
the story by swelling his narration at appropriate moments. It's like
blowing into a balloon. ". . . [T]hey have raised the fancies of credulous people to such height . . ." What height? Here is the verbal
mimic of it: ". . . they have formed companies, chose committees,
appointed officers, shares, and books, raised great stocks, and cried

up an empty notion to that degree . . ." The story continues, after the bust comes, with the narrated consequences, naturally brief, since this is a summation sentence: ". . . they leave the cloud to vanish of itself, and the poor purchasers to quarrel with one another, and go to law about settlements, transferrings, and some bone or other thrown among 'em . . ." As stories insist, there is a fine moral here, suitable for the sermon already in germ.

My statement of the gist resembles only Defoe's bare bones, though bones disposed in narrative motion, but it is the flesh that makes the sentence of its time and by this author, that gives it weight and, above all, its energy and sardonic cast of mind. The teller of the tale, the disposer of clauses, is evident at every halt we make for a comma.

In short, neither story (which can be told in many media and in many ways) nor meaning (which can be expressed with similar flexibility) are active elements in literary work. Narration and signification, on the other hand, are fundamental functions.

[10]
Chester Himes. *Run Man Run* (1995).

He turned the knob. It turned. He pushed the door and it opened.

Here are three sentences each of which is almost wholly consumed by meaning—that is, they are all core. They have no fruit, no flesh. Together they do fit into a story, and together they take on that "tough guy" tone so popular in detective fiction. The effort is inept and halfhearted. "He tried the knob. It turned. He pushed the door. It opened." Even the improvement achieved by eliminating the careless repetition is negligible.

[11]
William Bartram From *Travels* (1791).

The morning pleasant, we decamped early: proceeding on, rising gently for several miles, over sandy, gravelly ridges, we found ourselves in an elevated, high, open, airy region, somewhat rocky, on the backs of the ridges, which presented to view, on every side, the most drear, solitary, desert waste I had ever beheld; groups of bare rocks emerging out of the naked gravel and drifts of white sand; the grass thinly scattered and but few trees; the pines, oaks, olives, and sideroxylons, poor, misshapen, and tattered; scarce an animal to be seen, or noise heard, save the symphony of the Western breeze, through the bristly pine leaves, or solitary sandcricket's screech, or at best the more social converse of the frogs, in solemn chorus with the swift breezes, brought from distant fens and forests.

THE JOURNEY (to the view)

on the backs of the ridges,

somewhat rocky

region,

airy

open,

high,

in an elevated,

we found ourselves

gravelly ridges,

over sandy,

for several miles,

rising gently

proceeding on,

we decamped early:

The morning pleasant,

JUDGMENT (of the view)

	on		drear		I
which presented to view	every	the most	solitary	waste	had beheld
	side		desert		ever

DEPICTION (of the view, as viewed)

groups of bare rocks   emerging out
of the naked gravel and drifts of white sand;
the grass thinly scattered and but few trees;

the pines,   poor,
oaks,   misshapen,
olives,   and tattered;
and sideroxylons,

DEPICTION (what can be heard while view is viewed)
scarce an animal to be seen,
or noise heard,
save the symphony of the western breeze,
through the bristly pine trees,
or solitary sandcricket's screech
or at best the more social converse of the frogs,
in solemn chorus with the swift breezes,
brought from distant fens and forests.

This is a classic example of the scroll sentence. Its intention is to model a journey. Having fixed the time of departure—"The morning pleasant"—the sentence gets going—"we decamped early"—then throwing its tense into the progressive past it rises over ridges to an elevated rocky region, where a view presents itself that is judged to be that of a dreary wasteland. As if to prove it, there follows a description of the experience, initially of sights, then of sounds: rocks, gravel, sand, a patch here and there of grass, a few pines, oaks, olives, and sideroxylons (a kind of ironwood)—with a breeze, a sand cricket, some frogs whose singing seems to have been borne from the fens by the wind. We came; we saw; we pondered.

This sentence sometimes moves to the beat of its explorers' encounters, that is, in terms of its denotations; but when depictions are required, it arranges the simultaneously present properties of the view into a serial order, thus ensuring that the final thing the hikers will feel is the breeze, another traveler.

[11]
Joseph Conrad. *Nostromo* (1904).

But not for long. Doña Emilia would be gone "up to the mountain" in a day or two, and her sleek carriage mules would have an easy time of it for another long spell. She had watched the erection of the **first** frame house put up on the lower mesa for an office and Don Pépé's quarters; she heard with a thrill of thankful emotion the **first** wagon-load of ore rattle down the then only shoot, she had stood by her husband's side perfectly silent when the **first** battery of only fifteen stamps was put in motion for the **first** time.

On the occasion when the fires under the **first** set of retorts in their shed had glowed far into the night she did not retire to rest on the rough cadre set up for her in the as yet bare frame house till she had seen the **first** spungy lump of silver yielded to the hazards of the world by the dark depths of the Gould Concession; she had laid her unmercenary hands, with an eagerness that made them tremble, upon the **first** silver ingot turned out still warm from the mould; and by her imaginative estimate of its power she endowed that lump of metal with a justificative conception, as though it were not a mere fact, but something far-reaching and impalpable, like the true expression of an emotion or the emergency of a principle.

I'll not go on about the Joseph Conrad sample, in part because so much might be said of this masterful paragraph, formed in the author's characteristic manner, as to require another paper. Here we have a true narrative time line, also shaped as a climb; that is, a lengthy project has been undertaken that Doña Emilia has overseen by regularly paying it a visit, so she has inspected it at stage 1 (first frame house), at stage 2 (first wagonload), at stage 3 (first battery), et cetera; but she has concentrated upon commencements, so Conrad has obliged her behavior by placing seven *first*s in the paragraph, four in its first sentence, three in its second. Consequently, although her actions (and the sentences) move on, she is always at a beginning. Her verbs also mark the progress of the mine: she is gone, she watches, she hears, she stands; then she sees, she lays, she endows. The narrative moves past the physical process of mining and smelting when the lady's imagination takes the first ingot, from a warm solidity that weighs upon her hand, all the way to principle, an unlikely place for silver.

Next. Stephen Dedalus and Leopold Bloom have stopped at a cabman's shelter, a small coffeehouse under the Loop Line Bridge, for a cuppa and a rest on their way home. And the hope that the coffee will sober Stephen up. After an appropriate period of such hospitality, Bloom sees that it is time to leave.

[12]
James Joyce. *Ulysses,* (1921).

To cut a long story short Bloom, grasping the situation, was the first to rise to his feet so as not to outstay their welcome having first and foremost, being as good as his word that he would foot the bill for the occasion, taken the wise precaution to unobtrusively motion to mine host as a parting shot a scarcely perceptible sign when the others were not looking to the effect that the amount due was forthcoming, making a grand total of fourpence (the amount he deposited unobtrusively in four coppers, literally the last of the Mohicans) he having previously spotted on the printed price list for all who ran to read opposite to him in unmistakable figures, coffee ad., confectionary do., and honestly well worth twice the money once in a way, as Wetherup used to remark.

Commonplaces------------------------------Narrative Events

1. to cut a long story short	authorial intervention
2. grasp the situation	subjective interpretation
3. rise to his feet	narrative action
4. don't outstay your welcome	rationale or justification
5. first and foremost	subjective evaluation
6. good as his word	characterization

7. foot the bill	promise, therefore a prediction
8. take the wise precaution	subjective evaluation
9. mine host	authorial archness
10. parting shot	subjective evaluation
11. scarcely perceptible sign	narrative action
12. to the effect that	subjective interpretation
13. amount due is forthcoming	subjective interpretation
14. grand total	characterization
15. literally the last of the Mohicans	authorial intervention, allusion
16. previously spotted	subjective interpretation
17. all who run can read	authorial intervention, allusion
18. honestly (in this context)	subjective interpretation
19. well worth it	subjective interpretation
20. worth twice the money	subjective interpretation
21. once in a way	subjective allusion
22. as [Wetherup] used to [remark] say	attribution

The sentence without its commonplaces:

> To be brief, Bloom, realizing they should not stay longer, was the first to rise, and having prudently and discreetly signaled to their host that he would pay the bill, quietly left his last four pennies, a sum—most reasonable—he knew was due, having earlier seen the price of their coffee and confection clearly printed on the menu.
>
> Bloom was the first to get up so that he might also be the first to motion (to the host) that the amount due was forthcoming.

The theme of the sentence is manners: Bloom rises so he and his companion will not have sat too long over their coffees and cake, and signals discreetly (*unobtrusively* is used twice) that he will pay the four pence due according to the menu. The sum, and the measure of his generosity, is a pittance.

The sentence is itself an odyssey, for Bloom and Dedalus are going home. They stop (by my count) at twenty-two commonplaces on their way. Other passages might also be considered for the list, such as "when others were not looking." Commonplaces are the goose down of good manners. They are remarks empty of content, hence never offensive; they conceal hypocrisy in an acceptable way, because, since they have no meaning in themselves anymore they cannot be deceptive. That is, we know what they mean ("how are you?"), but they do not mean what they say (I really don't want to know how you are). Yet they soothe and are expected. We have long forgotten that "to foot the bill," for instance, is to pay the sum at the bottom of it, though it could mean to kick a bird in the face. Bloom, we should hope, is already well above his feet when he rises to them. The principal advantage of the commonplace is that it is supremely self-effacing. It so lacks originality that it has no source. The person who utters a commonplace—to cut a long explanation short—has shifted into neutral.

The concluding cliché is not exactly as advertised. "Once in a way" mangles the trite, but hasn't triteness itself, except for Wetherup, who apparently says it often, as might be expected, because he was a onetime clerk in the Collector of Rates Office with John Joyce. "It's well worth twice the money once in a way," he'd invariably say. We well remember. On every visit. So, the skids greased, the pair slip off toward home, "[s]eeing that the ruse worked and the coast was clear," despite the fact that Stephen is still four sheets to the wind. When Stephen wonders why they place chairs upside down on tables in the café every night, Bloom makes no mention of the Shakers who had hangers on the wall for their ladder backs to cling to, but does say, "To sweep the floor in the morning." Routines of speech and behavior, good custom and propriety continue to control every action as Bloom skips nimbly to his companion's right, "a habit of his, by the by, the right side being, in classical idiom, his tender Achilles."

My culminating sentence, one that most clearly demonstrates what I've been trying to suggest, is appropriately from Henry James.

Henry James. From *Italian Hours* (1909). Spindle Diagram

To dwell in a city which, much as you grumble at it, is after all very fairly a modern city, with crowds, and shops and theaters and cafés and balls and receptions and dinner parties and all the modern confusion of social pleasures and pains; to have at your door the good and evil of it all; and yet to be able in half an hour to gallop away and leave it a hundred miles, a hundred years, behind, and to look at the tufted broom blowing on a lonely tower-top in the still blue air, and the pale pink asphodels trembling none the less for the stillness, and the shaggy-legged shepherds leaning on their sticks in motionless brotherhood with the heaps of ruin, and the scrambling goats and stagger-ing little lads treading out wild desert smells from the top of hollow-sounding mounds; and then, to come back through one of the great gates and a couple of hours later find yourself in the "world," dressed, introduced, entertained, inquiring, talk-ing about "Middlemarch" to a young English lady or listening to Neapolitan songs from a gentleman in a very low-cut shirt—all this is to lead in a manner a double life and to gather from the hurrying hours more impressions than a mind of modest capac-ity quite knows how to dispose of.

To dwell in a city which,
much as you grumble at it,
is after all very fairly a modern city;

                       with crowds
                       and shops
                       and theaters

THE CITY   and cafés
                       and balls
                       and receptions
                       and dinner parties
                       and all the modern confusion of social pleasures
                       and pains;
             to have at your door the good and evil of it all;

and yet
to be able in half an hour
to gallop away and leave it a hundred miles,
      a hundred years, behind,
and
to look at the tufted broom blowing on a lonely tower-
      top in the still blue air,
and
THE COUNTRY   the pale pink asphodels trembling
none the less   for the stillness,
and
   the shaggy-legged shepherds leaning on their sticks
in   motionless brotherhood with the heaps of
ruin,
and
   the scrambling goats and staggering little kids
   treading out wild desert smells from the top of
   hollow-sounding mounds;

and then
to come back through one of the great gates
   and a couple of hours later find yourself in the "world,"
           dressed,
           introduced,
THE CITY   entertained,
           inquiring,
           talking
   about "Middlemarch" to a young English lady
   or
           listening
to Neapolitan songs from a gentleman in a very low-cut
   shirt—

all this is
to lead in a manner a double life
and

to gather from the hurrying hours more impressions than a
mind of   modest capacity quite knows how to
dispose of.

James manages this quite complex sentence with the ease of a
waterslide. It takes its trip in a travel book; what could be more
appropriate? In front of us is what I call a spindle diagram, designed
to reveal the axes around which the phrases and the clauses turn,
usually a modest preposition or obliging conjunction, and therefore
generally a part of speech. In this case, it is both the infinitive and
the *and:* nine of the former and seventeen of the latter. *To,* as ver-
satile as it is, can stand at either side of a verb as comfortably as a
sentry: "to go to the dogs," "to declare to your beloved your love," "to
see to it," "to remodel to suit," and "I am about to dance to the music
to the movie *To Have and to Hold.*" James's city divides itself, like a
sonata, into a departure point—Rome, "to dwell in"—the country-
side nearby, "to gallop away" to, and a destination—Rome again, "to
come back" for. Each of these sections is followed by a bit of tempo-
rally characterized reflection. "To have at your door the good and evil
of it all, and yet to be able in half an hour to gallop away . . ." "and
then to come back through one of the great gates and a couple of
hours later find yourself in the world . . ." "all this is to lead in a manner a double life and to gather from the hurrying hours . . ." What?
impressions, of course, what else?

The city, described as you are about to leave it, receives eight
qualifiers, and regains them again when you return, while the coun-
tryside receives but four; however, these four are more redolent
with detail and make up in richness what they lack in numbers.
Although the Rome which we rejoin after our hundred-mile gallop is
Rome still, the city we left was given over entirely to public bustle—
theaters, cafés, and balls—whereas the city we recover is more privately social—chamber music and conversation. What we see in the
city is activity, but what we see in the country is still—shepherds,
towers—though we and our carriage are perhaps ajounce and ajolt

on the road, except for small natural movements which do not disturb the scenic serenity—trembling asphodels, for instance.

For the country is reserved James's most mouth-filling music: "the tufted broom blowing on a lonely tower-top in the still blue air," or "the scrambling goats and staggering little kids treading out wild desert smells from the top of hollow-sounding mounds." James is nonetheless a city man. The country is visited, but he is a happy grumbling part of the crowded streets and a participant in the hubbub of parties and receptions. He is not about to chase after a scrambling goat; nor is his sentence, though it ends very brashly with a preposition.

One could make many other observations about this sample of Henry James's magazine prose, among them the fact that *Middlemarch*—here entwined—is a country book and the songs are citified, but the narrative shape of the sentence is not just a nice touch or final flourish; it inscribes the verbal journey that the meaning also makes; the two travel together in the same coach, although the words are up top driving the horses, while their referents are sitting in the stage with hankies held daintily to their noses against the persistent dust.

THE AESTHETIC STRUCTURE OF
THE SENTENCE

Decades ago, when I was in the grades, the teacher of composition would occasionally go to the blackboard and write there a sentence of some appropriately simple kind for her students to worry like cats with their prey—for example, "The man at the door was an encyclopedia salesman," though, I suspect, my instructor chose a more succinctly spelled commodity. During the Great Depression such a neat but shabby-suited person would ring the bell oftener than anyone cared to remember. Then teacher would draw lines that tied various parts of her sentence together, "at the door" descending like a staircase from its noun. This moment made me happy. I was perhaps the only student in the class who relished diagramming; who could while away a happy hour picturing predicates docking at the ports of their subjects like ships. Levels one through six were called grammar schools then, attesting to the importance once placed upon the subject.

The idea of the sentence, I saw from these chalky demonstrations, was the disappearance of the words that comprised it into one compounded notion, namely whatever was designated by a large often smeared letter S on the board. *The* had scarcely slipped without any fuss into *man* when *at the door* folded up into the slightly fattened S on the slate as if swallowed by its shape. Meanwhile, *encyclopedia* was safely inside *salesman* and resting comfortably. The sentence offered no guarantee that the union of *doorsman* and *salesman* would ever be relevant for any other stoop. Its allegation was quite indefinite about all else except this one past-tense declaration.

Yet its time frame did determine certain circumstances. Had the verb (here, one weak as water) been in the present, I could have easily imagined a comfortable use: "Mabel, I think the man at the door is an encyclopedia salesman." But our sample sentence is not in an immediately functional mode, but rather in one of recollection and depiction. (Actually, even this is a pretension, because the sentence isn't being used, but merely being mentioned.) Moreover, its meaning is not captured by any easy refiguring, such as, "An encyclopedia salesman was at the door," because that blunt version fails to highlight the statement's sense of recognition: "O lord, the man at the door . . ." et cetera. There is absolutely no point in saying, "The man at the door," if you already know who he is. And if you know who he is, you probably won't utter an entire sentence, just, "Uh-oh, an encyclopedia salesman," in a warning whisper. Incidentally, is that warning a fragment or can we treat it as a sentence with copious elisions?

The teacher, to my mystification, did not give word order much attention, and she seemed to think that some sentences could be flipped like pancakes. She regarded with scornful indifference my claim that the news, "David slew Goliath," was seriously not the same as, "Goliath was slain by David," but that each registered joy or woe depending on whose side you were on. Grammarians were on the side of the parts of speech. Wherever it might find itself, an adverb was surely an adverb, the *-ly* a brand as on the flank of a steer, and in just that way her classifications went through the words of the alphabet, *aardvark* to *Zion,* declaring them to be articles or prepositions, nouns or verbs. If I wanted to insist on a difference between the two Davids-versus-Goliaths, beyond a simple change of voice, fine; but my opinion would not be a grammatical one. The syntax of the sentence—its form—was the issue, although no one said *syntax* back then.

Thus I learned that grammar was concerned with only one sort of structure that a sentence had to have to earn a period. Its aim was always clarity of communication. Nothing should leak out of, or fall idly into, the perfect sentence. It must not forget its way and wander in the wilderness. Later, after the steam engine's invention, we might say "lose its train of thought." In 1783, when Hugh Blair composed his lecture "Structure of Sentences," he listed their desirable properties as "1. Clearness and Precision. 2. Unity. 3. Strength. 4. Harmony." Yet we do not always share those goals when we speak or write, for we often desire to be devious, to mislead, conceal, confuse, or confound our audience; perhaps to persuade them to vote as we wish or to purchase our faulty vacuum cleaner or grant us a reputation for profundity. Much later, I came to believe that Hegel must have thought reality was a sentence, because everything that occurred in the world turned out to be a predicate of the absolute, and disappeared into it the way the steps to the front door did, or the standing man would if he left the stoop, having been invited in to wait at the end of the sentence, when he'd get to put, under someone else's care, the book of cut-rate erudition he had so long borne beneath his arm, weariness from previous refusals showing in his face, a weariness not unlike the weariness this sentence gives its listeners, and will its readers, too.

Hegel, of course, would not be the first to look at the world through the methods of its depiction. The Pythagoreans may have been originals at that. Aristotle's categories serve him as the grammar of being, and prove amazingly useful for an error of such magnitude. A sentence, the philosopher says, is a form of speech that has a beginning and an end within itself, and is of a length that can be readily grasped—two conditions that resemble those required of a tragedy: beginning, middle, end, and the unities of time and place that are imposed upon the action. Of course, to utter a rule is half on the way to breaking it. For instance, Laurence Sterne, who loved to cause metaphysical alarm in his readers, damaged the rule for time with this rip in the fabric of reality: "A cow broke in tomorrow morning to my Uncle Toby's fortifications." And E. E. Cummings, to continue along this line, begins a poem "anyone lived in a pretty how town / with up so floating many bells down." Grammarians are not taught to cope with this sort of thing. How do you diagram the "cowtown" that manages to live in the shadow of "how town," or set down the up so floating many bells? You don't, I'm sure Miss Duck (for that was her name) would say. The incorrect does not deserve the honor of a design.

Philosophers can often be classified in terms of their favorite parts of speech: there are those who believe that nouns designate the only reliable aspects of being; others, of a contrary view, who see those nouns as simply unkempt nests of qualities; and all are familiar with the Heraclitean people who embrace verbs as if you could make love to water while entirely on land. I have personally always preferred prepositions, particularly *of*, and especially, among its many meanings, those of possession and being possessed, of belonging and exclusion.

In that classroom I also encountered what was apparently a mind like mine: one that had to picture relations in some symbolic space if it hoped to understand them. Later, Venn diagrams would provide visible evidence for the soundness of the syllogism. The syllogism required a rewriting of any sentences offered to it so that they would fit neatly into a system that would facilitate the diagramming of its premises by means of overlapping hoops. Like a ticket machine, this logic did not accept sentences until they had been pressed flat, formed into propositions, and fed carefully through the appropriate slot. "David is the slayer of Goliath." According to some readers, of which I am one, this formula—S is P, with its quantifier and simplified copula—encouraged the concepts of Substance and Accident and gave them considerable legitimacy. The syllogism itself, apart from the fact that anything it could handle had to be uninteresting, encouraged a conflation of premises and their valid conclusion with the actions of causes and effects, supposing that between them there had to be a necessary connection simply because the propositions that expressed causality were that firmly linked.

Wittgenstein has even said that the structure of a true proposition mirrors the structure of its fact, but this is true only in fiction, where there are no other facts than those created by the prose, and no other relations either.

At a social function, the name tags may be folded at your plate or they may be pinned to your dress at the door. If properly posted Sir Gregory will remain the MP for Gladhampshire wherever he stands and as his name tag identifies him; otherwise that must be Lady Disgrace seated at the left hand of the host, as her place mark says, since that is where a person of such rank and compliant reputation is always to be found. The English sentence creates a predelineated space, like a table set for lunch, while a Latin one is satisfied that everybody knows their station and their duties wherever they may be positioned. In an English sentence, as Blair remarks, "the words or members most nearly related, should be placed in the Sentence, as near to each other as possible." Placing relations in such proximity with one another is not wise social advice.

When word ordering is insufficient for the organizing task at hand, one can fold the sentence back upon itself as line breaks do in verse, or by creating interior rhymes, and symmetrical structures bring it to heel; but now closeness must be redefined in terms of each word's placement anywhere on the page or its resemblance to others when read and heard in the head.

The favored name, in Blair's time, for the effect of a word on its neighbor was *qualify*, whereas today it is *modify*. The adverb, by its presence, does something to the meaning of a verb that the verb, by itself, is incapable of doing. The general assumption has been that though these qualifiers are subordinate to their objects, and must be considered to be fastened to them in some life-giving way (weariness cannot exist on its own), it is their presence alone that effects the change. That is to say, if the salesman is standing wearily at your front door, weariness will be like a car's paint job, and do its work on the poor fellow's posture without suffering, itself, any modification. This is, I think, a major mistake. If, out of all the kinds of standing, the adverb is pointing only to the weary ones, *standing,* in its turn, is picking out only those elements of posture that are appropriate, and certainly not all the ones the sentence—"'Wanna buy a book, ma'am,' the salesman said wearily"—is selecting; or, even more obviously, "The geese lit upon the pond, where they floated wearily about like lilies made of feathers."

Many adverbs and some adjectives have private as well as public sides. Here, only the posture of the salesman has been described as weary, so the reader must first go to the qualities one associates with the corresponding behavior of the body, and only then, if the inference is deemed safe, to the appropriate state of feeling, since a person may feign weariness, or hide it if he wishes to make a sale.

To dwell at this point a moment longer like those geese who now are resting on the palest patch of water: if it is a part of the syntax of the sentence that any adjective in it modify or qualify a noun, how it does so will depend not only upon the nature of the noun but also on the connections that the adjective has made with other portions of the text, provided, of course, there are such companions. It has been suggested that our salesman was shabby-suited, and given the general circumstances we might reasonably suppose that neatness was nevertheless likely. The salesman is poor but he is trying to make a good impression. Still, we can't be sure. If Mr. Micawber is the guy ringing the bell, we do know that he will be dressed as well as Mrs. Micawber can manage. So if this sentence were in *Copperfield,* the way the adjective modified its noun would be precisely determined: shabby but not as one who is homeless, rather as one who is poor but proud—even pompous. Sometimes the text will furnish details and particulars: "The frayed edges of his coat sleeves had been sewn shut so that the ravelings could no longer embarrass." At other times it may indicate that *shabby* alone is quite enough. The reader must read carefully and obey. Such links, such severances, are everywhere inevitable in literary work and, I should say, are formal properties of the sentence with the consequence that the sentence cannot be surgically lifted from its context like a liver to be transplanted. I call these possibilities *contextual tentacles,* because, though they reach out, they do not always grasp.

The placement of the man's shabbiness is as important as the suit's location—worn rather than still hung in a closet or flung over a chair. To say, "The suit was shabby," is to grant *shabby* its full powers as an adjective and to place special emphasis on the suit's condition (the *suit* goes to seek *shabby*); whereas if it is allowed to cozy up and be *shabby-suited* it will take on substantive, or nounlike, qualities. Then the sentence is on its way to omitting the suit—to say *shabby man* and be done with it. In addition, "The man at the door was a shabby encyclopedia salesman," casts aspersions on the poor soul's selling techniques, and *shabby*'s closeness to *encyclopedia* suggests a similarly low opinion of his merchandise. I shall stick with *shabby-suited*. Because it fits him.

Let our instructor in these matters be Samuel Beckett, who understands the general problem of word order and selection as well as anyone who cares. In his early novel *Watt,* Beckett reckons with the problem.

> With regard to the so important matter of Mr Knott's physical appearance, Watt had little or nothing to say. For one day Mr Knott would be tall, fat, pale and dark, and the next thin, small, flushed and fair, and the next sturdy, middlesized, yellow and ginger, and the next small, fat, pale and fair, and the next middlesized, flushed, thin and ginger, and the next tall, yellow, dark and sturdy, and the next fat, middlesized, ginger and pale, and the next tall, thin, dark and flushed, the next small, fair, sturdy and yellow . . . [in this way the permutations continue for a full two pages until, not even out of breath, we reach] . . . and the next small, fair, sturdy and pale, or so it seemed to Watt, to mention only the figure, stature, skin and hair.

To dwell on this point still a moment longer like a guest who will not say "good night": sentences must be understood to contain all sorts of unused syntactical space. These are places that could be filled with more words, but, in any specific instance, aren't. Instead of, "The man at the door was an encyclopedia salesman," we could have written, "The weary shabby-suited man at the door was an Encyclopaedia Britannica salesman." Between any adjective and its noun, more can nearly always be added. Sentences are like lattice-work, like fences, to be left open or prudently closed, their boards wide or narrow, pointy or level, the spaces between them, ditto. "The man was a salesman" is a short sentence that is as gappy as a badly buttoned blouse. An adjective that began its duties nearly in the arms of its noun can suddenly find itself removed almost to another room. Or if in a queue, a victim of violators. "The tall gaunt shabby-suited weary-looking man who suddenly appeared at my door after ringing its bell with a hand I identified as that of an old radioman because it sounded so like Morse, was, to my surprise, not an encyclopedia salesman, though I at first had taken him for that, but a Bible pusher whose stature and demeanor reminded me of my father, dead these many years, and a man of the book if there ever was one." Don't think we can't make this a novel. Words in a sentence are like stars in the heavens: close together only if viewed from a distance of many light-years.

Occasionally we are misled into thinking that some of these spaces have been adequately closed up. For instance, what room is left between *at* and *the* in the phrase "at the front door"? Well, a lot if we cheat a little. "The man at [rest at] the front door . . ." Without changing the order of the words we can begin our redesign with, "The man at rest at the first step leading to the front door was, to my dismay, a dismay I conveyed to my wife in a whisper, not just an encyclopedia salesman, but the same guy I turned away yesterday when he was selling brooms." Although the grammarian, as well as the logician, will find the original sentence and pull it out with pliers, to the ordinary reading eye that original unity will have disappeared. This is called *embedding*. There are two kinds. We simply place the sentence to be embedded, as it stands, in a larger whole, usually with material added fore and aft; or we segment the sentence and make intrusions all along its length.

Embedding is related to framing. Frame tales are famous: *A Thousand and One Nights, The Decameron, The Canterbury Tales.* At the level of the sentence it is called indirect address. "Seymour said that the man at the door was an encyclopedia salesman." At all times, the authority for statements, assertions, beliefs, and opinions is crucial. Gossip, the very lifeblood of the novel of manners, can do its damage regardless of its reliability, but that reliability is essential if we are ever to know what Millie has actually done with her life, besides running away with that fact-flogging encyclopedia salesman. Henry James, who is fundamentally an epistemological novelist, is always concerned with who said what, why, and with what authority. He would certainly be interested to know that Miss Duck, who wrote our initial example on the board, was one of Millie's aunts, an intimate of the family, who might very well know what her niece of only thirty-five had done, running away with a lowlife like that. What Seymour said made only half a frame; a full frame might go like this: "Seymour said that the man at the door was an encyclopedia salesman, but Joseph wasn't so sure, because Seymour owed Britannica a bundle and saw their emissaries hiding in his drawers."

These spaces and the relations established within them are nothing like the physical relations of things and properties in the world of reference. The weariness of the salesman inhabits his veins, his nerves, his bones; defeat and despair darken his consciousness; and his skin is as tired as his clothing. But the word *weariness* is not weary; nor is the little verb *was* even a bit bored because of the two spaces it has had to occupy (as *was*—as *wasn't*) in the salesman's last sentence. In addition, there are maybe a billion more instances of *was* and *wasn't* in use, and an inexhaustible number waiting their chance; another billion that were forgotten as soon as spoken, a billion more written, only to be erased or stricken or consumed by accidents, cruel indifference, or the elements.

My grammarian was using a prescribed notation to develop in

the blackboard's representational space a picture of relationships that cannot be normally observed. Yet I doubt if she realized the creative importance of such figurations (they were essential to the development of mathematics and symbolic logic; they revolutionized music) or appreciated the human mind's desire to spacialize whatever it wishes to understand. Time is not without a strong presence, although it, too, is always given a linear presentation. For instance, if a real man were standing there at the door, shabby and weary; his eyes, his nose, his turned-down mouth would be in simultaneous alignment, and given together to the world; but the sentence can give these characteristics to us only one item at a time, like keys and lipstick taken from a purse, and the salesman's self would be parceled out in pieces that might be supposed to fit together finally in a coherent form and face, like a jigsaw one might buy at the five-and-dime. For another instance, that initial *The* must wait until *at the door* has had a chance to fold up into *man* before it does its work, because it is being definite about "man-at-the-door" not *man* by itself, just as *at* must apply itself to "the-door" not *door* alone. Of course, conceptually, these relations are in instantaneous play, but the reader's eye and mind do not move quite that fast. Meanwhile, notationally, *the* is spoken, typed, or written in a sea of space between it and its noun. *Fainthearted,* for example, might pop in between them, or *weary,* or both, or more than both: "The weary fainthearted fat man at the door was, if I had read his look aright, a damned encyclopedia salesman." In this sentence we are forced to deal with epistemological disclaimers and heated evaluations in addition to descriptions that fly from one realm of being to another: in and out of the public world and then in and out of the salesman's consciousness like purple martins to and from their house.

By the way, the period that puts an end to any sentence—that says a sentence is a sentence—and was at one time used to name a sentence instead of saying *sentence*—is not an arbitrary mark, yet its presence must be justified, for any sentence whatever can be longer than it happens to be, running on like a kitchen tap. "The man at the door was an encyclopedia salesman / who stood there nervously shifting his weight from one foot to the other as if he needed to pee." A new addition, like a breezeway or a screened porch, will provide fresh entertainments. Arnold Schoenberg once advised John Cage to go back over what he was doing and see if it still worked if you added something. "See how it continues," he suggested, "how it flows." We know these things about sentences, as obvious as most noses on most faces, but we often choose not to remember them, or the noses either.

The similarity of logical form to grammatical form is generally acknowledged. However, these regulatory systems are not the same, nor do they have the same aims. Grammatical structures are superficial. They want and need to be as evident as gravy spills, because countless superficial people must use them, and because common speech loves vagueness and ambiguity. In an essay on the ontology of the sentence, I once gave up after listing thirteen uses for the preposition *of,* although, as a result, *of* became my favorite among my favorites, because it is, like *on* and *and* and *in,* so many different words. Grammar offers no clue to which *at* I have in "at the door." Is it the *at* of "at an impasse" or the *at* of "not at all"? My favorite syllogism, however, celebrates *in,* a real mischief maker. There is a pain in my foot. My foot is in my shoe. There is a pain in my shoe. The man with the pain in his shoe is not *at* an impasse, no, not *at* all, but simply *at* the front door.

The hypothetical nature of Aristotle's seemingly categorical, "All S is P," has now been unmasked by logicians and written, "If x is an S then x is a P," not something obvious on first consideration. When Aristotle forced verbs to act as nouns (turning *slew* into "the slayer of"), he did so on behalf of *ousia* and the simplification of the copula, which he understood in spatial terms as if he were using contemporary eyes: namely as connecting species to genus. Nouns (and adjectives after they had been made into nouns) were like classes that contained other classes that contained yet others until classes were reached that were so small and specific they had no differentiations (the *infima* species). These were the conceptually thick terms, since they told you so much more about themselves than nouns of greater scope and less density. What is common to all things may be profound but it can't be much.

Plato's Form of the Good, on the other hand, is the analytic embrace and dense compounding of every other Form, because, as the sun of the spiritual world, it not only makes each Form intelligible the way light makes material things visible, but it does so by granting them logical consequence—they flow like a fountain from it. Aristotle's Being is like Saturn who ate his children, but with such sluggish digestion they could be coughed up later, reborn just as they once were except they are now angry as hell; whereas Plato's Good (like the idea of One and the idea of One More that were once supposed to generate the whole of arithmetic) is never separate from its components but utterly made of them. For Plato the Idea of the Good is the ultimate subject. We should expect that from an Idealist. For Aristotle, however, Being is the predicate of predicates and true of every significant thing. For Aristotle, the man at the front door is no one much until he becomes shabby-suited and weary, while for Plato . . . can we see past those scuffed shoes and that overzealous tie? Do we understand? He is Man in all his calamitous glory.

Traditionally, then, the subject of a sentence has been viewed in three quite different ways: first, as an outlined object in a coloring book which the predicate obliges by crayoning in, making the apple green or red or yellow or spotty brown and rotten if the teacher is to be displeased (color the man weary); second, as a sorting box into which the predicate tosses the subject like a button, coin, or nail (where does Man go? One place the concept belongs is in the carton called Mortal along with forest ferns and hummingbirds); and third, as a stew to which predicates are added like ingredients asked for by a recipe, or as you might rub a goose with garlic (to the stock, *Man,* add a cup of salesmanship). Sometimes, whether the subject is regarded as a coloring book or a sorting box depends on whether the predicate is an adjective or a noun. Only in the third case is any semantic change to either term permitted to occur.

Plato thought of his Forms as blending much the way, if I read

him aright, colors are blended, and then splayed forth again, pris-
matically, as if white were indeed the fountain of all and not just the
froth. Some prefer to look at language chemically. For them, sentences are like compounds composed of elements whose connections create different emergent qualities while allowing the original
elements to retain their identities the way letters or even phonemes
do. Hydrogen does not resemble a gas when performing the magic
of water, though when it makes its escape from oxygen's grasp, it is
vaporous and volatile enough. The ultimate model for the sort of
mixing we mean may be music. There each note retains its identity
within the chord while sounding, with others, as one, and composing the onward rush of its narrative structure from recombinations,
repetitions, and all the elements of pitch placement and dynamics.

But words are too duplicitous for such comparisons to run their
course. Ford Madox Ford and Joseph Conrad agreed that writing
in English, as contrasted with writing in French, was like throwing
mud at a wall, but I think that most words are closets crammed
with suits, shirts, socks, and dresses, panties, hats, and gloves, and
I see words dressing themselves in the wardrobes of others, first of
all picking out this or that sense and then asking: will this skirt go
with that blouse? Does this tie match my shirt? Consider the little
unassuming functionary, *at,* that pinpoints times and places. The
sentence does not say what door our man is *at,* but the location
need not be spoken: any man at a side, closet, kitchen, or cellar
door would not be an encyclopedia salesman. The content of the
sentence establishes an unspoken occult context in which *front* has
a necessary though ghostly presence. This context is crowded. We
know that this sentence belongs to the Great Depression; that the
door in question is the front one; that someone outside or in the
house (whose existence is also presumed) has seen the man and
then identified him, probably for someone else, even a third man.

"The man at the door was an encyclopedia salesman" and "The
dog at the door was a Doberman pinscher" have the same grammatical form as "The flea on the dog was a nervous Nellie." Grammarians
have found these shoes too loose to be comfortable, and have tried

to tighten their forms by including other elements, such as insisting on an equivalent Depression-era placement and proper door selection for any other sentence said to have "the same form."

The syntactical spot filled by *man* might better have employed the word *fellow*, because then we could profitably alliterate: "The fellow at the front door was an encyclopedia salesman." Unfortunately, *fellow* is a bit demeaning, and we should have to decide whether we wanted to retain the initial anonymity of *man* or sacrifice him to euphony and its unifications. Of course, if we have determined on *shabby-suited* and dissed the poor wretch before he has even reached our door, then *fellow* he must be. "The shabby-suited fellow at the front door was a Fuller Brush salesman" would be only a step from perfection.

The philosophical rule we are invoking for the careful writer here is Leibniz's Principle of Sufficient Reason. In fact, the universe has insufficient reason; it is but an accident determined to happen, and human beings, who possess a little reason, rarely use it; however, works of art are governed by the question, "Why this, rather than that?" Why *fellow* rather than *man*, why put *shabby-suited* up front with *man* rather than right before *encyclopedia salesman*, why *weary* when *worn-out* will do? One odd result of the application of this principle, first employed, to my knowledge, by Plato in the *Timaeus*, is that it flies in the face of form. Form makes possible reproduction; form insists upon substitutions, multiplication: there are many heroic couplets, many valid arguments of the type called Barbara, lots of recordings of *Swan Lake*, oodles of Van Gogh's sunflowers; but only one such painting, one such Taj Mahal, one such text called *Tom Jones*. Form cares only about loyalty to its regulations. Banal sonnets can be as perfect as Milton's, and great ones as imperfect as Hopkins's. For philosophers, paradoxes like this are paradise.

Such equivalence is essential to the understanding of the fourth formal element of the sentence: its sound, and therefore the meters and rhythms of its words, the effect of assonance, consonance, gutturals, glottals, sibilants, fricatives, dentals, inflections, and other ties of the tongue that are often studied under the heading of *prosody,* including rhyme schemes and verse forms. Any sentence claiming a literary status should not be simply read or said but sung. Apart from genre rules and regulations, little is usually done to connect these patterns to other organizing principles or to assess either how—or how much—they affect the meaning of their host. Unfortunately, no two people are likely to scan a line or a sentence in the same way, except by mischance. Moreover, there is always present the desire to squeeze the meter of a poetic passage into obedient feet, as though they were those of Cinderella, and in the case of prose to ignore its rhythms altogether, as if it were improper for it to seem musical, feminine, and weak, when it is expected to be masculine, vigorous, and visual instead of auditory, seductive, and sensual. I made the immediately preceding sentence awkward to sharpen a point. The three properties (musical, feminine, and weak) set up the expectation of three others that would balance it (masculine, vigorous, and visual), but then I added another trio (auditory, seductive, and sensual) and hung it rather firmly on the line by repeating the alliteration pattern and near-rhyming *sensual* with *visual*; but now another group is called for in order to restore the equilibrium of the whole, since, hanging there in public view like undies taken from the wash, it threatens to bring the entire wardrobe into disrepute.

Sentences, especially extended ones, contain an unruly clutch of repetitive patterns and structural orders, some made for the concepts in advance of their choice the way syntax lies in wait for its vocabulary; some composed on the spot with the materialities of language; and these interact continuously with one another. Every repetition (a rhyme, for instance) pulls the knot of its joint significance tighter, drawing meanings that are often many words apart into conjunction, modification, closure, or, as Hardy puts it, chime.

The connections rhymes make are mainly copulative, not in the sense we associate with the copula *is*, which wants to say something factual, such as, "I think therefore I am," or, "In the fall the leaves are brown"; but in the carnal sense implied by the grounds for their conjunction, since they often have no other relation to boast of and are not, in their referents, very much alike (are *moon, spoon, loony, tune?*), but who are joined by the strength of their physical attraction. They are most frequently found in the company of the line break, where they tend to enlarge that breach by creating a sense of closure, snapping the purse shut. Nevertheless, a poem's sentences are folded back to a secondary beginning when the rhyme sends meaning in search of its twin.

In a masterfully awkward Thomas Hardy poem this very function of rhyme is the hidden subject. The scheme is insistent: a, a, a, a, b, b, a, a, a.

If It's Ever Spring Again
(song)

If it's ever spring again,
    Spring again,
I shall go where went I when
Down the moor-cock splashed, and hen,
Seeing me not, amid their flounder,
Standing with my arm around her;
If it's ever spring again,
    Spring again,
I shall go where went I then.

If it's ever summer-time,
    Summer-time,
With the hay crop at the prime,
And the cuckoos—two—in rhyme,
As they used to be, or seemed to,
We shall do as long we've dreamed to,
If it's ever summer-time,
    Summer-time,
With the hay, and bees achime.

    [from *Late Lyrics and Earlier*, 1922]

It is rarely observed how rhyme limits the poet's vocabulary, just as meter controls the choice of words and their order. Suppose the poet wrote, "If there are other summer days . . . summer days . . .

with the hay baled in its ripest phase . . ." Indeed, the *prime, time* anachronism is unfortunate, but in this poem it is essential. These lyrics, if written straight out as prose, would damp the drama of *Down*'s position, since everything in the line must splash upon the receiving hen—"Down the moor-cock splashed, and hen . . ."—in their amorous entanglement indifferent to height, to water, or to the poet's presence. The poem tells us, perhaps inadvertently, that neither the girl, held in the poem by the poet's arm, nor the hen, tacked to the line by a barely adhesive *and,* are of any great significance, though in summer-time the relationship, according to the pair of cuckoos, appears to have equalized.

The great stroke in this poem is the so-called awkward line with its inverted word order—"I shall go where went I when"—partly because it makes getting where it's going difficult (the stumble) and pointless (as if only to reach the rhyme), and partly because the *when* takes us to the edge of the poem, where we might fall into an endless wondering of, "What next?" if it weren't for the powerful upward pull of its rhyme with *again* and the tightness of the trio "where went when." In short, this line shouldn't have a strong closure, but it actually has a quite vigorous one, enough to help suspend *hen* as if in midair. Indeed, *Down* does the plummeting for the moorcock, as well as the hen, though her plunge is rather an afterthought, as I've suggested.

Lines that are wrenched suggest a powerful emotion has wrenched them, such as Hopkins's, "My own heart let me more have pity on; let / Me live to my sad self hereafter kind"; but even the slightest displacement of customary acts or values will do it. For instance, "We once were in love, made love and kissed without a harmful history," puts kissing after love and last in an amorous past blessed by brevity. "We had children, married, and met," has a similar, though more emphatic, backwardness. In the Hardy poem, the double rhyme (*around her*), by returning us to its previous partner (*flounder*), compares the tumultuous behavior of the fowls with the socially more acceptable gesture of possessive affection.

The Aesthetic Structure of the Sentence

Which brings us, perhaps with the relief of surprise, and the stimulus of suspicion, to the juncture of René Descartes with Samuel Beckett, with Beckett's riders and their bicycles, bicycles that are always breaking down, breakdowns that imperil the smooth machines we are supposed to be, minds riding around like ghosts (the critic's complaint was) steering only bits of wire, steel, and rubber wheels; for when the cuckoos chime they pop out of a chalet to do it at an appointed time; and so very similarly does the poetic—even prosy—line go quark, because even one word, standing alone in one of Beckett's barren chambers, replicates the philosopher's problem: the interaction of marks with minds, and minds with cries of *coo-coo*, of concepts riding about on meaningless and arbitrary sounds, something like Beckett's own chorus of frogs: "Krak! Krek! Krik! Krak!" for two unmelodious pages of *Watt*. If meaning, for the philosopher, tends to fly off into abstraction like steam, for the poet it tends to condense the way moisture bathes a cold glass. Although Beckett, following Descartes' lead, lets the body be a machine, the odd thing is that nowadays it is the computer that tries to behave like a mind, although in the absence of a body it remains more mindless than a monkey.

In the aesthetically interesting sentence, in any case, every materiality of language is employed to build a body for the meaning that will realize the union of thought and thing that paradise apparently forgot to promise us, and give consciousness the solid presence it constantly yearns for and will never quite realize. Over and over, we think that in the word we shall find the place where mind and matter meet. As Wallace Stevens writes:

The deepening need for words to express our thoughts and feelings which, we are sure, are all the truth that we shall ever experience, having no illusions, makes us listen to words when we hear them, loving them and feeling them, makes us search the sound of them, for a finality, a perfection, an unalterable vibration, which it is only within the power of the acutest poet to give them. Those of us who understand that words are thoughts and not only our own thoughts but the thoughts of men and women ignorant of what it is that they are thinking, must be conscious of this: that, above everything else, poetry is words; and that words, above everything else, are, in poetry, sounds.

Stevens is constantly endeavoring to "find the vital music [that] formulates the words," either rather blatantly, as if we were as dense-eared as a carving—"the miff-muff of water, the vocables / Of the wind, the glassily-sparkling particles / Of the mind"—or more smoothly, uniting a rhythm with a passage of thought, fashioning sweetmeat music to surround a phrase and its figure like cream poured over berries:

> And so I mocked her in magnificent measure.
> Or was it that I mocked myself alone?
> I wish that I might be a thinking stone.
> ["Le Monocle de Mon Oncle," from *Harmonium,* 1950]

Here, as often in Stevens, music leads meaning by several meters, but who could resist the lure of a line like, "The enormous gongs gave edges to their sounds," since it (cadence and image) suggests a sense that's at the same time secret, melodious, imperial, and sexy. The demands of sound and the impediments, apparently so arbitrary, that poets force themselves to hurdle also compel them to explore the meanings they had in mind, and enable them to discover in what they thought, more than they thought.

"The shabby-suited fellow at the front door was a Fuller Brush salesman." The rhythm of the sentence not only propels the sentence forward, it helps to organize its significant units—its phrases and clauses. The reader is made not merely to see the sentence, but to sound it, because it is now a small mouthful. These sounds are usually not those of ordinary speech, but the spectral mimicry of things that are said to the mind, heard only by the mind, in the arena of the mind—in the subvocal consciousness that exists during reading.

The Aesthetic Structure of the Sentence

This salesman's sentence seems quite sure of itself. It is direct; it is definite; it has no room for reservations. Yet without altering a word, its epistemological and ontological status can be radically altered. That is why I call these verbal instruments *transformative operators*. For instance, we could lower the sentence's degree of assurance. "[I thought that] the fellow at the front door was a Fuller Brush salesman." "[I guessed that] the shabby-suited fellow at the front door was a Fuller Brush salesman [but Gertrude was of quite a different opinion]." Amphibolously: "[Harold said that if] the shabby-suited fellow at the front door was a Fuller Brush salesman [he was a monkey's uncle]." Or change tone and attitude: "[I certainly hoped] the shabby-suited fellow at the front door was a Fuller Brush salesman [otherwise I've just now bought a cat's brush to comb my beard]." "The shabby-suited fellow at the front door was a Fuller Brush salesman [but what if he were also the exhibitionist who has been frightening the neighborhood?]" More radically, we can put it in another realm of being. "[While seated before the fire in my dressing gown reading Descartes' *Meditations,* I dreamed I heard a knocking. Then a cuckoo popped out of its clockhouse to announce that] the shabby-suited fellow at the front door was a Fuller Brush salesman. [I realized, when I was awakened by my desire to answer his knocking, that I had been dreaming inside a dream not altogether mine.]"

Layers of reality, degrees of uncertainty, ranges of attitude, levels of society, depth of contextual connection, modulations of tone, the ramifications and complexities of concept, and, above all, the vocabulary of the denoted world must be taken into account, managed, and made the best of. As here, in this partially realized spindle diagram which displays the sound patterns around which the rhetorical center of these sentences turn:

It was the language of the house itself that spoke to him, writing out for him with surpassing breadth and freedom the associations and conceptions, the ideals and possibilities of the mistress. Never, he felt sure, had he seen

343

                        so many things
                        so unanimously ugly—
operatively, ominously so cruel. . . .

They constituted an order and abounded in rare material—precious
woods, metals, stuffs, stones.

He had never dreamed of anything
                        so fringed   and scalloped,
                        so buttoned   and corded,
        drawn everywhere so tight   and curled
        everywhere so thick.
He had never dreamed of   so much gilt   and glass,
                        so much satin   and plush,
                        so much rosewood and marble
                                            and malachite.

But it was above all the solid forms, the wasted finish, the misguided cost, the general attestation of morality and money, a
good conscience and a big balance. These things finally represented for him a portentous negation of his own world of
thought—of which, for that matter, in presence of them, he
became as for the first time hopelessly aware. They revealed it
to him by their merciless difference. [Henry James, *The Wings
of the Dove*]

There is no dimension of the sentence that is not operative here,
from the upper class Latinate word choice, the steady interruption
of qualifying phrases, the carefully constructed climax, the shocked
tone, both dismayed and outraged, the repetitive encircling of *and*
and *so,* and the helpful disclosure, as if for use in this essay, of the
language—both in its syntax and lexicon—of the world of human
things: the single teacup that speaks of former wealth and dashed
hopes; for Henry James is as much a master of that language as he
is of the urbane style of verbal social exchange with which he was
daily engaged. There is no more attentive prose than one of the Mas-

ter's sentences. The quality of what any one of them sees or feels is not only meticulously depicted, but placed in its proper sphere, and hefted for its proper weight, and seen through, realized, and measured as though each object were a little scene inside a glass globe, with snow that will obediently fall when its world is turned upside down.

I have suggested in other places that such sentences as these are containers of consciousness: a verbal consciousness, of course, one built of symbols, not sensations, yet one of perceptions all the same: perceptions followed by thoughts like tracking hounds, and infused throughout by the energies of memory and desire, the moods emotions foster, and the reach, through imagery and other juxtapositions, of imagination: six elements that I would substitute for Blair's selection (though our choices overlap and never negate); and also properties that the forms I have been discussing are designed to bring into being or enhance; above all, to unify, as our awareness is unified when full and sharp and contemplative, despite the fact that this awareness is, at the same time, being urgently driven, like the scientific eye that searches greedily for clues to the nature of what it sees, yet, for just that reason, dares not miss, however microscopically tiny or cosmically distant, anything that might be significant.

The sentence must shelter its sense in sounds and arrange the furniture of that dwelling in an appealing pattern; but understanding how this is done is made difficult by the amorphous and variable term *form,* which, like so many words philosophers are fond of, is one moment firm and sharp and shining as a blade, while in the next helter-skelter in its applications, soon dull and tarnished and worn thin.

Why not admit that the sentence is a suitcase packed with all of these, for James is obedient as a servant to the rules of grammar, and yet has his own manner or style of address? His sentences are made of words whose spelling is prescribed, and of letters whose shapes not only endeavor to be recognized, but hope to look lovely. These words are in English, a form of mostly Frenchified Germanic

345

speech. His periods embody grammatical, musical, and rhetorical structures. They are continuously aware of the rank given words and their objects and actions in the social world: James would never write *stink* but rather refer to something possibly odiferous; he would not say *shat* in any company. Any of his sentences are immediately recognizable as such, and belong to rubrics innumerable; moreover, the various phrases, lengthy clauses, lists, and repetitions they contain are given the order, correlation, and symmetry that any high style requires. That is to say, they are formed to a fare-thee-well.

Primarily, a form consists of terms in a significant relation: a relation of communal belonging that gives rise to a quality or condition—a meaning, an emotional effect—that could not be realized otherwise. We can, as we read, feel it occurring, but how does it happen? I suspect there is no single cause or simple explanation. Yet it is a quality felt by any responsive reader and it constitutes the verbal consciousness that has been built by many different sorts of relations, and by the interconnections these systems have with one another—some dominate, others subordinate—but all in tune, as the strings of a guitar or violin must be; so that any word or phrase or clause that finds itself in such company would have chosen to be there. Like love, it is a free and freedom enhancing enslavement.

Perhaps this is metaphorical thinking at its worst, but it describes how writing feels when every word is fully active in the networks of its world. By *active* I do not mean "in use." By *active* I mean sensitive and alert to every possibility, even though many will, in this or that context, have to go unrealized. It means that avenues are open to be explored even when—this time—they are only viewed. A spare and simple-seeming style can be fully aware of what else might have served where it is serving, and a convoluted and apparently complex manner may be obtuse to every possibility but the flourish. If it is Mr. Micawber knocking at our door, we shall hear such posturing, but we shall be amused by it, because it is not the author but his character who is thusly revealing himself.

We are familiar with texts that bear like a banner some trope that modifies or distinguishes them. Richardson's *Clarissa Harlowe* pretends it is made of letters; Swift and Defoe both say their famous travelers kept a journal; Dickens insists that he has written David Copperfield's autobiography; Nabokov that the characters in his novel, *The Defense,* are pieces that move about on a chessboard, while Cortázar claims that his *Hopscotch* is the game itself. *Finnegans Wake* is a dream. John Barth's *Perseid* is inscribed on a column. Calvino's *Invisible Cities* follows a Dantesque path to hell that performs like a dance step a logarithmic spiral. One of my own novels is called *The Tunnel,* and has been dug to resemble one; a few others are mazes, or portraits, or pastorals, or symphonic movements, or fake confessions. Many of Beckett's paragraphs, even pages, resemble contrapuntal pieces, and poems are sometimes shaped to look like altars or angels' wings or leaves, or driving rain for Apollinaire, or pipes or lutes. Sentences cannot be quite so explicit, though I have depicted one of Mark Twain's diatribes against another river pilot ("He was a middle-aged long, slim, bony horse-faced ignorant, stingy, malicious, snarling fault-finding mote-magnifying tyrant") as a towboat pulling behind its noun a long row of barges bearing acidulous and pejorative adjectives.

A sentence can sometimes give its reader such a strong sense of its overall character that it provokes a flight of fancy, a metaphorical description: it's like a journey of discovery; it's like a coil of rope, a triumphal column; it's like a hallway or a chapel; it's like a spiral stair. To me, for instance, Sir Thomas Browne's triplet—"Grave stones tell truth scarce forty years. Generations pass while some trees stand, and old families last not three oaks"—with its relentlessly stressed syllables (seven strong to one weak in the first row, seven to two in the second course, and six to one in the last) resembles a wall. I can even locate spots (the weak stresses) where its stones have crumbled. Families come to pieces the way the word does.

Henry James builds a stairway with *old* as a riser in a sentence from *The Golden Bowl,* punning in addition on the word *decent* while depicting the decline of the West's several ages, and by deftly return-

347

ing our attention to the sentence's beginnings—one step forward, one-half back—with a marvelous row of Os, thereby obtaining a spiral effect: "Of decent old gold, old silver, old bronze, of old chased and jeweled artistry were the objects that, successively produced, had ended by numerously dotting the counter. . . ." Nor dare I omit James Joyce's use of the same sound in his magnificent conclusion to *Finnegans Wake,* as the waters of the River Liffey finally make their return to the sea, and Joyce, too, completes his cycle of life.

SPINDLE DIAGRAM—SOUND AND RHYTHM PATTERN
From James Joyce, *Finnegans Wake,* conclusion.

		[oh]				
And	it's	old				
and		old				
	it's		sad			
and		old				
	it's		sad			
and				weary		

[that]	I	go			back	to you,
	my	cold				father,
	my	cold	mad	feary		father,

till	the		near	sight	
of	the		mere	size	of him,

	the		moyles	
and			moyles	of it,

		moan-
		an-
		oan-
		ing,

| makes me | seasilt |
| | saltsick |

| and   I | rush, |
| my only, | into your arms. |

Finally, here is an example of how Stanley Elkin gives his subject matter a form admirably suited to it by imitating the actions of an elevator, and beginning at the parking garage level, B2.

THE ELEVATOR
From Stanley Elkin, *The Franchiser* (1976).

in	the dark sand.	10
	the dark cigarette butts	9
	the dark silky stripes on the benches outside the elevators	8
of each	dark floor,	7
pressed against	the dark walls	6
on	the dark halved tables	5
in	their dark vases	4
and	dark flowers	3
	the dark lamps	2
	the darkened mezzanine and black ballrooms,	Mz
through	darkness, imagining, though it was day,	L
and sensed himself sucked up		B1
He pressed the button		B2

This is our floor. Time to get off at encyclopedias, brushes, and shabby suits.

A NOTE ON THE TYPE

This book was set in Fairfield, a typeface designed by the distinguished American artist and engraver Rudolph Ruzicka (1883–1978). In its structure Fairfield displays the sober and sane qualities of the master craftsman whose talents were dedicated to clarity. Ruzicka was born in Bohemia and came to America in 1894. He designed and illustrated many books, and was the creator of a considerable list of individual prints in a variety of techniques.

Typeset by Scribe, Philadelphia, Pennsylvania
Printed and bound by RR Donnelley, Harrisonburg, Virginia
Designed by Laura Crossin